'Make Germany Great Again'

'Make Germany Great Again'

How the German People Reacted to Nazisim

Andrew Sangster

Pen & Sword
MILITARY

First published in Great Britain in 2024 by
Pen & Sword Military
An imprint of Pen & Sword Books Limited
Yorkshire – Philadelphia

ISBN 978 1 03612 267 6

A CIP catalogue record for this book is
available from the British Library

Typeset by Mac Style
Printed in the UK by CPI Group (UK) Ltd, Croydon, CR0 4YY.

Pen & Sword Books Limited incorporates the imprints of After the Battle, Atlas, Archaeology, Aviation, Discovery, Family History, Fiction, History, Maritime, Military, Military Classics, Politics, Select, Transport, True Crime, Air World, Frontline Publishing, Leo Cooper, Remember When, Seaforth Publishing, The Praetorian Press, Wharncliffe Local History, Wharncliffe Transport, Wharncliffe True Crime and White Owl.

For a complete list of Pen & Sword titles please contact

PEN & SWORD BOOKS LIMITED
47 Church Street, Barnsley, South Yorkshire, S70 2AS, England
E-mail: enquiries@pen-and-sword.co.uk
Website: www.pen-and-sword.co.uk
or
PEN AND SWORD BOOKS
1950 Lawrence Road, Havertown, PA 19083, USA
E-mail: uspen-and-sword@casematepublishers.com
Website: www.penandswordbooks.com

Contents

Acknowledgements

Over the years I have been very grateful to those who work and administer the various archives, and for the work of fellow historians with their various insights and perceptions.

However, I am exceptionally grateful to my wife, Carol Ann, for her incredible patience as I disappear into archives and rarely emerge from my study. I am also grateful for the support and encouragement of my friend and colleague the Revd Dr Canon Peter Doll, Vice-Dean of Norwich Cathedral.

The Revd Dr Andrew Sangster

Preface

The years of 1919–1945 in Germany were turbulent, and from 1939 this affected most of Europe and many other parts of the globe. The 1939 war generated considerable suffering, hatred, a desire for revenge, and the figure of between 50 to 55 million deaths during the war would be seen by some as a conservative estimation. In post-war Germany, divided by the victors and being regarded as a pariah state once again, there was a deep confusion of feelings and memories, not least as the de-Nazification courts became widespread, as if the German mind-set had to be re-programmed. It is probably true that the pain of these years hung like an unpleasant shadow right up to 1989–90 when Germany re-found its unity. After 1945 many people held their tongues and locked away their secrets, as bias and boiling revenge simmered for a long time. In the post-war era historians and other commentators were busy writing about the causes and course of the war which is basically a careful accumulation of verifiable facts and figures. It was also widely acceptable and easy to tear apart the Nazi regime, and then elevate or denigrate some military commanders and political leaders.

The New York Times of 5 September 1939, noted that the day before that Chamberlain had said that 'the fight was not against the German people, but solely against the tyrannical regime which had betrayed its own people and the whole western civilisation.' However, the Allies soon introduced the term 'collective guilt' which was heaped upon the entire German population, and this took some considerable time for any sense of objectivity to be found. At the time of writing this study, nearly 80 years have passed since the end of the war, and this exploration has set out to explore the reaction of Germans to Nazism, attempting to avoid any sense of Pharisaic judgment and hypocrisy. The question may be asked as to why bother, what can this prove or how can it be useful. The answer was not just a matter of setting the record as straight as humanly possible, but although we generally fail to learn from history, this study may well ring bells with many readers as we see what is happening in our world today. The features of a charismatic politician leading people into the abyss of war, imprisoning their own citizens in a police state, instructing them what to think, indoctrinating the young, and thereby creating a repressed society living in fear, this can all happen again. Even in traditional democratic countries there is today the danger of a populist leader who may or may not have criminal leanings, leading a country astray. The Jewish historian Zimmermann, a specialist in German history, once said in an interview that history is more than telling a story, because a historian needs to infer from the past about the present. Any student of German history during this vexed period will be aware of how the Weimar Democratic Republic collapsed, and the danger of propaganda in the hands of a man like Joseph Goebbels led by a populist politician like Hitler should be well-known. History does not move in a cyclic pattern, but it warns that events can often be repeated if the warnings from the past are not heeded.

In terms of German public reaction to the Nazi regime there are no reliable or available statistics, no trustworthy electoral papers, because the presence of a bullying brownshirt Nazi hovering at the polling station could be all too influential. This study can only be an estimation which is based on various texts, diaries written at the time, historical common sense, and some knowledge of human society and nature. Having spent decades pondering this subject, it can be stated that any community of people during such a turbulent period can have a change of mind, as the promises of a better future disintegrate into mayhem and chaos.

Given this factor it means that in terms of a broad reflection German society had various groupings. The first identifiable cluster would be the seemingly large number of Nazi supporters, but this group reflects two sub-elements. The first element was the group whose enthusiasm faded over the years as Nazi behaviour and reality came to light, while the second sub-element was the fanatic who believed in Nazism to the end of the war and for some even beyond 1945. Another significant cluster were those who remained silent for different reasons, varying from people who always kept their politics to themselves, to those who never ever bothered to vote, and those too terrified to express an opinion either for fear of falling out with their neighbours, or being drawn to the attention of the Gestapo. The last vast cluster also has its sub-divisions, namely those who opposed the regime but kept it to themselves and their diaries, those who opposed by protest, but by 1933 many of these were already in so-called protective custody in Dachau and other camps. Others within this group resisted even to the extreme of wanting Hitler dead or a coup d'état. In 1945 with the discovery of the barbaric slaughter in the concentration camps and other massacre sites, it was all too easy to announce collective guilt, but it was far from the truth, which this study does not pretend to resolve, but will raise questions in this jigsaw of the many different reactions.

Any one generation can be influenced by its recent past, so the book starts with Germany's pre-Nazi history to illustrate how a national 'mind-set' can develop, and why the Nazi regime was so popular in its early years. It will use two everyday diarists to paint the various and different reactions of the German public, outline the power of propaganda, and the suppression of possible opposition by sheer fear, when living in a controlled police state. It will explore those who resisted from individuals to groups of young teenagers, educated undergraduates, to Churchmen, senior politicians, civil servants, and the military. When watching archival film footage of mass rallies, a wrong image is often perceived that every German was there, when many more were elsewhere and often in prison camps.

This study could be perceived as potentially contentious but that is not the intention, it is a search for the truth of how a nation of good and often clever people were led down the road to self-destruction, and the knowledge that it was not the first time in history a criminal type of leader had assumed power, and the warning that it could happen again, even in traditional democracies.

Foreword

German history from the modern period (1870) has resulted in two world wars, the first devastating in the loss of life and economic stability, the second resulting in the Second World War with the Nazi regime noted for its evil brutality and the Holocaust. How this arose has often been asked, and where the focus should be placed for responsibility remains a vexed question. A. J. P. Taylor claimed that the Third Reich 'was also a system which represented the deepest wishes of the German people…It was a tyranny imposed upon the German people by themselves'.[1] This claim made by a well-known and famous historian has many justified critics, and it has raised many questions. It has proved a popular stamping ground to claim that Germans had always held the propensity to dominate as early as the late eighteenth century, which the leaders of the monarchical Empire exploited, but this amounts to a crude attack on the German personality, and it is necessary to examine the political structures under which the people existed and were influenced. It took time for the English-speaking world to know that not every German was a fanatical Nazi, and to realise there was considerable resistance by many Germans against the regime, which still remains little known to many. This book starts its exploration long before Hitler's appearance in 1933, to try and understand why so many Germans gave him support and not forget the others who made many efforts to resist.

The period of modern Germany history from 1870 onwards was marked by a growing sense of nationalism, influenced by racial bigotry and a sense of national superiority. This attitude was not just a German characteristic, but it was widespread among many European countries and elsewhere. In the 1870 Franco-Prussian war, it had been the French who attacked the German Federation trying to assert their dominance in Europe. Britain, not so interested in Europe, was busy consolidating its overseas colonies with pink coloured maps in schoolrooms, showing the extent of the British Empire. Russia under the Tsarists also sought expansion, not least in pressing south towards the sub-continent of India to the concern of the British, who were by the turn of the century fighting to retain South Africa under British control. Nationalism as seen in Europe (and elsewhere) was more than mere patriotism as it encapsulated political superiority and the right and desire to dominate others. Racialism was rife, especially over skin colour and anti-Semitism, all regarded as indicators of superiority of one ethnic group over another.

This all raises questions as to who influenced the German people, who gave them the directions which many of them, but not all, eventually followed. A country whether governed by a monarch, a dictator, a communist committee, or a democratic government tends to follow the leader even when some may be in doubt, giving rise to the dangerous cliché 'of my country right or wrong'. Few countries have a public totally united behind their leaders except in extreme emergency. During the interbellum years in Britain there was Oswald Mosley leading a growing fascist movement, an active Communist Party, anti-Semitism existed, Church divisions and bigotry prevailed, as did skin-colour racism. France was politically swinging between the left and right-wings, the Dreyfus affair indicated along with French colonial attitudes that racism was rife. The question must be asked as to what was so different with the Germans, that in Taylor's view they wished the tyranny upon themselves.

To try and work through this delicate and complex problem, the first task is to explore in the opening chapter Germany's history under the authoritarian controlled Empire, the defeat in the First World War, and its consequences on German life, followed by the attempt at democratic government and why it failed, and try to understand the rise of Nazism in what was seen as a civilised and cultured country. This survey indicates the political indoctrinations the German public lived under, but it is therefore essential to see why the democratic process failed, and how Hitler rose to power. He did not have the total public support often proposed by many historians, otherwise the introduction of 1933 concentration camps for thousands of opponents would not have been deemed as essential, even by the Nazi regime.

Into this equation is explored the nature of political indoctrination and the fear of opposing a police state which was paranoid about potential enemies. It was a major factor which subdued many potential opponents, along with the control of the press and media to influence the German public. It would appear that the political leaders dictated the direction, and many followed the proposed route like lambs, but not all Germans agreed, and this book seeks to challenge Taylor's claim that the German public was totally in favour of the Nazi regime. This study attempts to understand why and how the German people were cajoled by the Nazi Party (NSDAP) in the first place, how many continued to be influenced by government propaganda, but not all. There were many who disagreed, some who opposed in a passive style, others who resisted at a local level, and a critical few who plotted and planned for the overthrow of the regime. This exploration will attempt to investigate public attitudes by looking at significant German diaries of the day, the machinations of senior people, and even at student protests and teenage rebellions. When the Allies spoke of Collective Guilt in 1945, it led in West Germany to many attempts to recognise the importance of the 'resisters', whereas in the GDR, Eastern Germany, they remained ardent in tracking down Nazis and accusing West Germany of harbouring war criminals. Over the last few decades as a united Germany has become a new and respected country, these issues appear to be of interest only to historians. However, it remains important to try and understand why a vast number of people supported a clearly evil regime and not to forget those who opposed and resisted, because it could happen again anywhere in the world.

It is critical to explore how and why the Nazi regime initially appeared to dazzle much of the German public, first through Hitler's promises, then hammered home by Goebbel's propaganda machine, and controlled by the fear and terror organised by Himmler. This section must be followed by the sensitive issue of the way the Jews were treated, exploring why so many Germans seemed to support this, and how the Jewish people reacted, raising the question as to whether they were led like lambs to the slaughter.

In the chapter which surveys the diverse types of resistance groups and some lead personalties, it is necessary to grapple with the 'mindset' of the day as times in Germany have dramatically changed. Previewing German history in Chapter One is important as it helps in understanding why many Germans thought the way they did. The central feature of being 'Prussian' had its ups and downs, the blind obedience to military orders has been criticised (albeit that it is not just a Prussian trait) but there was a powerful sense of Protestant and Catholic shared ethics, and a belief that order could be established through morality.

Being called English, French, or American can carry varying undertones of a judgemental nature, but the previous history of a country has an influence on its next generation. There was once a joke in a forgotten satirical magazine that when various nations decided to do a joint study on the elephant, the Germans wrote about its role in war, the French wrote on its love life, the Italians saw it as an item for artists, the English wrote on its use in sport, and the philosophic Russians queried whether it existed. It was an amusing joke as there is a human tendency to see the next-door neighbour as fitting a pattern, and while it is true that a country's history may influence the up-and-coming generation there is no definable answer, as in Nazi Germany there were many who resisted and many others who opposed, but most were silenced by the fear of the police state.

Three chapters are devoted to surveying some individuals and groups who opposed and refused to support the Nazi regime. They did so on the grounds that the new regime was taking the country down the wrong route, by what amounted to an organised gang of political gangsters. There were individuals, student movements, traditional German conservatives, middle and left-wing groups who eventually found common ground in opposing Hitler. They were often divided on how to accomplish the downfall of Nazism and the post-war type of government in the proposed post-Hitler years. There were many connections with the military as it was generally understood that a serious coup d'état could only be accomplished by the military. Their motives were also widely mixed, ranging from the moral abhorrence to the regime, to military reasons of either avoiding war or later, defeat. Their motives were often mixed making it a kaleidoscope of motives and intentions. The end result was one of total confusion and eventual failure, but the sacrifice made by many in opposing Nazism helped restore some German dignity in the post-war years, and it is best seen in this light. The tragedy of history is that because we fail to learn from its lessons, the problems of human conduct can be too often repeated.

Chapter One

Failure of German Leadership 1870–1945

Author's notes: *In this first chapter Germany is explored as a nation from 1870, because a country's recent history frequently influences the mindset of the next generation. The Germans had lived very much under a form of monarchical despotism whose influence was deeply felt. Germany had many divisive problems as they changed from an agricultural base to industrialisation. A new social structure appeared with an emerging and often educated middleclass, there were sharp religious problems between German Protestants and Roman Catholics, there was a degree of anti-Semitism, a growth of nationalism, and as they entered the First World War all this was similar to other European countries. Until 1918 Prussian tradition had been the highly influential factor, almost to the point of deification of the military class with its stress on loyalty and obedience.*

The defeat in the First World War led Germany towards what could have been a better future with the democratic Weimar Republic. However, many traditionalists resented this change, made angry and bitter by the demands of the Versailles Treaty, the impact of which was severe, not least in the humiliation, but in the resultant hunger and poverty which many Germans suffered, coupled with ridiculous inflation and a financial world disaster. There were too many political parties, the constant fear of revolution, fighting on the streets between the extremists persisted, and with the benefit of hindsight it is not difficult to see why the possibility of a democratic government fell after just one decade. The army, despite its disputed defeat in 1918, tended to remain staunchly right-wing despite the pretence of keeping above politics. Under General von Seeckt it reorganised itself in a clandestine fashion and continued down this course despite Seeckt's dismissal, leaving a reorganised military recognised as being both new and potentially powerful.

It is essential to understand what made the Nazi Party so attractive from the point of view of the German electorate. In these early years German people were looking for positive leadership, economic recovery, and employment, which the NSDAP promised, all this with a better German community with a special appeal to the younger generation, backed by a well organised and pro-active propaganda. The Weimar Republic had collapsed just as Hitler's electoral support increased, but he moved swifty with his charismatic persona, and with the backing of the unholy trinity of the bully Göring, the persuasive Goebbels, and the dangerous Himmler, he was soon the dictator of Germany, welcomed by many, but not all.

Despite modern popular belief that Hitler had the total backing of the German people, many were critical and bitterly opposed, and a few examples of very early resistance are noted. The elements of fear, the early appearance of concentration camps in 1933, the Gestapo, the Night of the Long Knives, Kristallnacht, all sent out warnings to those critics who had survived. In addition to this important factor the only information and news the public received was that which was dictated by Goebbels, and foreign broadcasts were soon made illegal. The chapter concludes with signs of early resistance, but a large number had been hoodwinked by the NSDAP promises.

The Days of Empire, 1870–1918

In every country each generation attempts to shape its future, often in ways different from the past, and this was not just a German issue but a feature for every country. Given the circumstances of German history in the first half of the twentieth century, and especially the period of the Nazi regime, it seems worthwhile to study and explore the influences which bore down on the German public, shaping their attitudes and opinions. The experiences of any new generation are to one degree or another, influenced by its immediate predecessors, the style of leadership, the social views of the day, and even the influence of the economic sphere of life. Historically the influences of the past, with the benefit of hindsight may appear obvious, but they are less so when living at the time, which is a factor which cannot be ignored.

To understand the German generation which supported Nazism, it is necessary to make a brief exploration of modern German history, as the shadows of the past may not dominate but carry considerable influence. While countries like France, Russia, Britain had existed almost from medieval times, Germany as a country was new, having once been a series of small states, city states, and keen on maintaining their independence, and linked by the German language, but not all of them. This was the hope of Otto von Bismarck, the well-known German Chancellor who had no time for liberal views. During the time of Germany consisting of small states they had been dominated or influenced by the Austrian Empire, subject to the King of Poland, many spoke French, and it was not the King *of* Prussia but the King *in* Prussia. Germany started to formulate a political identity following the Napoleonic Wars with the German Confederation, called Germany from 1871 on Bismark's order. Following the Franco-Prussian War some parts of Germany such as Alsace and Lorraine were basically French, and although many spoke German, they tended to prefer the French form of government. Also, many Polish speakers found themselves designated German which was far from welcome. Some of the other states were equally unhappy about their change of circumstances because of their history of independence.

The problem of 'being internally and externally incomplete proved to be the heaviest burden which the Empire had to bear and from the outset hindered its further development'.[1] There have been times, which still persist, when the Irish, Welsh, and Scots prefer their original names and background and not to be called British and certainly not English. The new Germany largely depended on Bismarck's driving force who dominated the government until Wilhelm II wanted the power in his hands. During these early stages various political parties emerged but no sound parliamentary principles were established. It should be noted that even to this day the United Kingdom is not that united. As the Welsh language and Gaelic persist, being German was not just a matter of a common language. There were many developing similarities with other countries as Germany came together as a major entity in central Europe.

Not every potential citizen was pleased with the emergence of the new country and there were groups which tended to find themselves less than welcome. Roman Catholics and Jews were a focus of distaste, and women were regarded as home keepers, and their natural citizenship raised questions. However, Germany was not alone, the suffragette movement in Britain was yet to gain force, France had to face the consequence of the Dreyfus affair, because as in Britain there was often social bigotry against Jews; anti-Semitism in one form or another was widely prevalent in Europe. In Britain there was also an anti-Catholic strain, and when George V was crowned in May 1910, he had insisted that the anti-Roman Catholic wording of the Accession had to be changed. The sense of a national community developed in Germany during the final decades of the nineteenth century, but it was little different from many of its European neighbours.

Most of Europe's major countries experienced the rise of nationalism often in an aggressive form, there were racial and religious bigotries in one form or another, not just between various faiths but within the divided Christian church. Germany because of its sheer size and position in central Europe was a politically sensitive area, which could and did have some serious sway on shaping the world today. Many have seen the central power of Germany as a link between the East and Western zones of Europe, but Germany wanted to choose its own path and not just be a bridge linking the geographical extremes.

In the final decades of the nineteenth century and the entry into the next, the so-called balance of power in Europe remained unstable with the rise and fall of states. The old power of the Ottoman empire had been described as the sick man of Europe, which was more a comment on loss of its economic rather than military power. Russia remained under the Tsars, but it was well known this vast country was suffering potential revolution, the Austrian power was in decline, Italy was weak and still living in its own shadow of the Roman Empire.

Prussia was rising in power, but all of Europe was finding their own way forward in terms of the growing industrialisation, nationalism, and basically preparing for what may be called the modernised world. Each country had its own social problems to cope with, including, as mentioned above divided faiths, ethnic bigotries, social classes, the place of women, all simmering below the surface as each country tried to find its developing identity for the next century.

As a forming major country, Germany had a valuable heritage of intellectual thinkers acknowledged worldwide. Men like Immanuel Kant, Georg Hegel, and Friedrich Nietzsche were world famous for their philosophical works. The German states had produced some of the world's best musicians, their churches had famous missionaries helping overseas, playwrights, authors, all amounting to a formidable bookshelf of progressive intellectuals. It has been proposed that German national identity started to form because of the Napoleonic Wars, and there is little doubt that major wars not only change the world, but for all those nations involved, it helped formulate their national attitudes forming their specific identity. The impact of war can never be ignored. It could be argued that the First World War was followed by a brief pause before restarting with the Second World War, leading to the Cold War with its ramifications, with the emerging superpowers remaining prominent into the twenty-first century. There are obvious similarities in each country, but Germany's vast geographical position made it central to the various power players in Europe. This underlined the fact that although a country may have some of the best intellects, the power and authority for the future remained in the hands of the few who governed, be they dynastic rulers or politicians.

The governing bodies, dynastic, dictatorial, or democratic, not only have a major impact in terms of international relationships, but also at the social level in their own country, a feature long recognised. As in any country it is necessary to try and understand how the rulers impact on their own society at every level, from the economics not just of a country but its inhabitants, the organisation of its social structure at an everyday level. During the Bismarckian era Germany was rapidly changing from being an agricultural country to industrialisation, as had happened in Britain. This process of change brought urbanisation and the working classes with all the traditional aspects of religious faith, ethnic and gender bias playing their roles, with all these traits being experienced in other European countries. Germany was a new country on the scene from 1871 but its problems and issues were shared by other much older countries. The sudden industrial growth in Germany has sometimes been linked with the violent course of their history, and although there may be a glimmer of explanation in this possibility it was not unique to Germany. Such rapid growth in economics and industrialisation often led to social instability with life changing results in all classes of society, producing monied classes alongside extreme poverty. In Germany, most workers had lived on agricultural land in small villages and towns, but with the industrialisation the towns and industrial cities grew exponentially, as did the standard of living for a few. The changes caused by industrialisation were not unique to Germany, but they tended to happen a trifle later than for example in Britain. As the working classes gathered together in larger conglomerations than required by agriculture, it led to occasional revolts, some threats of revolutions as working men (and soon women) wondered why their workload often left them into extreme poverty, while others further up the social ladder became enriched. It often transpired that the 'working-class unrest' often influenced the political leaders. This clash in the social class structure was not unique to Germany, and it still remains a constant and vexed issue.

One of the main characteristics of pre-First World War was the rampant growth of aggressive nationalism which asserted one country over another, and often minority groups such as Jews suffered. As noted, in France there had been the outrageous Dreyfus affair, in Russia there had been pogroms, some in Poland, while in Germany and Britain Jews suffered from social snobbery, but they were generally accepted living normal everyday lives. As there were Church divisions of Roman Catholic and various strains of Protestantism, so among the Jews there existed the Orthodox Jewish elements and the more liberal Reform groupings, and many, as amongst so-called Christians, those who were merely nominal and had little or no faith in a supreme creator. The social snobbery aspect could not be brushed aside as it often excluded Jews from high positions, and until 1910 no Jews were allowed to serve in the Prussian army, often contemptuously dismissed as foreigners or Jews.

Being Jewish in early German history was not as conspicuous as the division of Roman Catholic and Protestant, as the Catholic tradition was often seen as being too universal and not German, and at times there was a high degree of enmity between the two groups. When the Protestant League was founded in 1886, although regarded as a support to the Protestant Churches, in reality it was more anti-Roman Catholic, and as such non-Protestants were less likely to make educational or career advances. As has often been noted by many historians and sociologists, the Protestant wing has long been associated with economic and social growth. Nevertheless, in the pre-Great War era Catholics started to become associated with central political parties and carried some influence, and in 1904 managed to overturn the regulations forbidding Jesuits from entering Germany. However, because of its connection with Rome 'the Centre Party was seen as a papist party and internationalist in outlook'.[2]

Despite some nationalistic inbuilt anti-Catholic bigotry and some simmering anti-Semitism and a distaste for foreigners, there were emerging more pressing matters in terms of economics and the abject poverty of some social classes. The Socialists had recognised this major impact on German society, and their efforts for change were bolstered by a series of poor harvests in the first decade of the twentieth century, and the way the taxation policies of the rulers tended to hit the poorest. These factors gave the Socialists more strength than they had hitherto ever dreamed about, not least because they mirrored the concerns of a large proportion of the population. The fear among the German upper echelons was that the Socialists seemed to be mirroring the unrest in Russia. Germany was dominated by the aristocratic landowners (the Junkers) who continued to rule the roost during the Wilhelmine era, and much of this tradition tended to rest on the power and influence of Prussia, whose role was deeply influential. Progressive and liberal influences were often focused on education, welfare, and the taxing system but never resulted in any sound political triumph. Against Prussian traditionalism there was never any serious hope of success. There had always been a tendency to tax the workers leaving the upper echelons in a tax-free haven, Britain differed here which led to a safer economy. However, from this social cooking pot the middle-classes evolved (*Mittelstand*) known as the 'black-coated', whereas in Britain they were 'white-collared' workers, and the public sector expanded, very much as in many countries. Bismarck fought fiercely against any form of social democracy, and the new middle-class tended to support him because of their fear of 'red anarchy'.

As always, whether in the medieval period, the modern era and to this day most of a nation's life was directed or dictated by the leadership of the country, which from a historical perspective appeared to be lacking in Germany despite its vast intellectual resources. Bismarck was dismissed in 1890 because Wilhelm wanted to be in overall charge. At the elite level in Germany, the Emperor Wilhelm 'himself suffered from what today would probably be diagnosed as a histrionic personality disorder'.[3] He always needed to be the centre of attention, enjoyed the drama, believed his opinions to be always right, and needed continuous approbation to keep him happy. The problem was that this form of governmental leadership bit deep into the national psyche. Many studies have been written on the subject of Wilhelm, many blaming his withered left arm, but he reflected the time when a dynasty still stood above all other governmental procedures. He was the grandson of Queen Victoria and undoubtedly saw himself in the theatre of royal rule. When his uncle, the British King Edward VII visited him, it was abundantly clear that Edward disliked his German nephew, always concerned that he would cause a war in Europe. There were some who even blamed Edward VII for creating a paranoia about Germany which helped create the tensions erupting in the Great War, but his perceptions about his German nephew were probably more correct with the benefit of hindsight. Although admired for the grand position the Kaiser held, it was probably true that most Germans never realised how badly they were governed, many having been brought up in the Prussian tradition of loyalty and obedience, which was their political summary of the ten commandments. From 1871 the Kaiser's Empire had sought national unity, but as it happened that unity had to come from the top, not least because of all the unified states, Prussia was the largest and most influential, and this was all part of Wilhelm's character and background. There may have been 22 princes and three free cities making up a federal state, 'but the predominance of Prussia was overwhelming and many of the goals of the liberal and democratic movements remained unachieved', despite the fact it was technically a federal state.'[4] This suited Wilhelm II, and some leading figures considered him a brilliant and natural leader in the world of international politics, and his close connection to the British Royal Family probably boosted this sense of self-confidence. Because of whom he was, he always chose weaker men, especially the Chancellors who accepted his instructions and opinions without objection. However, during this historical period there was a constant problem with the national economy. Wilhelm's obsessive love for the military, meant financial demands from the Army and Navy were regarded as essential, although it often meant more poverty for workers. Such was Wilhem's character the military commanders could meet the Kaiser directly without the presence of the Chancellor of the day. On the other hand, the worker-movements agitated for a fairer society but were bound by the Prussian elite. Nevertheless, the domestic issues of this era were the continual fights and wranglings against social democracy gaining any ground.

Within the international sphere Germany faced a series of alliances, not least the links between France, Russia, and Britain, whereas Germany's two traditional allies of Austria and Italy were hardly strong and weaker than in previous years. Wilhelm had an overactive interest in asserting himself and Germany as being militarily strong, although he had never led in any battle or experienced warfare first hand. Occasionally he made serious blunders, not least by offering support to President Kruger of the Transvaal during the Boer War, and then congratulating him and wanting to send German troops, confirming the suspicions of Edward VII.[5] This was a mistake because if there were any hope of a better alliance it could have been Britain, already linked by the monarchies. It was well-known that Britain had more interest in its colonies than the machinations on the continent, that Britain feared Russian expansion for this reason, and Britain and France were often at loggerheads on colonial matters. There was little chance of working together because Wilhelm had his own imperialist ambitions in the hope of seeing Germany as a world power, but in terms of years he was late to the party. It was because of this that he wanted a navy large enough to combat, if necessary, the British Royal Navy.

This produced what was called the Tirpitz plan (after Admiral Alfred von Tirpitz), gaining a formidable budget to increase the number of battleships and was naturally aimed at British sea-power. This added yet another thread to the complex tapestry he produced, which seemed to alienate and warn the British that despite family relationships, Germany was becoming a potential threat. It was enough for the British to start a new process in strengthening their navy, which at the time was the largest in the world. None of this was helped by the Schlieffen plan (Alfred von Schlieffen, Chief of Staff from 1891) which, as is well known, was a plan to invade France via the neutral countries of Belgium and the Netherlands, gaining a formidable coastline which would evidently encourage Britain to assist the French. In short this was paving the way to war, which was unnecessary, and a generation later Adolf Hitler would pick up the same reins.

There seems little doubt that Wilhelm's world policy (*Weltpolitik*) represented the problem of an irresponsible national leader, but it was not just the German Kaiser. Many of the European countries were ruled by an elite who were all too 'willing to gamble on a war to fuse their divided societies into unified nations'.[6] Imperial ambitions, rampant nationalism, capitalism became some of the critical ingredients which turned the new twentieth century into a period of war. How far Germany was guilty can be disputed for a long time. There had already been many pre-war tensions such as the gunboat episodes, colonial conflicts, failures of Germany and Britain to work together, and diplomacy had failed. Bismarck had always ignored the colony grabbing issue being more interested in the European scenario, but Wilhelm II regarded this as part of world-policy to establish Germany's reputation as a major power. In terms of Germany's colonial aspirations, the 'Kaiser's aggressive speeches and the brutality shown by the 'Expeditions-corps' and the *Schutztruppen* (colonial troops) in putting down uprisings in the colonies damaged German standing in the world'.[7]

Germany did not start the Great War (1914–18) which had its initial fuse in the Austrian-Serbian conflict, but Wilhelm appeared overly enthusiastic, and he had plenty of support but was now dependent on a seriously weakened Austria as a partner. Russia was in support of Serbia, the French hoped to influence Austria to seek some form of mediation, but the roulette wheel was already spinning, and when, on 3 August 1914, Germany invaded the low countries to penetrate France, this led to Britain declaring war. Wilhelm had proved to be enthusiastically bellicose, but the causes were more widespread as were the various elites in other countries who welcomed war. The German and French arms race and the naval rivalry with Britian were all part of the causation of this war, along with Russia's aggressive approach in the Balkans.

As with other European countries the public had mixed feelings about a major European war. There were those who expressed patriotic fervour stirred by the prevalent nationalism of the day, and those who were anxious and not so disposed to fighting their neighbours. In July 1914 there were major peace demonstrations, some rushed to join the army, some sought exemption, there was food hoarding, money was removed from the banks, and unemployment increased dramatically. There were similar reactions in the other involved countries. This war was not a local event and it meant, as elsewhere, the mobilisation of every aspect of the country's life. As the pain of war was felt in every home public attitude changed and there was social and industrial unrest. Kaiser Wilhelm II was soon marginalised both from political and military planning, eventually leading to his unavoidable abdication and flight. The failure on the battlefield took time to emerge, but the economic disaster was too much for the public to tolerate.

Volumes have been written on the First World War, but it is important in exploring Germany's modern background to understand the way the war influenced the future development of social and political history in Germany. Precise figures are difficult to establish but it is generally agreed that at least two million German soldiers died, many of whom could never be identified. As in Britain, France and elsewhere, all involved countries were distressed by the war, with families and the public in most countries all felt traumatised by the catastrophic experience. Germany's defeat was so unexpected by the country's leaders and people, bringing into focus the questions of the country's identity, its traditions, questioning the belief of its military supremacy, and raising questions over leadership. As the war raged on some of these issues were already simmering below the surface, creating a fracture between the pre-war and war generation, not least because many saw the leadership problems of Imperial Germany as the cause of failure and suffering. The question arose as to whether the war was caused by problems of leadership and whether change was needed. Some wondered whether it would lead Germany in a new direction, or whether its past would continue to influence the country into a more dangerous future, and many started to ask these questions as the war rolled on, for what must have been felt for ever. It was not a local war which could be finished by a single battle or victory, but like the American Civil War had become one of long-lasting attrition. In the emotional surge to fight, few politicians in the Reichstag had influence in such matters, as foreign relationships, because of Bismarck's heritage, this form of leadership had to be decided only at the very top.

In the initial stages it appeared the German military were winning, bolstering the belief that the Prussian rule of arms was the best in the world. There were two areas of conflict with Paul von Hindenburg and Eric von Ludendorff succeeding in the east, while Germany faced what appeared to be a bloody stalemate in the west. Falkenhayn had failed to bring France to heel, the British stood alongside the French, and there was always the fear the Americans would arrive. The Germans had not collaborated well with their allies with little communication with the Austrians, and Italy left the Triple Alliance in 1915. The naval conflict prepared long in advance failed, and although having some success at the Battle of Jutland the German navy stayed in port thereafter because of the Royal Navy strength, who were also causing serious economic problems for Germany by blocking imports. It was no better for the German Army who were spending more time on defence. The problem was that there had been no serious planning for a long bitter war, and soldiers' lives were being sacrificed at an exponential rate as the months passed. This included the lack of economic foresight and there was a considerable lack of food supplies and other essential resources. This was also true of other countries, but Germany was fighting in the east and the west, to the south a weak Austria and a defecting Italy, and the British Royal Navy still ruled the waves despite German U-boats. The once angry German unions were patriotic and ruled out strikes, but as in the west the industrial companies profited, and were hardly taxed, as in pre-war days. The agricultural industry was hit by poor harvests, and with the conscription to arms there were fewer workers; prices rose as did inflation. This was no longer the anticipated war fought elsewhere, waiting for the return of a victorious army, this type of warfare touched upon the lives of every member of the German population, both the personal suffering of family deaths and in the economic collapse. The initial feelings in all countries that the war was necessary and welcomed soon started to fade. When opposition started to surface it was shut down as fast as possible and countered by encouraging patriotism and publishing letters from frontline soldiers, which soon stopped as the letters later reflected a life the propagandist experts dare not use. In May 1916 there was a major protest meeting in Berlin based on 'bread, freedom, peace' but the ringleaders were soon arrested. Other protesting demonstrators soon followed this effort being mainly concerned about the starvation levels. It was not long before Germans at the front were calling themselves 'front [line] pigs', (*frontschein*).

The faith and racist bigotry continued with Protestant and Catholic regiments, with their denominational padres all preaching victory, condemning the enemy, and many Catholics hoping this would heal the long breach between themselves and the Protestants, which looked hopeful, until Pope Benedict XV wisely called for a negotiated peace. There were also Jewish regiments with some Jewish officers, and an estimated 12,000 died fighting for their country. Unlike their opponents the Germans did not deploy female doctors and nurses, again reflecting the attitudes of the Prussian dominated Empire. However, on the home front women were soon employed in industry out of sheer necessity. Nevertheless, the German army, despite essential shortages, did not mutiny like some French or disappear as the Russians managed, or fall apart as some elements of the Austrian army. However, as the ongoing crisis made it clear that Germany could not win, many Germans were happy to call it a day, and 'many others surrendered, disappeared during transport or while on leave, or pretended injury or illness. As many as 750,000 to one million may have avoided battle during the final months of the war, a covert military strike'.[8] The battlefront was appearing to be a lost cause, but at home the economic failures made food so short there were serious malnutrition problems in the civilian population.

On the political front Ludendorff has been described as forming a military dictatorship, which for some felt that this was the only solution, although he was not a dictator. He and Hindenburg tended to reflect a popularity achieved by the sacrifices of the army, and the success they had managed in the eastern sector. A right-wing party was encouraged to grow (nearly one million members) demanding annexation of territories with extremists living off racial prejudice and anti-Semitism, some of the leading figures were Protestant clergy, and one of the members was Anton Drexel, the founder of the Nazi Party. They were supported by the government with funding, indicating that a clear link was being formed, reflecting the days of the empire.

Ludendorff at first wanted the proposed armistice accepted and then changed his mind. When it was clear the western allies had to be met, Ludendorff was compelled to resign and on 9 November 1918, he was replaced by General Karl Groener, who with Hindenburg, informed Wilhelm II that he had to go, and on 11 November 1918, the war finished.

The German population of this generation had experienced many changes in their lives, many aspects of which were common to other countries, but the political experience of being governed or controlled by an aristocratic leadership was a major factor, which was more a feature of the Russian way of life, and who by this time had revolted successfully against this form of control. France had extricated itself from the aristocracy after their 1789 revolution, and Britain had developed a form of democracy based on a constitutional monarchy, but with a House of Lords. The early twentieth century underlined that national politics is extraordinarily complex and with no easy answer. France had experienced the rise of Napoleon after the revolution, Britain felt the influence of the old class patriots who were now part of the wealthy landowning class, Russia's bold attempt at communism rapidly degenerated into a form of totalitarian state as it had been under the Tsars. In Italy and Spain as the years unfolded Mussolini and Franco would be dictators, and for many years ongoing into this century the nature of how man governs its own country remains a major issue. In America there was some hope, with a vast number of fleeing European refugees seeking a better way of life, but the wealthy also held sway.

There seems no doubt that the German population experience had been deeply influenced first by being a new country, then living under a despotic regime controlled by a Prussian monarchy, first led by Bismarck and then in the hands of Wilhelm II. There seems no doubt that this Prussian monarch, supported by the inbred sense of unquestionable Prussian loyalty, lacked any leadership direction as his life revolved around himself and not the people; he would have been better suited for a more primitive tribal leadership. His sense of self-importance and grandeur was supported by the Prussian demand of loyalty even though he led the wider population into a state of total collapse. As such the German public were brought up on a diet of monarchical despotism which gave them the agony of the First World War and the collapse of 1918 leaving them in an even more delicate and bewildering complex situation. This period of 1870–1918 is all part of a vast jigsaw which should help in providing a form of corporate 'mind-set', or 'frame of mind' which indicates established attitudes concerning values and a general political outlook.

Post 1918, The Weimar Republic

Despite the difficulties of poor political leadership, Germany in 1914 appeared a well-balanced and wealthy country, but after losing the war the monarchy was replaced with a new democratic government, followed by economic depression and financial collapse, not helped by a world-shattering financial collapse a few years later. At times Germany was in a state of chaos, riots, and generally unsettled at the political level. Their old leaders and military commanders had been seriously discredited, and it was accepted the system of government had to change, with the Social Democrats carrying the greatest support in the electorate. They made it known they wanted to make social and economic changes, while underlining they were not copying the Russian revolution, namely they were not communists. When elections were held for a Constitutional National Assembly, they were the major party with Friedrich Ebert as the President of the Reich, and a parliamentary democracy was thereby founded. There were too many parties and often dominance could only be achieved by temporary political alliance. The Social Democrats under Ebert tried to stop Germany plunging into a civil war and avoid starvation. They also led the way in allowing women to vote which clearly indicated the intentions of forming a sound democratic system and a good social order.

However, their first task was the vexed question of the Treaty of Versailles, dictated by the victors, and which amounted to Germany ceding some of its territories which weakened the Germany economy.* The demand for reparations increased the gathering economic turmoil, which was not helped by the German currency devalued by war debts. The most obnoxious clause related to German War-Guilt, which was rejected by nearly every German. It would take time for the West to understand the anger caused by this particular expression of guilt. Later in 1939 John Colville, one of Churchill's Private Secretaries, anticipating an early British victory in the Second World War, noted in his diary there should be no *guilt clause* in the next final peace treaty.[9] It was immediately apparent that many Germans took this guilt clause as a personal insult and not without justification. It was felt by most that Germany had come to the support of Austria from where the First World War had its origins, and other nations had excitedly joined the fray. It is difficult not to have some sympathy for the Germans at being pinpointed with this guilt clause. The German representatives at the international meeting had strongly opposed the clause, but they had no option and carried the blame at home, being accused of being political puppets. The Versailles Treaty was universally condemned in Germany making it the one political issue on which there was common German accord. As Churchill later wrote, it was 'natural that a proud people vanquished in war should strive to rearm themselves as soon as possible'.[10] Churchill was writing with the benefit of hindsight, but the 1919 Daily Herald cartoonist, named Will Dyson, had sketched a picture of the Versailles gathering, with a baby crying in the corner with the label '1940 Class [conscript]'.[11] It was a highly perceptive political cartoon which underlined that the more astute could foresee what might happen as a result of the Versailles Treaty. As noted above, the new German government had no option but to accept the terms of Versailles, and thereafter carried the blame for the appalling consequences.

The anger was widespread in Germany, and the army felt they had not been defeated but betrayed, and the myth of 'the stab in the back' (*Dolchstosslegende*), mainly blaming the wealthy Jews, which soon found its roots in German thinking, but with no justification. The Weimar politicians also suffered, as they had no choice, but the blame was laid at their feet. As early as 13 March 1920 right-wing extremists produced the Kapp-Putsch in Berlin wanting to abolish parliamentary democracy, and many accustomed to the old regime continued to fight the principle of a democratic republic. It all led to a growth of right-wing fury, assassinations, (Walther Rathenau was killed by right-wing extremists in June 1922) with growing hostility between the right and left-wing parties. With the benefit of hindsight, it was clear that the influence of the Wilhelmine years

* These territories included: Alsace and Lorraine, North Schleswig, Posen, West Prussia, part of Silesia. The Saar district was placed under French control for 15 years.

was still prevalent, and the Versailles Treaty had not helped. For the general population it was not only entering a period of poverty and hunger, but it must have felt deeply depressing, their humiliated country seemingly sinking into the world of impoverishment and having a pariah status. The hatred engendered during the First World War turned the so-called armistice into an issue of revenge and blaming. The problem was money, as all countries were in debt and every country owed money to others, having informed their respective publics that the day would come when the enemy would have to pay.

As early as the 1920 Reichstag elections, the gathering forces of the right-wing reflecting anti-republican feelings were evident, and it was not helped by the economic poverty across Germany as living standards plummeted. The reparations could not be met, with French and Belgium troops occupying the Ruhr in January 1923, and the German government offering passive resistance, by instructing industrial and other keyworkers not to cooperate. Even the Allies started to recognise that in its current state Germany could not pay the demanded reparations. There were attempts made at an international level to bring financial stability (Dawes Plan of 1924 and later the Young Plan 1929) recognising that only a stable economy could repay the required debts, and for a time this seemed to work both at a national and individual level. As the 1920s developed there was some hope that industrial and social restoration was underway, often helped by foreign investment, which was soon shattered with the world's economic collapse-crisis of 1929. These early problems, from the Versailles Treaty to economic chaos, alienated some Germans while others started to lose confidence in the new system which led to vast changes in the voting patterns. Right-wing traditionalist parties of different forms appeared, which given Germany's background since 1870 was not that surprising, but this was also reflected on the left-wing of the political divide especially the German Communist Party (KPD) which had emerged from the Spartakus League (Marxist revolutionary movement) and played a key role between 1918 and 1933. In the middle area stood those who aimed at civil liberties based on Christian principles.

The inflation and starvation levels in Germany touched everyone's lives, especially the workers and those of low income. It led to the cartoon of a man leaving a wheelbarrow full of money on the street, when he returned the money was still there, but the wheelbarrow had been stolen. In France and Britain poverty and unemployment were rife, but not as serious as that touching the German population. In January 1923 it took 18,000 marks to buy one USA dollar, by July it as 353,000 and continued to rise until November when it rose to 4.2 trillion, turning the national currency into meaningless paperwork.[12] There were signs of hope of international acceptance and growth when the

Paris Air Traffic Agreement allowed the newly formed Lufthansa into their organisation. Germany had not slipped back intellectually, and in '1920, fully 44 per cent of all scientific publications in the world were written in German'.[13] One of the major interests during this era was the study of eugenics stimulated by population policies. There had been severe losses of people during the war years, there was a decline in the birthrate, and concern about the role of women. German eugenics started to focus on how to produce a healthier population, raising questions of sterilisation, abortion, and race. When the Nazis came to power even a young woman born deaf from deaf parents was obliged to be sterilised, despite the fact she was an intelligent woman of German birth.[14] It was, morally, a potentially dangerous area and attempts to pass eugenic laws were unsuccessful. This form of study was not confined to Germany and was of later interest to the Nazi regime in its immoral pursuit of a pure but mythical Aryan race. As elsewhere in the world the role of women as home and family makers or workers or being in the professions was coming under scrutiny. The new Weimar Republic had shown considerable forward thinking by granting women the vote.

The Political Jigsaw Puzzle

The Weimar Republic under Gustav Stresemann worked hard at its foreign policy and soon Germany was not treated as a pariah state and helped put the memory of war on the shelf. There were international agreements, reductions in reparations, and Germany was regaining some status. However, the domestic political scene was not helped by the wranglings of the many political parties which often joined forces to oppose government measures, and in 1928 the fifteenth government of the Republic collapsed over a mundane issue relating to schools.

The question of politicians wrangling for power was somewhat novel to Germany, but it was a feature of politics, not only in Germany but in other democratic states. A couple of years before he died Max Weber (a sociologist, historian, political economist, and outstanding intellectual of his day) explained that 'competition among party machines leads to an emphasis on the demagogic effect of the leader's personality, on his will and particularly on his speech'.[15] This feature of politics is still apparent to this day, as many voters tend to turn towards the so-called charismatic leader. In Germany there were many different parties, some divided by minor differences of approach or because of their respective leaders, but the greatest rift was between the two extremes of the left and right-wings, who held strong appeals to the public because they were fervent in their approaches, and their policies were easily definable. The right-wing as exemplified by the NSDAP (Nazi Party) made a point of appealing to the younger generation infusing them with the promise of hope in the future because they were the party of youthful vigour. This was a useful ploy in what is best called a growing mass society, providing enthusiastic promises and ideals which could be easily grasped. It was not too surprising that with the impact of the immediate past, the Fatherland Party grew rapidly before it shut down. Often the government of the day could exercise control over public thinking with its control over what information it chose to make public, but growing political parties were able to challenge this feature of public opinion. The main fear for the Weimar government tended to be the left-wing threat with its neighbour Russia casting what was regarded as a dark shadow across central Europe. It was because of this that Ebert had asked the army to maintain order and thus the arrival of the *Freikorps* (Free Corps) mainly controlled by demobilised officers and enlisted men. This had the effect of alienating many of the government's supporters who disliked the thought of the military acting in a police role, not least because it was well-known that many senior commanders in the military were themselves deeply right-wing, still influenced by the Empire days. There were often attempted coups, with a failed bid to march on Berlin, and Hitler's well-known abortive attempt in the Munich putsch.

The days of the old Empire continued to cast its shadows over the next post-war generation during the days of the republic. The emergence of the class structure with workers and middle-class was more apparent, as were the old issues of Roman Catholics and Jews, which effected the voting patterns, and it has often been suggested that one of the Weimar Republic's main weaknesses was its failure to resolve these problems. Anti-Semitism with the new ridiculous claim of the 'stab in the back' tended to increase this unfair bigotry, and it was often reflected in German literature and even some films. Goebbels soon recognised this as a useful tool and mobilised it as a supporting ploy for the NSDAP. It had once been propagated by radical nationalists and it was revitalised by the Nazis, and there were soon violent attacks on Jews. Under the influence of the NSDAP and later the Nazi regime, supporters often accepted the legal discrimination against Jews, even if they did not appreciate the violence used against them. It was morally wrong and deeply obnoxious, but tragically racialism was worldwide. Apartheid was a feature of some American states, anti-Semitism was prevalent at various levels in many European countries, Russia, Poland, France, and Britain. This writer as a boy in the 1950s saw a notice for renting, but with the added note of 'No Irish, No Blacks, and No Dogs'. The Weimar Republic did not assert anti-Semitism, but its weakness enabled the rise of Nazism which made it a national policy, influencing the public with its vile propaganda. During the First World War German Jews had fought and died, and most of them considered themselves as German born and bred, and the Weimar period gave them some space to find their feet, but the failure of the republic brought irreparable damage on them as a community. In the same way the Catholics had been isolated, but they were as divided themselves as to where they stood; some remained right-wing, others supported the centre parties. If anything, the Church hierarchy leaned towards the right-wing but opposed the extremes, seeking a more authoritarian type of rule, and it was known that many Catholic clergy were anti-Semitic.[16]

From the point of view of the working classes, they were attracted between the Socialist and Communist parties, but there was a high degree of enmity between these two camps, not least because it was known by many that Moscow influenced the communists. The KPD (German Communist Party) was revolutionary in outlook wanting the overthrow of capitalism and always contemplating violence and civil war. Despite its success (especially in 1928) the KPD was excluded from government because of its fear of Bolshevism. The conservative elements, as usual, tended to live in the rural areas, knowing that the instability of economics and the social unrest was changing their ways of life and expectations. They appeared in a lost world, many not appreciating the Republic but rejecting the past, concerned about democracy yet with no outstanding viable ideas for the future. There was also a distinctive and widening gap between the variety of the conservative leaders and their people, giving the impression of being lost in an alien world, making them vulnerable to the influence of other parties. There were so many parties fluctuating in their relationships, that even the Socialist Party were by 1932 out of government. The Liberals failed to grow, the Centre appeared lost and vacillating, and the extremes started to muster strength.

The resentment of what was happening in a once proud country was continually fermenting, especially regarding the military, indicating the authority of the past had not vanished, epitomised after Ebert's death by the election of Field Marshal von Hindenburg as President, who was openly loyal to the abdicated Kaiser.* Germany was divided and unaccustomed to the new political system, and not helped after a period of economic recovery when the world had to face the 1929 economic crisis, which further induced a sharp 'radicalisation and polarisation in politics, which gradually crippled the democratic institutions'.[17] It was the economic crisis of 1929 which helped the re-election of Hindenburg. He was a deeply biased traditional man who appeared confused and tended to listen to military advisers such as Wilhelm Groener and Kurt von Schleicher, having 'become convinced that only a government above the parties would have the

* The President was elected for a term of seven years.

necessary determination to confront the deepening crisis', which was a dangerous step away from democracy.[18]

The extreme political wings were helped by the collapsing state of the middle-class who were fractured and losing direction. From 1930 onwards there was no longer a republican parliamentary majority. This meant the government depending on the Chancellor who acted on emergency decrees making him independent from the elected body, making that office of major importance. When the Reichstag could not reach a voting agreement the power fell to the Chancellor, and the new Weimar system started to look more like the governmental system during the Kaiser's time. More elections did not help the deflated system, and many Germans started to despair and started to look to some form or authoritarian leadership. The right-wing managed to form a political alliance which re-elected Hindenburg as President in 1931, who decided to put his trust in the strong anti-republican Adolf Hitler, leader of the National Socialist German Workers Party, the NSDAP, mistakenly believing a mere corporal could be controlled and contained.

It was not just the loss of the war which turned Germany upside down, but the demands of the reparations caused such misery, that it increased the support for the right-wing who had turned to witch-hunting those democrats who had been obliged to sign the treaty, and for accepting the massive demand of reparations and the guilt clause. The ensuing poverty and mayhem played into the hands of the right-wing extremists who were opposed by their opposite numbers on the left-wing. Historians hold varying views, but there seems little doubt in this writer's mind that the imposition of the Versailles Treaty by a revengeful West helped pave the way to chaos and assist the utilisation of those elitest traditions of the Prussian period by the Nazi regime. It should be noted that this is just one view, first supported by John Maynard Keynes the famous economist who promptly condemned the treaty, but others argued the debt was realistic and Germany was simply averse to paying the bill, and 'yet there was always a good deal of suspicion (especially in France) that German protestations of insolvency were fraudulent, or at least exaggerated'.[19]

The Weimar Republic had started with the best if not idyllic motives to establish a sound democratic system, but it could not cope with the financial burdens which meant, understandably, a loss of confidence by the public. Heinrich Brüning of the Centre Party was named as Chancellor in 1930, but his policies failed, and the Communists grew in numbers and poverty and unemployment increased, and he was dubbed the 'hunger Chancellor'. Brüning was replaced by Franz von Papen surrounded by what has been dubbed the 'cabinet of barons'. Papen withdrew Parliament's powers and changed the electoral laws and there was no more genuine republic. Hitler manipulated the jigsaw elements of the political powers, and when Hindenburg dismissed von Papen, he was followed by von Schleicher who was also dismissed, and Hitler formed the national government. The bewildered German public had experienced the bad rule of the German Empire, suffered the humiliation of defeat and the economic consequences, and it was a time in German history when no one could be sure who was in government and whether life would improve. For many it must have felt as if Hitler were the new political messiah with all his promises and his ability to persuade others.

It is perhaps easy to criticise the Weimar Republic as being too flimsy, their ideals were high and expectations for a better future were genuine. From the very start they had been obliged to face the Treaty of Versailles which transpired to be a matter of dictation by the victors, and the 'demobilisation of roughly six million soldiers who flooded into Germany…the abrupt termination of wartime production; the huge overhang of war-related debt' to say nothing about the loss of territory and facing first a national financial collapse, only to be followed by the 1929 world market failure.[20] Under these circumstances it was perhaps not too surprising that the Weimar Republic started to disintegrate. Another factor appeared to be that the German electorate, because of the economic crisis and ensuing poverty soon deemed the new system to be failing and turned to the right-wing, with its apparent adherence to the old imperial days. Others have claimed that the Weimar Republic had pushed the boundaries of welfare too much leading to financial damage. This would be like accusing an individual of being too compassionate and kind, but personal poverty in the masses could not be ignored. The impact on the post-war generation was immense in terms of suffering, and the population, as in many countries, turned to a leader who promised a better future. In July 1931 the Hoover Moratorium suspended the international debts, and a year later at the Lausanne Conference the German reparations were cancelled, but it was too late for those who were impoverished and unemployed.

The Nazi Party had promised an end to divisions, talked of a folk-community instead of a class-society, and rebuilding Germany, and they must have appeared as a lifeline to many Germans. It has, however, been proposed that the Weimar Republic had entered a self-destruction mode long before Hitler had grown in electoral strength. The economic crisis had cracked the basic structure of a democratic republic which had always faced those who objected to its existence. Parliamentary process had finished when Brüning had accepted the Chancellorship without a parliamentary majority and soon Hitler had been given the opportunity to finish the job in 1933, when the conservative elements supported him.[21]

The Military and Politics, Post-1918

Technically the German military commanders have always claimed they were not involved in politics, and in post-Second World War memoirs they always persist in this claim. They may not have cast votes in elections, but like any normal human being they had views and opinions and would have discussed them. Some have argued, with possible justification, that there were those in the military who never moved away from the mindset of the Empire days, resented the democratic effort, and they waited for an authoritative leader to which they were accustomed.

Defeat in 1918 for them and many Germans was humiliating, and despite the Versailles Treaty restrictions reducing the Germany navy and limiting the army to 100,000 men, they almost instantly started to re-organise their military in a clandestine fashion. The leading figure in this scenario was General von Seeckt, who curiously was anti-Semitic, although his wife was Jewish. The defeat and humiliation of the Treaty of Versailles drove many military officers towards the right-wing, where they had always stood being part of the Empire, mainly because it appeared to offer the best route to recovery.

Seeckt was probably the most important post-Great War general who deeply influenced what happened in the German military in the interwar years, and his influence on others was considerable. Seeckt 'succeeded in rebuilding its [the army's] spirit by making each regiment the tradition-bearer of several of the old, which he intended would be reborn in better times, and by teaching the officers that they were the guardians of Germany's past and future greatness'.[22] Many future generals and field marshals (the classical example being Field Marshal Albert Kesselring) came under his pervasive influence. Seeckt organised co-operation with Russia for military development, which was technically illegal because it contravened the Versailles Treaty. Not only did they agree to build planes, train pilots, and army officers, they also established a German/Russian joint stock company Bersol, near Samara, to build a chemical factory in order to make poison gas.[23] Seeckt's singular aim was for 'Germany to recapture the prestige, powers and territories of which it had been stripped'.[24] When in Russia, because no tanks could be built they trained with mocked-up cars and small lorries. Later German pilots would train with the Italian air force, which in those days was regarded as one of the best in the world.

Seeckt, who had a major influence on the emerging German military commanders, had been a member of the delegation in Paris, and constantly worked against the treaty, never wavering in his conviction 'that Germany needed to recapture the prestige, powers and territories of which it had been stripped'.[25] Like the Russians he distrusted Poland believing co-operation with the Bolsheviks would help Germany. There were trade arrangements between the two countries, both regarded as pariah states, but Seeckt and his staff were engaged in top-secret collaboration. The Soviets needed to rebuild their military, and the Germans needed space and secrecy for the same reason. Such was the growing relationship that the Dawes Plan was viewed by the Soviet leadership as a bribe, to bring Germany back under western influence.[26]

Many officers saw rearmament as a natural part of a recovery process, but being of military background, they often regarded war as a resolution to problems. The German right-wing distrust of the communists or anything near the left-wing or even the central parties, emphasised the cynical attitude of Seeckt, and many other senior officers, in seeking Russian collaboration. Despite co-operating with Russia for training programmes, they feared the Bolsheviks, although the Soviets later became a partner in the Polish war of 1939, and soon a victim in the long-planned Operation *Barbarossa*. The work done in Russia and Germany at this time set the stage, so 'when Hitler came to power in 1933, he found all the technical preparations for rearmament ready, thanks to the *Reichswehr*', the official name for the Germany military during this time.[27]

Seeckt, who would eventually arrive at the judgement that Hitler's personality was distasteful, influenced other future commanders to obey in blind obedience the elected politicians, and behave as one 'who took care to keep out of politics'.[28] Seeckt was a dominant and persuasive man who influenced his many army officers, with an attitude towards the Weimar Republic which 'ranged from an angry denial of its legitimacy at worst to lukewarm support at best, a tragic state of affairs that contributed in no small way to the downfall of the republic and the rise of Adolf Hitler.'[29]

Many regarded Seeckt as a model for the younger generation of officers, the driving force behind the Luftwaffe's origins, and it may be claimed that he was 'the real founder of the new German Air Force; already in 1920 he was convinced that military aviation would someday be revived in Germany...he therefore secreted a small group of regular officers...in the various sections which dealt with aviation in his ministry...notably Felmy, Sperrle, Wever, Kesselring and Stumpf."[30] He never looked for top pilots because 'he needed planners and builders, not aces'.[31] Given the state of post-war Germany 'von Seeckt was known as *the sphinx* within the Army because of his arrogant secretiveness, and he seemed to have a hopeless task', but he succeeded.[32]

Liddel-Hart proposed that although Seeckt died three years before the war, and retired ten years before that, he remained the single German general who had the greatest influence on the Second World War.[33] Seeckt's authority during this period of reconstruction was immense. 'His polished manners and pleasant personality contrasted with the domineering Prussians such as Ludendorff, making him a more attractive proposition to the leaders of the new Republic. He appeared to keep the army out of politics, but he pursued an aggressive Right-wing nationalist agenda 'cloaking his military development schemes, as well as the half-veiled political activities in which numerous officers of the older school indulged'.[34] Seeckt's military manuals were based on the German Army being more than 100,000, and centred on the premise that every action should be based on surprise; this contrasted with the French manuals, which reflected the slow moving tactics of the First War. Above all Seeckt re-established the army and eventually 'removed the danger presented [to the army] by the *Freikorps* by dissolving it'.[35]

Seeckt encouraged all officers to be non-political. but it could be argued that 'the Seeckt-pattern professional became a modern Pontius Pilate, washing his hands of all responsibility for the orders to be executed'.[36] The concept of the non-political-soldier can be carried too far: General Siegfried Westphal wrote that 'the soldiers' political ignorance rendered them blind to the satanic side of his [Hitler's] character and actions'.[37] The officer class did not vote and it has been argued that 'political isolation encouraged political naivety, with many senior officers becoming apolitical rather than unpolitical'.[38] In his time, Bismarck was well aware that army officers, though pretending to be non-political, formed camarillas to influence the monarchy 'as they did in Russia or Prussia ... in such extreme cases officer politics takes the form of conspiracy.'[39] Attitudes towards the military and politics has always been divided, from Seeckt's apparent no contact, to the political commissars of the Soviet Union, to a later commentator like Janowitz, stating that the 'military commander must develop more political orientation, in order to explain the goals of military activities to his staff and subordinates'.[40] Seeckt and his officers' views were fundamentally dishonest, because it was a pretence that they had no interest in politics, when they were a secret cabal, often described as a state within a state.

Many senior German commanders always looked back with self-serving reflections, often trying to convince post-1945 listeners that they were politically neutral. Seeckt was undoubtedly involved in political intrigue, and quite capable of manipulating politicians. A traditional monarchist, he laid the foundations of a strong *Reichswehr*, and concealed the forbidden leadership of the outlawed General Staff, under the ubiquitous name of *Truppenamt* (Troop Office). An elitist, Seeckt surrounded himself with the best. He frequently ignored the Weimar government, and 'took major military decisions without going to the Reichstag', but he made a political blunder in allowing the eldest son of the German Crown-Prince to take part in an army manoeuvre, and this finished him in 1926.[41]

Seeckt left behind many senior officers deeply influenced by his careful diplomatic manoeuvrings and pleasant personality, who followed his line of pretending to have no interest in politics. Seeckt had found nothing 'incongruous in pledging the support of the armed forces to the Weimar Republic and in making it clear that he would not permit the army to interfere or become enmeshed in the sphere of domestic politics'.[42]

Seeckt with his chosen disciples worked with the aim of establishing an army containing 102 divisions, a breaching of the Versailles Treaty, which many regarded as patriotic. During the Weimar Republic, and through all the political strife as Hitler brokered his way to power, Seeckt's officers were rebuilding a technically advanced and efficient war-machine. Part of their planning was the preparation of Seeckt's insistence on surprise and speed, combined with air power. The core of Seeckt's strategy 'was founded on the harnessing of modern technology to armed warfare, and the utilisation of motorised armoured vehicles supported by self-propelled guns, aircraft and infantry'.[43] *Blitzkrieg* as a means of warfare remained effective until the Allies grasped its nature; 'it was a tactical innovation rather than a revolutionary form of warfare'.[44] Seeckt, and his military followers produced a professional expertise which would be used by a corrupt regime which by the early 1930s was in the ascendancy.

Seeckt's influence in the military was undeniable, but he was no Nazi, and it has been noted that after once meeting Hitler in 1923, he said 'we are one in our aim; only our paths were different'.[45] It was also noteworthy that he had little time for Hitler finding him somewhat tasteless. After his dismissal in 1926 he worked as the German liaison officer in China and died in 1936. In terms of this study, it underlined that under Seeckt's influence the German military tended to follow his lead which reflected his adherence to the old Empire, which had led to his dismissal in 1926. This clearly indicated the right-wing influence which persisted in the military despite the pretence of having no political views. The proud Prussian tradition was thereby kept alive in the German military, and their traditional efficiency helped build a force which was sound and would be used by the extreme right-wing. Generally, it meant that many senior military officers could influence their men even though seemingly they ignored politics, and with the dangerous Prussian rule of obeying all orders and being of a right-wing nature by their politics concealed within their structure.

1933–39 Why the Nazis were Popular

To call someone a Nazi today is the worst possible insult anywhere in the world, based on the policy of the Holocaust, countless massacres, widespread destruction, and the sheer unbelievable brutality of the regime. As such the question must be asked as to how they came to power. The above exploration of pre-1933 Germany indicated a country first controlled by a monarchical despotism and defeat in a major war, followed by serious weaknesses in the Weimar's economic and social efforts, mainly caused by an economy wrecked by demands for reparations and rocked by the global economic crisis of 1929. Poverty was rife and a feeling of hatred was brewing against those held responsible, namely the lead politicians of the republic. This soon became the rallying call for those in opposition to the government and democracy. Hitler came to power because these weaknesses and the political machinations of the day portrayed him as a possible saviour for a country in distress. It has been argued it was negative language which brought him to power, namely that they were supported because of what they opposed rather than what they favoured.[46] The NSDAP started to form a formidable majority by 1930 with over 13 million supporters, especially among the young badly hit by unemployment and lack of prospects. They also found support among many in the middle-classes and many traditional areas who were distressed by what they perceived as their lives being ruined by political mayhem, and therefore seeking any form of direct leadership. It appeared that the other parties of the centre and left had failed to understand this major wish of the population. The Nazis capitalised on the old so-called values such as the place of women in the homes and the culpability of Jews, which the Weimar ideals had tried to rectify, especially with the status of women. It was as if people wanted a return to the old days when memories seemed to suggest 'it was better in the past'. The NSDAP made extravagant promises on economic growth and made this a priority in their early years. The SA (Brown Shirts) street battles with the communists also brought in some support from those who feared Bolshevism as it was appearing in Russia.

There is no question that the NSDAP was well organised, young, pro-active, and supported by a clever if not astute propaganda machine led by Goebbels. They appealed to the young of the day with their youth organisations and used this as a means of influence. The Hitler Youth was enjoyable for many youngsters, even though it was soon clear that it was not the Boy Scout movement, but a potential training ground for indoctrinating Nazi views and a means of building up the military. The Nazis were good at staging public events, the cost of which indicated they were finding support from the monied classes, many of them suffering from the same delusion as some people at the top of society who believed that Hitler could be controlled, much of this driven by economic instability. The same had happened in Russia where poverty and a class-ridden society governed by the elite had led to Communism, another fear which the NSDAP managed to calm such concerns because they were strongly right-wing. For many Germans, such were the circumstances of the day, only the Nazis appeared to offer hope for a better future. It is all too easy with the benefit of hindsight to see it was a mistake, but Max Weber's argument that the demagogic effect of the leader's personality was critical was true in 1930, and it remains a worldwide feature of political life to this day. Nevertheless, during the 1930s the Nazi regime grew in popularity, and had many important visitors from abroad including foreign national figure heads and statesmen, as well as hosting the 1936 Berlin Olympics giving the public a sense that Germany was becoming internationally important again.

When, in the post-war years of the Second World War, the brutality and sheer evil of the Nazi regime became widely known reactions in Germany differed, sometimes they were met by grim silence, some by embarrassment, and some with shock because many remained ignorant of the precise details of Nazi atrocity. It must not be forgotten that in its election campaigns and propaganda the NSDAP were not mentioning a war or genocide, but economic uplift, an end to unemployment, and a sense of community. Even the promise to overturn the Versailles Treaty attracted a larger vote from retired nationalists, because for the average German it was so utterly unfair. Even an appeal to the masses to change the morals and culture of the perverted Weimar culture, whose night clubs were no different from Paris, New York, and London. The Nazis even courted the Churches, especially the Protestant denomination. They had support from the young with promises of a better future, the wealthy classes saw the possibility of profit from their economic ideas, and the middle-class sought the promised security. It is known that some support came from a dissatisfied working class who voted for them, but none of this support was able to foresee the concealed horrors that the NSDAP would bring upon the country, until it was too late.

In his book on the history of modern Germany, Frank Tipton takes time to explore the reactions of a man and woman in 1965 who had lived during the Nazi years.[47] They had much in common, both denied any direct allegiance, both accepted the Jews had been badly treated but added 'they had done bad things', both had enjoyed the youth movements and its camaraderie, for the man this was again emphasised when fighting on the Eastern front, and both saw the economy improve and both explained they had only heard Hitler on the radio. In the new post-war generation, they were trying to distant themselves from the past, they had still accepted the Nazi propaganda about Jews built on the post-war Great War claim of the 'stab in the back'. They had enjoyed the Nazi youth activities not realising then or later they were designed to capture the younger generation's allegiance, and they had recognised the benefits of economic improvement. For both of them it was now a closed era, and the door was shut on the past. This writer taught young German teenagers 25 years after the Second World War finished, and he can recall that none of them knew much about the war, and from their curiosity knew it was not just grim silence. As this exploration unfolds it will try and understand the German public and individual reactions to the Nazi regime both among supporters and the critics, but first it is necessary to outline the Nazi rise to total power.

Life in Germany under Nazi Rule, 1933–39

Despite the views of a few historians there can be little doubt that life in Germany during the 1930s was dominated by the dictator Adolf Hitler. Many Germans had seen him as redeeming the so-called values of a Germany, of 'make Germany Great Again' and bringing in wealth and raising living standards. His ability at giving speeches, his assertive personality all brought hope for a better future. Curiously, Hitler rarely read governmental papers nor wrote any, always happy to dictate his views to others and issue verbal commands. He and his cabal always built the picture that he was virtually infallible, and even Hitler believed that Providence protected him, although whether he saw this as divine intervention is unlikely. He used plebiscites as his main platform to prove he had the backing of the people, first in the German withdrawal from the League of Nations in October 1933. These plebiscites, overlooked by the security police, gave the impression of total national backing. This clever political device soon made it clear to those conservative-minded elite that Hitler could be controlled was a total fallacy. Papen had boasted that Hitler would be no problem, intimating he would be like putty in their hands, one of the grossest political prognostications ever made. During the early years of his rule, Hitler made many public appearances exhibiting himself to the devoted crowds, nearly always organised by Goebbels, who arranged the turnout was maximum with excited supporters waving swastika flags, and then the films of this public rapture were sent out worldwide. It was not until the Second World War turned against Germany and the strategic bombing of cities occurred, that many people became more cynical about their Führer, but by this time he was not in the public eye but always in one of his map rooms.

However, in the early years many thought he had been true to his word, especially in the economic sphere when life suddenly improved as promised. The Nazis established a job creation programme which included public work schemes which did little with the economic situation, but it lowered the unemployment rate by offering wages which certainly increased Nazi popularity. By 1936 most of the unemployed were back at work and over the next few years the economy appeared to boom.[48] Hjalmar Schacht was president of the Reichsbank in 1931 and by March 1933 was the economics minister and brought forth more expertise than his Nazi overlords could muster. Their only concern was directing the investments to political and later military ends. Women were persuaded to leave employment and many unemployed were 'directed' to work in agriculture, with the special intention of moving young people away into a safer political environment. Meanwhile Fritz Todt was responsible for the massive motorway projects across Germany which created a major work programme, with Todt cleverly arguing that it had major economic benefits and would be of use for the rapid movement of the military. Under Göring a four-year plan was established, a form of state-planned economy as in Russia. As a consequence, Schacht lost his position and was replaced by Walter Funk. Schacht also lost his position in the Reichsbank (1939) as the Nazi regime, having boosted the people's morale, took full control. To the average citizen life seemed to have improved in this critical sphere on employment and income, and Hitler appeared to many as a man of his word.

The morally unacceptable attack on Jews was welcomed by many, by some because they had been taken in by Streicher's anti-Semitic articles and cartoons, for others because they had believed the ridiculous 'stab in the back' myth. Others took on board the Nazi propaganda that Jews were mainly Bolshevist, sub-human, enemies of the state and corrupt, and were supported by a worldwide conspiracy of International Jewry. Such was the power of modern propaganda many thought the Jew was a dangerous element in the world. The attacks on Jewish shops and businesses epitomised by *Kristallnacht* were welcomed by some German businesses and shop keepers as it increased their profit margins, and many were simply jealous because hard working Jews appeared to be better off. When Jews were removed from positions in government offices, the medical professions, and universities there were some who saw this as a possibility for prompt promotion to replace them. It was little wonder that the Nuremberg Race Laws were accepted, and those who did not like what was happening found it best to stay quiet for fear of being denounced to the Gestapo. It was all portrayed as part of the German effort to crush the enemy on the inside, the *Volksfeind*.

In a similar vein, the Nazi regime rapidly fastened onto the so-called science of eugenics, often based on medical grounds of eliminating hereditary illnesses, both physical and mental. It was given the safety umbrella of science and medicine, but it would rapidly lead to the immoral concept of creating the pure Aryan race, not only eliminating the sub-human Jews, but anyone who might breed further problems.

At a social level Goebbels was the prime mover even in what should be considered good art, good music and what literature should be read, having books written by Jews banned with having bonfires of such works making it more like the English Guy Fawke's night. Many young people by fault of age were often deeply impressionable, inculcated with Nazi ideas through the organised youth movements created and controlled by the regime, and they were swept along by a misplaced idealism.

The general public knew little of the military machinations, and many followed the regime willingly. If the past wants an answer from the present, many German people had been hoodwinked by a seeming economic recovery, and virtually brainwashed by a propaganda machine, even allowing themselves to be convinced that their Jewish next-door neighbour was an infectious disease. The impressionable young, the greedy, and many others had been caught up in an idealism which was corrupt. There was little by the early 1930s that those who were critical of the growing Nazi dominance could do. If they objected their lives could be ruined if not destroyed. The supposed untouchable judiciary, normally a separate entity within the state to ensure fairness, was subject to the Führer's instructions, and no judge had any right to question Hitler's judgements and opinions, and there was no right of appeal against decisions made by the People's Court (*Volksgerichtshof*) in April 1934. In 1936 the normal criminal police were blended into the Security Police, the SS police under Himmler had unrestricted powers, and it was widely known that the Gestapo would knock on a door if a neighbour had overheard any criticism of the Nazi regime. The Night of the Long Knives, the growth of concentration camps for the regime's opponents was known about, and there were a growing number of accounts of serious bullying of individuals regarded as Nazi critics.

In the remains of the Reich SS Leadership and the Reich Main Security Office (Albrechtstrasse) stands today an exhibition of the relics and photographs and documents of these years. There is a photograph of a local councillor of the SPD being taken into custody by the SA in a humiliating procession watched by a curious crowd (2 May 1933), and on the next page a lorry full of prominent Social Democrats being taken into protective custody.[49] This is rapidly followed by a photograph of a cinema owner called Karl Kiesewetter who had criticised the NSDAP and who was denounced and paraded through the streets carrying the sign 'I have insulted the government'.[50] The catalogue which reflects the exhibition is packed tight with such pictures, including one journalist who was a newspaper editor along with a KPD member being released from protective custody to prove they were not ill-treated, but the photograph revealed both men had black eyes and had been brutally beaten. They were well dressed to look good, but the photograph revealed the unpleasant truth.

The Nazi regime had convinced many people of a better economic future, hope for a renewed Germany, a united people and Goebbels ensured it was all covered with smiles and flowers and seemingly good will. Many joined the Party for a better future, and some because it was useful if not necessary to make any progress. Quite recently on the news (6 October 2023) the Dutch government confirmed that Prince Bernhard (a one-time German aristocrat and the prince consort for many decades after the Second World War) had been a Nazi Party member, but probably because he found it necessary to be associated with them on the grounds that 'at the start you had to take part a little way in one way or another', because had he opposed it would have been difficult to pass the university examinations.

Prince Bernhard's original NSDAP membership card.

It did not take long for those people who were opposed to the NSDAP to understand they were in serious danger if they spoke openly or even confided in a so-called friend or neighbour. From the very start of the Nazi rise to power, they had supporters, but the opposition which existed was silenced by the Nazi exercise of fear and terror; the German people had been divided into supporters and those terrified into submission, whether as a young aristocrat like Prince Berhard or a shopkeeper.

Rise of the Führer state

Hitler demanded another election to prove the public were behind him and his projected policies, and he moved swifty and without any subtlety. For him it was a political matter to gain total power, whereas for the German people it was about overcoming the economic and political crisis which had confronted the Republic after 1929, and which had rapidly led to the abolition of the democratic system. It was the single-mindedness and organisational skills which had marked the NSDAP as offering some hope for the future, in a country sharply divided in opinions, with so many parties unable to find a common ground which seemed to rule out any form of consensus, so the republic lost its basis for power to the delight of those elements which always opposed it as a workable system.

There is no question that Hitler had some form of charismatic hold over those he met and managed to display this when addressing crowds seeking a better future. When the original NSDAP leader Gregor Strasser had resigned in December 1932, Hitler had radically changed the Party, focusing on its propaganda to gain power on the grounds of creating a new Germany based on his charismatic leadership. He was virtually creating a cult around himself which attracted a probable third of the people which grew with the clever use of propaganda. Hitler used his personality as the focus of attention and attraction. This charismatic hold was almost magnetic, and years later during the war it was still prominent, known by some cynics as the 'command bug' when he was able to impress, bolster, and convince military commanders facing battlefield defeat.

He had produced his own cabal, the unholy trinity of Göring, Goebbels, and Himmler. All three of these top Nazi leaders tried to build their own empires within the state, Göring being the one who made most progress with the economy, police, and Luftwaffe under his control, Goebbels interested his sense of self-importance in the world of propaganda and needing total control of anything 'going public'. Himmler grew the various divisions of the SS making him one of the most feared men. Himmler assumed he was the most important but Goebbels and Göring were politically astute regarding the political machinations of this time. Some historians have tried to argue that Hitler was not the major causative force, but this seems almost fatuous given the nature of his strongly warped personality which many mistakenly believed they could use. Hitler appeared as an authoritative figure at a time when other alternatives appeared to have failed, presenting himself as a man with a mission offering hope.

Göring as minister without portfolio took control of the police, instructing them to ignore political neutrality and use their weapons against anyone who appeared anti-government. All the policing later became Himmler's responsibility, but in the initial stages it was Göring who established the Gestapo, dismissing any potential problems and appointing his own trusted SA and SS men with orders to suppress any left-wing organisations with force, while Goebbels masterminded the propaganda machine. These two elements had a critical impact on the public front. For some the violence against the opposition introduced the element of fear, a few may have seen it as justified recrimination, but the warning bells were already sounding. It would not be long before other parties, starting with the communists, would be declared illegal, and any form of opposition outlawed. To oppose the Nazi regime was rapidly becoming dangerous and the element of fear amongst many must not be forgotten, as it would drive some to side with the Nazis for safety, and for others a discreet silence was the only option. If one imagines the same situation in Britain, that if in voting Liberal one's life was threatened, only to find such an action had police and government support, it would reveal much about the feelings of many under the Nazi regime.

In his detailed history of resistance, the German historian Peter Hoffmann indicates that, while the Nazi regime had tightened its grip on the nation already, many small pockets of resistance were being established. He draws attention to an Ernst Niekisch who in 1926 founded a 'Journal for socialist and national-revolutionary Policy, called *Der Widerstand* [Resistance]…and in 1932 Niekisch published a pamphlet, Hitler – a German disaster'.[51] He continued until 1934 when the paper was banned, and in 1937 was imprisoned and not released until 1945. It must not be forgotten that during the 1930s there were many Germans who had not been incarcerated who continued active opposition by refusing to fly the Swastika or refused the Nazi salute. Another example was Walter Löwenheim who brought out publications attacking the regime, which could be found in English and French editions. However, in 1935 the arrests increased as the power of the Gestapo grew in tracking down so-called dissidents. Another little-known active resister Hoffman draws to attention was Dr Joseph (Beppo) Römer, a soldier from the Great War and commander of the Free Corps Oberland.[52] Apparently there is little information about him apart from the fact he was active in opposing first the NSDAP and then the Nazi regime. He was arrested in 1933, and again in 1934 and sent to Dachau; by the influence of old comrades he was released in 1939. He was eventually executed in 1942 followed an attempted assassination charge. Perhaps the most interesting aspect of this early active resister was the number of contacts he made with various opposition groups at all levels of society, including the Foreign Office and senior military commanders. There were many who had the courage to oppose the regime, and probably many more unknown today but who paid the price of opposition. These people actively opposed the regime, in some cases resisted, but at this stage it could only be protest as active resistance was simply impossible.

One of the major factors in making the regime virtually untouchable was Goebbel's oversight of propaganda and control of the media, radio and newspaper rapidly falling into his domain. The public heard only what the growing Nazi control wanted them to hear, and this would soon develop into a total control over the thinking of the masses. It may sound overly trifle, but in many societies, it is often the case that some people think that if it is in the papers or announced on the radio it must be true, only the more astute tend to question government news. Whether the Nazis burned down the Reichstag is open to dispute, it may well have caught the Nazis by surprise, but when it was announced, the NSDAP grasped the occasion, and when they claimed the Communists had done this, it was believed.

Hitler had managed to convince Hindenburg to sign an early nineteenth century Presidential Decree for the Reich Government to assume control in all federal states, noting that any disagreement would result in the death penalty, thereby ending the federal structure. Despite a few seeing the warning signs, the 5 March 1933 election saw the Nazi vote increase their seats to 288, not quite the required majority, suggesting they had yet to gain full public acceptance, often taken for granted by some historians that it was achieved. Hitler came to the idea of the Enabling Act which granted the government emergency powers for four years, which meant by-passing the President. The curious matter was that the leader of the Catholic Centre Party supported this move in the anticipation that Hitler would prove to be moderate, thus creating a blunder based on hope. It could be claimed that it was a mistake based on lack of foresight, but many civilised people would have found the imminent future impossibly difficult to believe. The use of outright violence had been noted by many, especially following what was called the Potempa case, a place in Silesia where in 1932 some brown shirts (SA) had kicked to death one of their political opponents in front of his mother, and the felons were given life imprisonment and death sentences. The Nazi leaders gave their support to the felons and in the following March they were amnestied. It was a forewarning that criminality on behalf of the NSDAP was acceptable.

The Enabling Act freed Hitler from any constitutional or parliamentary control. As such the Reichstag became a mere institution enabling Hitler to announce decisions, and seemingly justify his foreign policies such as remilitarising the Rhineland in 1936, as this appeared to offer legitimacy to his actions. This gave the new government total freedom with no parliamentary or constitutional restraints. The arrival of a dictatorship or totalitarian regime was a novelty which produced little opposition because for many it felt that strength, even if it required a degree of violence, was necessary for the state. There was one brave response from Otto Wels chairman of the Social Democrats who protested in the Reichstag, accusing the NSDAP of clinging to power by all methods. There were some areas and individuals who resisted at a local level, but they were soon stopped by governmental initiatives. The Burgomaster (Mayor) of Leipzig, Carl Goerdeler, who will be mentioned later in the text, stopped the swastika being raised, as in his opinion, it was not the national symbol. He also stopped some attacks on Jewish citizens, probably, at this stage, unaware of the dangers involved in contradicting the new Nazi regime. The Reichstag members, even before the fire made them redundant, were under extreme Nazi pressure.

No one in the many parties would have foreseen that by 14 July 1933, the NSDAP would be the only legal party allowed in Germany. On 30 June 1934 (Night of the Long Knives) several hundred opponents of the regime were murdered by Hitler's orders, and two months later after Hindenburg's death, Hitler combined his office as Chancellor with the Presidency and became the Führer, and the military swore an oath of allegiance to him. Many have pointed out that this was no different to the oath sworn in Britain to the monarch and the president of the USA, which while true enough, Hitler's full name seemed to make it more personal. However, it was undeniable that it was Hitler's way of stating that he was the one and only leader, and to challenge that was to break the oath. Either way, Germany was now a totalitarian state led by a dictator, which for some felt menacing, for others a sense of fear, but for many there remained the hope the new leader would fulfil his promises of economic recovery. The sense of pervasive fear was felt by those who held different views and as early as 1933 concentration camps such as Dachau (near Munich) were established to imprison and inhumanely treat Hitler's political opponents and anyone who had criticised the NSDAP. When Rudolf Breitscheid the Social Democrat clapped with joy on the news that Hitler was to be Chancellor, mainly on the grounds that he would expose who he really was, he met his end in Buchenwald.[53] Many of Hitler's opponents had little time to think before they found themselves incarcerated. The well-known Spandau, a onetime military prison, was used by the Gestapo to imprison and torture any critics of the new regime. The concentration camps grew rapidly and soon incarcerated not only political opponents but many others especially the Jews, with well-known consequences. Those who were fortunate enough to be freed were sworn to silence which was noted by others and created another strand of fear.

Anti-Semitism had increased after the First World War, had simmered during the Weimar Republic, but was used by the Nazis to enforce their racial hatred and the infamous desire for a so-called pure Aryan race, for the Nazi theory of the *Volksfeind* (enemy of the people) condemning them under the 'Jewish-Bolshevik ruling class'.[54] Amongst the intended victims were also politically minded clergy, Jehovah Witnesses, Freemasons, homosexuals and ordinary common criminals, and anyone the Nazi regime regarded as a threat or distasteful and were regarded as public enemies. Hitler had outlined his thinking in his tedious political biography of *Mein Kampf* including his views on the Aryan race, *lebensraum* (living space) and his foreign policy plans. Jews were shifted from public office, educational establishments, the judiciary, hospitals, and even had their names removed from First World War memorials. They were not allowed on park seats, barred from some park areas, bars, and public baths, to save, it was claimed, the purity of German blood. By the same prejudice Jews were not allowed to marry Germans, and the infamous Nuremberg Race Laws of 15 September 1935 confirmed this obscenity. A few years later in November 1938 occurred *Kristallnacht* (Crystal Night), stirred up by a young Jew killing a German diplomat in Paris, which led in Germany to Jewish shops, businesses, and synagogues being destroyed, all linked to the so-called threat of the Bolshevist Jew.

Goebbels' control over the news and propaganda propelled many Germans to believe what the government said must have been true. As will be noted in the following chapters, the Goebbels' propaganda machine, backed by Gestapo and SS Security Servies, had a lasting effect on the German public's mindset to the end of the Second World War. The bigotry against Jews increased and was more than supplemented by Julius Streicher who started his newspaper *Der Stürmer* (Stormer, Striker or Attacker) in 1923–24 with his vitriolic attack on Jews, depicting them as sexual predators against German women, with pornographic and revolting cartoons often portraying Jews as rats. The historian Richard Evans described it as a paper of screaming headlines, full of sexual innuendo, racist caricatures, with accusations of ritual murders by Jews with pornographic stories of Jewish men seducing German girls.[55] Streicher blamed the Jews for losing the war, creating the depression, unemployment, inflation, ritual murder, white-slave traders, and anything else his repulsive imagination could produce. In any population there are those of low intelligence, ill-educated, and others prone to believe anything which appears in print, and fear of having critical views made known, silenced many more. The public soon learnt that every single organisation, club, and individual was under some form of political surveillance, and that ardent Nazi supporters, although close neighbours and even family, might report them for their views.

Chapter Two

German Public Reaction to Nazism

Author's Notes: *This chapter proved difficult to write as available evidence is confusing, at times questionable, and mainly depends upon historical common sense and an understanding of human nature. After the war there was a tendency to place collective guilt upon all German people which, with the benefit of hindsight, was an error of judgement. However, why 40 per cent of the public voted for Hitler and supported him during the war years is curious, albeit this support diminished somewhat as the years unfolded. How so many Germans found Nazism attractive needs exploration.*

The question of rampant nationalism is studied as it laid the base for many attitudes in and outside Germany, especially irredentist nationalism, and ethnicity. This exploration is followed by the intense indoctrination within the Hitler Youth where a generation was deeply influenced with Nazi views, although a few teenagers rejected the teaching, which will be explored in a later chapter.

Goebbels the man and his post as head of propaganda is examined because he was good at his job which meant telling lies, prefabricating false accounts, and generally persuading the German people of the value, as he saw it, of the Nazi regime and treating Hitler as a deity. His influence through the world of propaganda was dangerously impressive, persuading many Germans that Nazism was the German answer and hope.

The next section of this chapter explains why, when the propaganda was not believed, most people accepted everything they read or heard because they lived in a society dominated by fear. The central figure was Himmler who eventually controlled all the police, including his own SS security branch (SD), the Gestapo, and even the Kripo, the criminal branch. It was because of the frightening reputation he projected that individuals dared not speak out, make jokes of the regime, or dare criticise the Nazi government. Germany had rapidly become a repressed society with little freewill unless they were prepared to sacrifice their freedom or their lives, including the same threat to their families. The masses of workers are finally explored to try and understand how such vast numbers could be controlled, and the answer tends to correspond in every German home of all German classes, sheer fear. The sense of repression coupled by terror stalked not only the workplaces, but the streets with the constant threat of denunciation for a passing remark. The question must be asked as how the reader would have reacted living under such a regime.

Introduction

The image of German society under the Nazi regime is at times confusing like a jigsaw with too many pieces to make sense. There are images of unbelievable adoration of the figure of Hitler, almost as if he were a deity, but coupled with ones of fear with images of the Gestapo, the SS security wing (SD) and the sheer barbarities of the concentration camps. It is equally difficult to look behind the façade and see the various levels of opposition which varied from silent distaste to passive and then active resistance. In Europe during the early twentieth century there were three main political ideologies, the democratic society, fascism developing mainly in Germany, Italy, and Spain, and communism with its main base in Russia. Soviet communism under Stalin soon became a form of totalitarianism, but in its Marxist origins with its complex inner logic and detailed reasons for existence, it differed vastly from the ideals of National Socialism of the NSDAP. Nazism had no real political aims, apart from Hitler's personal obsession with anti-Semitism, and 'one sees that for Hitler ideology was nothing more than slogans…the programme of the NSDAP consists of clichés which are hardly original'.[1] Hitler had made his appeal to the traditional nationalistic middle class of the 'old world' and to the growing anti-Semitics of that period. This had no intellectual foundation, but its presentation and sense of dynamic agitation allowed it to grow rapidly in popularity. Nationalism had been rife for years in Europe and elsewhere, it was part of Germany's history since 1870 as outlined in Chapter One, and there is no doubt that Hitler took this as his main bandwagon, and nationalism must be briefly explored to keep this view in context.

Nationalism

Studying the nature of nationalism during this period with any degree of objectivity tends to indicate that a severe form of nationalism, namely aggressive and racial nationalism scarred European history, with ramifications which endure to this day. It was more than patriotism, as nationalism raised issues of land, ethnic race, language, and became aggressive and dangerous as it still is today. After 1945 the term was frequently used in a disapproving fashion, but it is often forgotten that the word has many shades. It has been associated with fascism and brutal military conflict, but it raises 'questions that need analysing…they should not be taken as foregone conclusions'.[2] The nationalism of this period can be clearly seen in the post-Great War successor states, when it displaced ethnic or minority groups caused by the post-war upheavals to counter the revisionist nationalism of the defeated states, and the entangled relationship between nationalism and fascism.[3] This was the hub of much of Hitler's thinking.

The surrounding political and military events of the period 1914–1945 tended to shape the thinking of nations emerging into a highly dislocated world; a disruption caused not just by suffering of the Great War, but the Treaty of Versailles' machinations which changed the map of Europe, punishing the losers and rewarding the victors according to the ideas of the major successful powers. The result of map-changing was the situation in which many ethnic groups found themselves trapped, often as minority groups, in a new nation. The well-known Rabbi Hugo Gryn once said that over a period of twenty years he lived in three different countries but never moved from his home-village: this was a feature for many people during this turbulent time, especially in Eastern and Central Europe.* Hitler grasped this with all its emotional attachments and made this his rallying call for 'making Germany great again', knowing a substantial part of the defeated Germany would rally to this call.

Post 1918 was a period which had intended to be a rebuilding following the conflagration of the Great War, during which little regard had been given to these ethnic groups within the evolving new states, who had suddenly become foreigners in a strange land. 'These nationalistic projects were fuelled in part, by the irredentist nationalism of the defeated states'.[4] The word irredentism indicated that political and often popular belief that a country had the inherent right to reclaim their territory lost in war or claimed by powerful neighbours, which had once been part of their natural and legal landscape. This form of irredentist nationalism was and remains a global problem and has been the cause of many serious conflicts to this day. The revised states of Romania, Poland and Czechoslovakia were all sharply aware that Germany, Hungary, and Russia (in 1924 the USSR) believed they had claims on the revised territories, which led to immediate violent clashes, and eventually to what could be described as a European civil war.

In Germany Adolf Hitler, as dictator, used aggressive nationalism to the full extent, but although he often appears as the initiator of this policy, it was more a matter of him inheriting many of the main strands. As early as the 1880s, not long after Germany's unification, it had been decided that citizenship or naturalisation depended on ethnic background, which effectively blocked Eastern Jews. This was Prussian-led and 'recent research on popular associations (i.e., choral societies and so forth) in the late nineteenth century suggests such organic understanding of nationhood was neither confined to the political class nor the conservative fringes of society'.[5] They were seemingly concerned about Germans living outside their national borders, and this gave the appearance

* Hugo Gryn (1930–96) was born in Berehovo in Carpathian, which was then in Czechoslovakia, and now in the Ukraine.

that irredentism was prevalent even before the outbreak of the Great War. This underpinned a strong nationalistic tendency and served as a pretext for a Greater Germany. It was a desire for a unified race of people ready to battle against external foes and enemies within. Before Hitler had published his thinking on *lebensraum,* research on this subject had already started. The Nazis took over an inheritance which had been planted partly before the Great War and certainly entrenched after the Treaty of Versailles. The growing sense of irredentist nationalism was used by Hitler as an excuse for invasion of territories which many supported at all levels; even overseas there was a small degree of sympathy, but less so when it continued with the attempted total domination of Europe. It was a claim based on justification or natural rights. Even the anti-Nazi Ulrich von Hassell noted in his diary that because the Polish negotiator had failed to appear 'there was nothing left for Germany but to take action to *secure its rights*'.[6] There was an assumption made by this anti-Nazi diplomat that Germany had right of occupation of other territories because of the invalidity of the Versailles Treaty. This was a nationalistic view shared by many, especially amongst the conservative military.

From his early days Hitler had become imbued with the popular theme that Germany was threatened by inferior races and alien influences. Prior to 1933 this had not been overly used simply because Hitler was sensitive to those members of the public who were not in sympathy with these attitudes. He influenced men like Gregor Strasser who thought the Party to be more important than race, and even Göbbels who as a young man had shown few signs of serious anti-Semitism. There was considerable interest amongst German scientists and anthropologists to regard ethnic origins as biological. It was no surprise that the Nuremberg Race Laws were inaugurated as Hitler in *Mein Kampf* had argued for the preservation of the race; a feature his servant Himmler took to heart.* There was talk of exporting all Jews to Madagascar, but as Poland fell, ghettoes and concentration camps became the norm for so-called sub-humans, including some Slavs, but other Slavs were utilised in running the camps. It will be debated for a long time as to when the extermination camps became an active policy; many believe it was the euthanasia programme time, but whatever

* In 1940 Himmler took a tour of Poland to establish German areas of settlement (although few Germans were happy with the idea of moving to Poland) and he noticed that many Poles looked Aryan; for him this meant they were blue-eyed and fair-haired. There began a sifting of children looking for those who could be taken from their families and raised as German. German Aryan women known as *Brown Sisters* would patrol the streets looking for likely candidates. A Dr Erhard Wetzel wrote that racially the Poles contained the same racial strains as Germans. This was all pseudo-science but Himmler believed this nonsense.

the view there is little question that it came from Hitler, transmitted through his henchmen, and based on racist Nationalism.

Racism, fascism, nationalistic irredentism, followed by expansionism were all components of the Nazi regime, and it was this form of aggressive nationalism which found a natural habitat for expression in Nazi propaganda. It was not the same in all nations, each had its own agenda and shape, but the dangerous driving force was the growth of Nazi fanaticism in their projection of nationhood as a superior race. Hitler's warped thinking made Germany the most dangerous, but Italy and Japan (with Stalin later) were also seeking territorial expansion with anachronistic notions of imperial glory. Wealth and resources also played their part. Hitler's economic four-year plans and his theory of *lebensraum* were driven by money. Some countries were better off than others, the larger empires had trade facilities, and others greater resources. Hitler understood Germany needed oil, rubber, copper and iron ore, and the desire for what the neighbours possessed remained for him a powerful driving force. The very word *lebensraum* was both economic and population driven because Germany had the fourth-highest population density of the world's major economies, but with less farming space. It was the primitive maxim that the other man's field is greener. Italy had taken space in Abyssinia, Japan was making incursions into its immediate neighbour's land, so Hitler looked east as Italy went south and the Japanese moved west. All these countries were nationalistically inspired and used the theme of nationalism to justify policies and inspire their populations.

This was all Hitler's major selling theme with his obsession with the Jews remaining central to his warped thinking processes. Many in different countries felt the same way, and at times it was popular to look at Jewish success in the financial world with such figures as the Rothschilds, and believe they were making money at the expense of others. This was not necessarily racial but just downright resentful suspicion. The French writer Alphonse Toussenel (1840s) who leaned towards the left-wing saw Jewish financiers as a new form of feudalism, but it took little time for the criticism to descend to calling them parasites. In Germany Otto Böckel called them the 'Kings of Our Time' (1886) also attacking their financial success. At the turn of the century, it was not just their economic ability, which was causing resentment, but they were also becoming extraordinarily successful in many of the professions. Nevertheless, their wealth was resented, and it is 'noteworthy that 31 per cent of the richest families in Germany were Jewish and 22 per cent of all Prussian millionaires'.[7] This along with their dominance in the professions caused a degree of resentment amongst those who were incapable of achieving the same success. This economic and professional jealousy of success prompted the German Catholic magazine *Germania* to issue the warning 'do not buy from Jews' (1876). In the late 1870s an anti-Semitic priest called Adolf Stoecker demanded Jews should be excluded from the teaching and the legal professions.[8] It could be argued that Hitler had focused his appeals on time old traditions, but his extreme barbarity more than matched that of Genghis Khan. Hitler wanted an ethnically homogenous Germany and wanted Jews and Slavs out of the way to make room for German settlers. This was expressed in the slogan *Ein Volk, Ein Riech, Ein Führer*, 'one people, one empire, one leader' which for many had a highly attractive ring, and through the machinations of clever propaganda the Nazis managed to convince much of the German public.

Indoctrinating German Youth

The NSDAP made a major effort to win to their side German children and teenagers, indoctrinating them with Nazi ideology and attitudes. Hitler once said in a speech:

> My great educative work, I am beginning with the young. We older ones are used up…my teaching is hard. Weakness has to be knocked out of them. In my *Ordensburgen* [schools for elite Nazi children] a youth will grow up before whom the world will shrink back. A violent active, dominating, intrepid, brutal youth – that is what I am after.[9]

It was abundantly clear how Hitler expected German children to become either soldiers or ardent Nazis members. The youth of the 1930s and early 1940s were indoctrinated not only at schools, where it was unwise for teachers not to be Party members, and children were expected to join the Hitler Youth, with genders always being kept separate. It is easy to teach a line of politics with subjects like history, religious studies, literature, but the Nazi curriculum even managed to put its policies into mathematics; for example, two questions:

1) In a given circle with an 8 cm diameter draw a swastika.
2) A Modern night bomber can carry 1,0800 incendiary bombs. For a stretch of how far can it spread these bombs, if travelling at a speed of 250 kilometres per hour, if it drops a bomb every second?[10]

It was noted that in one primary school in their assembly room, there was a large notice over the stage with the lettering 'We are born to die for Germany' and the headmaster announced that 'we must give our faithful heart to the Führer since he is Germany's liberator and greatest hero, that our whole life belongs to him'.[11] School teachers were scrutinised by Nazi Party officials to ensure they were adhering to government instructions, and even some pupils where it was suspected that home or clergy were exercising a different influence, and all schools were instructed to make sure their pupils joined the Hitler Youth.

The Hitler Youth under Baldur von Schirach, who led this organisation between 1931–1940, projected the message of unity amongst German youngsters. In their camps, they would enjoy the hikes and bonfires as the Nazi message, along with its pomp and ceremony, were continuously pumped into their minds. It did not take long for coercion to apply, and the pressure to join became more heavily applied, and the most junior of the ranks of the young were designed to teach obedience to commands. It was made exciting by marching to drums carrying Nazi banners and provided the adrenaline most youngsters enjoy. It was not a boy scout movement as the older members were soon imitating the military. They attended mass meetings where Hitler sometimes made an appearance, and it was all too easy, given their youth, to be mesmerised by the Führer whom they were expected to reverence. For many it was an escape from their humdrum existence at home and a place where they could meet new and exciting friends, and they were treated as important. For the teenagers gliding clubs proliferated, as potential pilots were considered necessary. It also gave many the opportunity to assert themselves with the seeming power provided by their uniform. In one incident at the Paulsen Grammar School some pupils objected to the waste of time in homework of translating the classics, when they claimed they had Hitler Youth duties. When one teacher insisted, the Hitler Youth members in the school had their 16-year-old *Gruppenführer* go to the headmaster and insist the teacher should be dismissed. From that point pupils did not have to do homework if they were engaged on Hitler Youth duties.[12] The number of Hitler Youth grew formidably from 107,956 members in 1932 to 3.5 million in 1934. Whether it was in the classroom or around the Hitler Youth campfire German children were indoctrinated with Nazism, and instructed to report on anyone who was critical of the regime, including parents, and there were many occurrences of this happening, undoubtedly causing deep regret to many such youngsters in their later years. The effort of making young people dedicated Nazis and prepared to join the military worked later as many joined the armed forces as dedicated fanatics. However, despite the vast numbers there were restless youngsters who resented the idea of being told what to do and what to think, perhaps causing the modern reader to reflect on difficult teenagers who want to deviate as not being so bad. They made their protests in their youthful way and will be commented on in the chapter dealing with opponents and resisters.

Goebbels' Influence on the wider German Public

It has often been noted with much justification that although Hitler with his nationalistic and racial views was the source of power, that the dynamic driving force for the NSDAP came through Nazi propaganda headed by Joseph Goebbels. He is one of the main characters in this account of how Hitler and the Nazi regime managed to bolster the German masses and indoctrinate them in the wonders of National Socialism.

Goebbels cleverly hoodwinked the German public with his propaganda. They were criminalised for listening to foreign broadcasts, and they were only allowed to listen to what the regime wanted them to hear. Goebbels was clever with staging events and organising the thought processes of the masses. On 18 February 1943 he gave a major speech at the Sports Palace with some 14,000 invited guests, knowing that it would be broadcast across the country to millions of Germans. In the speech he was demanding a popular response to supporting a total war as the tide was turning against the Germans. As a nationwide broadcast it lasted nearly two hours. Goebbels asked questions of his audience and they replied with roars of approval and cheering. This response was important because millions of Germans were listening in on their radio sets or over a public address system. The whole event was orchestrated with carefully selected and fanatical Party members in the crowd, roaring their approval at the right time, prompting Goebbels to tell Albert Speer that 'this had been politically the best-trained audience in Germany'.[13] Even a sceptical listener to the speech would have been impressed by the vocal support of the massive audience, and only the most astute may have wondered whether it was a carefully staged event. The vast majority would have been impressed by the vocal support, not knowing that it came from chosen Nazi members, and Goebbels was cynical enough to tell Speer that it was basically a 'setup' for him to convey the Nazi message of victory in a war which was beginning to fail. The German public were being deliberately misled.

Goebbels deserves attention because of his influence on the public and supporting their adoration of Hitler; as such it is important to understand this man. Stephen Roberts, an Australian academic, visited Germany on a sabbatical tour and authored the book *The House that Hitler Built*, published in 1937. It allows the reader to observe an intelligent man's judgement uncluttered by the war years, the Holocaust, and the aftermath. He met Goebbels and wrote 'the outstanding feature about Göbbels is his searing contempt for humanity. One feels that he despises the human race and looks on people as so many ants to be managed or stamped on. His attitude may easily be explained by a mixture of tortured nerves and acute resentment-psychosis, due to his physical defects'.[14]

This was an interesting observation, and as this brief survey of Göbbels unravels he presents as a highly intelligent man who looked down on everyone except Hitler. Göbbels was to divide humanity into three types, Germans, Jews and the rest of mankind. He always obeyed his master and attempted to crush everyone who he perceived as an enemy of the regime. Roberts saw Göbbels clearly for what he was in the mid-1930s, and he wrote that 'he should call Göbbels the most dangerous man in Europe, precisely because he is so diabolically clever and so frankly Machiavellian in his views of mankind and the methods he would employ'.[15] The historian Kershaw wrote 'He was one of the most intelligent Nazi leaders, possessed of a cruel wit, ruthless and dynamic, organisationally able, a fervent Hitler acolyte who is in his mastery of propaganda managed to combine utter cynicism with extreme brutal ideological fanaticism'.[16]

Goebbel's propaganda played an immense role in influencing the German public so a few moments should be given to explain who he was. As a young man he had taken his Roman Catholic faith seriously, and his father even projected that he might become a priest. He was hindered by his club foot but from his youth he wanted some standing in the world. His first girlfriend was a Jewess, and this did not seem to be a problem for him, he had other girlfriends, and according to many accounts, when he rose to power became a sex addict. Although Göbbels as a young man was given help by Jewish scholars and received funds for his education from the Catholic Church, this all changed with his fastening onto the NSDAP and his worship of Hitler. Göbbels followed his master's voice and turned his vehement propaganda against Jewish people, and against the Church, but with more caution with the latter because of its international status.

Göbbels later alleged he joined the Nazi Party in 1923, but there is little evidence for this, and it is unlikely that he did not meet Hitler until 12 July 1925.[17] A year later Göbbels wrote in his diary 'Hitler is coming. I venerate and love him'.[18] His later dubious assertions included that he wrote to Hitler when he was incarcerated in Landsberg prison, but his early union with the Nazi Party is all part of the fabric of lies he built up so cleverly in later life; a characteristic of the man's ability to be blatantly dishonest.

For Goebbels the NSDAP became his means of status, and his hopes rose when he was asked to edit a new political magazine the *Nationalsozialistische Briefe*. He started to feel important and his skills at oratory were applauded, which he frequently commented on in his diary. Later he was to claim that if he told his audience to jump from the fourth floor some may have done so, but most would have done it for Hitler.[19] Hitler had the animal power which appealed to the people who followed him. Göbbels was clever but intellectual, but 'his loyalty to Hitler was without doubt linked sub-consciously to the same instinct to gain power and glory for himself'.[20] Göbbels was soon elevated to the position of Minister for Propaganda and Public Enlightenment which virtually gave him control over what the public heard and watched.

He was especially interested in what he termed cultural politics. He instituted a prize-giving system whereby pro-Nazis were given the prizes followed by the habitual drumming of the propaganda machine. Eventually he took control of the radio, working on the accepted view that for the Nazis the spoken word carried more weight than the written. It would prove to be a productive source for Göbbels' propaganda, which for Göbbels was using lies and deceit to spread the power of the Nazi Party. He had hardly been in post a few days before Göbbels was addressing hundreds of broadcasting employees commenting in his diary that 'many of them would have to go'.[21] Göbbels avoided using Hitler on the radio until he had rehearsed him; the radio lacked his magnetism and force, 'in fact his voice sounded rather unpleasant'.[22]

Göbbels wanted to take control not only of the arts and all forms of communication but the education of Germany. He finally secured Göring's agreement that he should be in charge even of playhouses and theatres. He was disappointed that Göring maintained his authority in this area over Prussia.[23] This broad spectrum of control over every aspect of German intellectual life illustrated Göbbels' desire to accumulate power over the mind of the nation, as well as increasing his personal status.

Göbbels' main and personal interest was the film industry about which he was obsessive, but 'he had to reckon with Hitler, who was a great film fan and very critical into the bargain'.[24] Göbbels with all his usual energy and bigotry praised some films, denounced others, and was always on the outlook for films which could be utilised for propaganda production, though he promised to leave room for genuine but safe entertainment.

In his pursuit to dominate the German mind through his own brand of education he encouraged the German Students Association to clean out public libraries of what he deemed to be trash. Most of the books were Jewish authors, Communists, and included such names as Marx, Trotsky, Wolff, Freud, Remarque, and hundreds of other classics. There was the infamous book-burning episode on 10 May 1933 in the Opernplatz in Berlin and in other places. Göbbels 'from now on was to put German culture into a Nazi straitjacket'.[25]

It was 'neither technically nor, from the point of view of personnel, practically possible to destroy the democratic press and replace it by a Nazi press monopoly, as a few extremists would have liked to have done'.[26] Göbbels thought he would handle the situation and took extreme measures to control the press, even proving dangerous for sports writers.

As early as September 1933 Göbbels produced the law to create the Reich Chamber of Culture, and in October the Journalists' Law which transformed them into servants of the State. It was a clever way of not only controlling people but ensuring they had to heed the demands of the new government. The once famous Journalist Conference was taken over, and as early as October 1933 any journalist or worker within journalism had to be Aryan and married to an Aryan. The press had rapidly become an organ of the state, but Göbbels 'had to fight for twelve years to obtain complete control of the press, which he was only able to achieve shortly before the collapse of the Third Reich'.[27] It was much more difficult for Göbbels to carry this influence overseas and his relationships with the foreign press never worked well. He frequently expounded his habitual outright lies and the foreign press were quick to point out his various fabrications. He used his power to expel many foreign journalists and many left because they were informed that their lives might be at risk.

Goebbels sold the Nazi themes and did it in such a way that the listeners felt proud to be part of the glorious future he painted. In a speech given at the Reich Chamber of Culture and reported in the paper *Völkischer Beobachter* (16 November 1933) he said:

> The revolution we have carried out, is a total one. It has gripped all areas of public life and changed them from the foundations up. It has completely altered and formed anew the connections of people to each other, the connection of people to the state and to questions of existence…the system we overthrew was most deeply characterised in Liberalism. If Liberalism was derived from the individual and placed the single person at the centre of everything, then we have replaced the individual by the Volk and the single person by the community.[28]

He painted the success of the NSDAP in glowing colours while demanding the abolition of individuality and the subordination of everything to the service of the nation. This boiled down to stating that the NSDAP leaders were now in total control.

When the USA was attacked at Pearl Harbor and Hitler declared war on America Göbbels appeared happy, but he was no fool and recognised the same combination which had won in 1918. The lie was broadcast that America was the aggressor. He hoped that the USA would be too busy fighting in the Far East to be of any help to Britain or Russia. Göbbels proclaimed 'they are fighting the war with figures of fantasy. Who can take it seriously when they say they will launch fifteen new merchant ships in a month – or is it a day?'[29] Anyone with a realistic knowledge of life outside their own country would have known that this ridiculing of America's industrial capability was a nonsensical lie.

Göbbels turned his mind to Total War with his theme of a tough home policy which included a form of labour conscription for women and closing down businesses which had nothing to do with the war effort. This was really Göring's responsibility but as always Göbbels treated it as if it were his sole initiative. It was at this stage that Göbbels entered what the biographer Reimann called his Frederician period, it had to be all or nothing.[30]

In the latter part of the war Göbbels tried every form of propaganda, but generally there were three main threads: the retaliatory theme, total war, and a political solution by seeking peace on one of the two fronts. Once the Allies crossed the Rhine 'he was clear-sighted enough to see that Germany's last hope of a political settlement had collapsed'.[31] Even so, such were the strains of hope and fear at times that even for Göbbels 'reality and illusion were closely interwoven'.[32]

Even after his death Göbbels' propaganda and lies were still proving effective. When in Italy the Supreme Commander Alexander reported to the Russians that the Germans had made peace overtures, he was taken aback by the Russian response of querulous suspicion. 'Göbbels and his agents had spread thoroughly, continuously, and convincingly the lie that the Western Allies would, sooner or later join forces with the Germans and march against the Russians'.[33] This played into Stalin's paranoid mind; Göbbels' ability in the craft of propaganda outlived him.

The most relevant factor for this study was his influence over the public mind. He organised the public rallies and receptions for Hitler with bands and drums as if announcing the second coming. He encouraged through speeches, radio broadcasts and leaflets first the belief that Hitler would make Germany great again, that Germans were to be united as one great traditional family, that the future was bright and sparkling under the Nazi regime. He forecast victory after victory, and as the war turned was happy to lie, and encouraged the people to accept hardship in total war because their efforts would bring victory. As the regime crumbled, he continued to encourage people with the rumour of wonder-weapons, lied about the enemy and their successes, derided men like Churchill the alcoholic and Roosevelt the Jew-lover, about Germany protecting Europe from Bolshevism, and always talked of ultimate victory. As with today there are always people who tend to believe what is in the newspapers, heard over the radio, and especially when, as Goebbels managed, to speak and write with such authority. He indoctrinated the public with the belief that Hitler was what Germany needed, that Hitler would always win despite the difficulties of war. Not everyone believed him and jokes about Goebbels abounded but always in secret, and the explanation for this follows in the next section of this chapter.

Subjugation by Fear

While much of the German public was taken in by Hitler and Goebbel's propaganda encouraging them to support the NSDAP and later the Nazi regime, others were not sure. Having seen the determined way that opponents of the regime disappeared, many into concentration camps, there was a constant fear of being denounced for opposing Hitler which meant three possibilities: imprisonment, death, or 'to be disappeared'. It was all too easy to express a view and find oneself denounced and interrogated by the Gestapo, and this became a frequent occurrence. Moltke's wife [to be mentioned later] in her memoirs noted that 'In the years when Germans denounced each other by the thousands – even within families – and in so doing often brought each other into life-threatening danger'.[34] This is a factor often overlooked in studies exploring the German reaction to Nazism. While it is true many fastened onto the Nazi claims of the *Volk*, one people, racially pure, the dominant ethnic stock with plans of territorial rights, other Germans had their doubts. There is little safe evidence to provide any form of statistical analysis, or even a broad picture, but the bits and pieces of information cannot be ignored any more than common sense. Post-war there were many claims made by citizens who wanted to free themselves from the taint of the publicly exposed horror of the Nazi regime. This happened in the de-Nazification courts, even in military commanders' memoirs and other publications, they distanced themselves from the Nazi regime, but the dust has now settled leaving a scar on German history.

However, there is no doubting that after 1933 German society was repressed, and while some revelled in the Nazi regime it was obvious that many landed up in the first concentration camps, and this was widely known leaving untold numbers living in fear of being treated the same way. Within a few weeks of the NSDAP coming to power a 'nationwide system of concentration camps, staffed by Party radicals, sprang up across the nation. By late July 1933, the Rhineland alone had 27,000 people in so-called protective custody'.[35]

Denouncement as mentioned above was a fear for many, and there are many references to inspired Hitler youth members informing on their family members, of colleagues passing on information, and strangers in a bomb shelter complaining of anti-Nazi comments. As Klemperer mentioned in his diary there was a deep fear of being interviewed by the Gestapo, who to this day are recalled for their brutality. To this day the word Gestapo is used to indicate a sense of terror.

Denouncing family and colleagues applied across a broad spectrum of life including even members of the SS in which Himmler took an invasive interest. When he heard that a senior officer's fiancée had been seen socially misbehaving, he wrote to the officer asking that 'you question whether your fiancée actually did go into a café with other men. If she did, then break off the engagement. Be clear that the youth of your fiancée does not excuse her of blame whatsoever', concluding the letter advising him to break off the engagement.[36] All potential spouses of SS men were vetted, but this letter displayed the nature of Himmler as an unpleasant control freak, who thought he was in control off even personal minutiae.

The Gestapo, the *Geheime Staatspolizei* (State Secret Police) was different from the ordinary criminal police insofar that its focus of attention was basically on opponents of the regime. It started life in Prussia under Göring in 1933 who combined various agencies, but by April 1934 the responsibility was passed on to Heinrich Himmler who was appointed head of the German Police by Hitler in 1936. The Gestapo became an office within the *Sicherheitpolizei* (Security Police), and from 1939 the Reich Security Main Office (RSHA) administered it as all part of Himmler's infamous SD (Security Service). Germany had become a police state, and the Gestapo and Himmler struck fear across later occupied Europe, but from 1933 in Germany itself. Everyone with the exception of Hitler were careful or wary of Himmler, and even Göring was once concerned about what Himmler's files held on him. The man Himmler needs some exploration to understand how he generated such fear.

He was once described in this way:

> Cleanliness was a fetish with him, and he gargled and washed himself throughout the day. He was a man of exact habits, parsimonious, neat, and careful, and blessed with no originality, common sense, or intuition...in the acid words of SS General Paul Hausser, who had helped him organise the Waffen-SS, the one-time chicken farmer was a 'fantastic idealist with both feet planted several inches above the earth, a right queer bird'.[37]

As with Göbbels, Himmler had read Hitler's *Mein Kampf* and found it contained, for him, many truths. He steered himself away from his once loved Catholicism, reading books on spiritualism, anti-Jesuit books, and anti-Semitic books which were widely common in those days. In 1927 he was made deputy head of the SS. According to the official record Himmler had joined the SS in 1925 and his number was 168. It was probably at this stage that Hitler recognised Himmler's organisational skills, and Himmler became a lifelong disciple of Hitler.

In 1931 the new Race Office was introduced demanding racial purity, which included strict guidelines in marriage.* It was rigid, and rule number four read,

---

* He employed teams of genealogists, with a research centre; many of the documents still survive. See Manvell R and Fraenkel, *Heinrich Himmler* (London: Skyhorse Publishing, 2007) p.58

'Marriage consent will be granted and denied solely and exclusively on the criteria of race and hereditary health'.[38] There had been marriage permission regulations within the traditional army, but they were less stringent. Himmler had chosen the infamous Reinhard Heydrich as a form of deputy.* There had been rumours that Heydrich had a Jewish background but despite this, or because of this, he was rabidly anti-Semitic. 'It is of course quite impossible to say that Nazi, German, and even world history would have followed a different course without the Himmler-Heydrich axis at the hinge of events, but it is hard to imagine that it could have been quite the same'.[39] Heydrich became Himmler's man as Himmler was Hitler's man. Heydrich under Himmler's guidance started to infiltrate every occupation from other government departments to the police and military; he did this with a series of hidden agents sometimes popularly known as V-men. The organisation started to grow exponentially and during the spring and summer of 1932 numbers grew from 25,000 to over 40,000. Heydrich was to become powerful within the Nazi regime, though Himmler was always the dominant head who 'kept out of sight, the spider silently operating at the centre of his web'.[40]

Using the notorious index-card list potential enemies were rounded up, and it was in some derelict ammunition works in Dachau that Himmler established the first official concentration camp, opened on 22 March 1933. Göring had been ruthless setting up what were called 'wild' concentration camps within his area, but 'Göring's barbarous vigour was one aspect of Nazi cruelty; Himmler's attention to the details of brutality was another'.[41] The camps were officially meant for political offenders, but this also included Jewish people; they enlarged rapidly with over a hundred sub-camps. New departments were established covering surveillance, suppression of internal enemies, including communism, trade unions, subversion, reactionaries, Austrian affairs, concentration camps, surveillance of the NSDAP and its organisations. It was in 1936 when Himmler was made Chief of the German Police that he managed to unify the various systems.

When opponents who survived the concentration camps were released, they were sworn to silence, and it worked; sheer fear made opposition weak because it was too dangerous to raise some subjects. Political parties soon disappeared and immediately the NSDAP was the only party in Germany. There were some

* Heydrich was a dismissed naval officer; the reasons for his dismissal are many but unclear. The most mentioned were his problems with women but there may have been political reasons. He had been a friend of Canaris and undoubtedly this also influenced his interest in the secret services. It should be noted the day Heydrich was officially dismissed from the Navy the day after he joined the NSDAP.

who questioned Himmler's methods, but any challenges were rendered useless because he had Hitler's total support.

Himmler strengthened Heydrich's position by promoting him to the Head of the SD and raised its status to an independent Office. Himmler's new organisation included counterespionage with Canaris, now a Rear-Admiral and once a good friend of Heydrich, which meant there were better communications between the Abwehr and the Gestapo than there had been previously.* Hess as the deputy Führer announced that the SD was to become the NSDAP's official intelligence service, and arising from this proclamation Himmler out-manoeuvred others in the internal power struggles.

From his earliest of days Himmler always singled out Freemasons for attack; they were part of his traditional rhetoric against Jews, Bolsheviks, and clergy. Because of the Nazi hostility all Freemason lodges had disappeared by 1933. It also appeared that to be a Freemason did not necessarily involve protective custody. The SD had kept a list of Freemasons but when they moved to Berlin in 1935, they set up a museum of Freemasonry which clearly showed that it belonged to the past and was of no consequence.

Himmler (and other Nazis) were deep into eugenics, with Himmler seeking the so-called pure Aryan, itself a non-sensical myth which had little to do with German history. Unlike any of the Nazi leaders such as Hitler, Göring, Goebbels, and Himmler, the true Aryan was fair-haired, blue-eyed, and well built. It did not take long before there was a scrutiny of people the Nazi society considered unworthy of German society. They were often referred to as anti-socials, parasites, racially unfit, and encompassed beggars, tramps, alcoholics, gypsies, and anyone considered biologically doubtful in mind or body. Many landed up in concentration camps to perish behind the anonymity of the barbed wire, some were exterminated, and many others sterilized. It should have been no surprise as Hitler had said as early as 1932–4 that if he were going to send 'the flower of the German nation into the hell of war…spilling precious German blood…then surely I have the right to remove millions of an inferior race that breeds like vermin'.[42] It was a cruel attitude towards other ethnic groups, those who had different life-styles, the physically deformed, and the intellectually handicapped. The policy, when known, must have sent a sense of sheer fear through many German families and their communities.

* The relationship between Canaris and Heydrich is difficult to ascertain. Longerich appears to paint the picture of a genuine friendship while Manvell describes it as 'uneasy', see Manvell R and Fraenkel, *Heinrich Himmler* (London: Skyhorse Publishing, 2007 p.55). It was probably the case that it changed as Canaris became more uncertain about the direction the NSDAP was taking as the years progressed.

The Jews, as well as being regarded as ethnically inferior, were also regarded as the intellectual opposition against the regime. During the early and mid-1930s, the most prolific anti-Semitic diatribe tended to arise from Göbbels, Grohé, and Streicher. Himmler tended to leave anti-Semitic measures to Heydrich, but he was nevertheless central to the criminality of anti-Semitism. From 1935, the Gestapo started to take in the details of Jewish people and their addresses; this was the sinister beginning of the vicious Jewish persecution carried out by the Gestapo and the SD.

Himmler had a particular hatred against his old Catholic Church, more so than the Protestants. His attacks upon Christianity were vociferous and he accused Christian doctrine of being at the centre of the country's weaknesses. As early as 1934 the SS were banned from joining any Christian groups. Members of the SS were expected to believe in a god, but not of the Christian variety but of Himmler's puerile mythological leanings. The Catholic Church had set up in July 1933 a Concordat with the Vatican, which was intended to guarantee the existence of the Catholic Church. Nevertheless, Himmler, Hess and Rosenberg remained bitterly opposed to the Church. Himmler was content to leave Heydrich to deal with Church matters, but in 1935 the Nazi regime started a series of well-publicized court cases with added press matter attacking the churches. Some of the cases involved currency laws, but the most difficult were those involving sexual misdemeanors, which Goebbels revelled in. From 1935 onwards, this also involved investigations into homosexuality all of which continued until the Olympics, paused for a moment, and then started again after the Games had finished. Catholic Youth and other organizations were restricted and later outlawed. The Catholic Church tended to be the main denomination targeted.

The Jehovah Witnesses suffered the most because they refused to adopt or adapt to Nazi demands, and later refused to fight. As early as 1933 they were excluded from public services in Prussia, and Bible students were banned. Despite this attack, the Jehovah Witnesses continued to evangelise, and the Gestapo stepped up its investigation and many Jehovah Witnesses were placed in protective custody in the camps, and the organisation was temporarily destroyed. A Jehovah Witness called August Dickmann in Sachsenhausen concentration camp received call-up papers, which he refused as a matter of principle. Himmler was asked for the punishment to go ahead as an example to the rest, and all the camp inmates saw his execution on 15 September 1939, and soon an article appeared in the press announcing his death because he refused to do his duty as a solider.[43]

Himmler was all powerful within the regime, he had produced the Waffen SS, the Death Head guards for the camps, the Security Department which included the Gestapo, and the traditional SS to guard the Führer. Unlike Göring and Goebbels he was not a well-known public figure, but it was always accepted that he was the orchestrating shadow behind the recriminations, and with much justification his name was feared. In chasing down and destroying the perceived enemies of the Reich, the Criminal Police (Kripo) were utilised. By 1936, Himmler was talking about a national community without criminals. In 1937 he transformed the Kripo into the Reich Criminal Police Department from which control could be exercised centrally. The Gestapo and Kripo sometimes worked together but often in competition. In 1937 with his newly vamped and centralised Kripo, Himmler decided to increase the number of offenders in preventative custody. In 1937 he ordered the arrest of some 2,000 habitual criminals, and preventative custody soon became the norm. He linked criminology to biology and genetics, and if any asocial group appeared, they were in imminent danger of arrest.*

This was further extended to work-shy people, and then to gypsies. The gypsies soon attracted special attention and were known as the gypsy plague. The gypsy fraternity, traditionally divided between the Roma and Sinti groups, came under racial scrutiny. Many simply disappeared into the camps. Himmler 'regarded them as particularly subversive because of their itinerant lifestyle, their alleged criminality and their aversion to regular, conventional employment'.[44]

Amongst the other plagues and diseases Himmler identified were abortionists and homosexuals. He presented to his various leaders statistics intended to show the seriousness of the situation in both perceived offences. The statistics were completely unreliable and were made to look as if Germany were heading for self-destruction. It was all a matter of preserving the German stock since both 'illnesses and plagues' resulted in fewer children. A considerable amount of work was done on paragraph 175 of the Penal Code dealing with homosexuality (such victims were sometimes known as 175ers) and Himmler set about an all-out attack on homosexuals. He accused them of being soft, pathological liars, lazy, prone to blackmail, too prone to talk and generally dangerous for the Reich.

In January 1937 he had given an extended radio broadcast on homosexuality and abortion. He informed his audience there were an estimated three to four million homosexuals in Germany and the *Volk* was in danger of being destroyed by this epidemic. He claimed it was not a private matter stating 'nothing in the sphere of sex was the private affair of an individual'.[45] He expounded that homosexuality was unproductive and the trouble was that a senior homosexual would surround himself with like-minded subordinates.

* This biological-genetic source for criminality was also researched in other countries including America.

Using the same excuse that homosexuality did not produce German children, so he made a major attack against abortion. As he travelled through Germany, he also claimed women had been subjugated by years of denigration by the Church, which was run by a priesthood of homosexuals. It was nothing less than a tirade of hatred in which he called for the cleansing of the nation by attacking Jews, Bolshevists, homosexuals, clergy, and all enemies of the German nation. Having been made Head of Police he evidently saw this position as being the country's supervisor not just in law but in his brand of morals as well. During the Weimar Republic Berlin had become what some might describe as a tolerant society, others as debased if not debauched, and it was clear which approach Himmler took.*

He revelled in accusing the male orientated Church priesthood as being homosexual and deviant. Such was the vociferous nature of his attack that some historians have wondered if it were an attack on his own problems given that he was a virgin until his mid-twenties.[46] For some extraordinary reason he suddenly announced that actors and artists were to be left alone (undoubtedly Hitler's influence), but during the war this pursuit stopped being a priority.

He started to pontificate upon the Nordic race as facing struggles with those lesser beings from the East. Because of the alleged natural relationship between Jewish thinking and communism, the so-called Bolshevik-Jew took on the theme of the racist war, moving from the Germanic to the Greater Germanic Empire to include all other blood-related peoples. If, he explained, there were signs of distinctive leadership in the East, it was because that person had a Germanic strain, and that person must be won over, or killed.

This policy of expansion increased the brutality against the Jewish people. It had started in Vienna with particularly violent attacks against individuals. Adolf Eichmann was sent to Vienna to persuade Bürckel to establish an Agency for Jewish emigration; the process was to be financed by confiscated Jewish property. The process of Aryanization of property and business was crude State theft.** Heydrich's team were so effective in this aspect Himmler had little need to interfere, but he remained the driving force.

Himmler issued direct and precise orders that when civilians committed crimes, they were not to waste time by placing culprits before a military court, but they were to be shot at once, and collective violent measures against suspect communities were also permissible. The Jews and Bolsheviks were criminal enough to be dealt with immediately. There is little doubt that the Eastern

---

* An excellent musical drama film is *Cabaret* produced in 1972 by Bob Fosse and illustrated Berlin at this time in an illustrative way.

** Aryanisation was an expression coined during the Nazi era.

war, *Barbarossa*, was understood by all the leading Nazi members to be an ideological and a racist war of annihilation. Himmler sent out a directive which was complex but clearly outlined that any official of the Communist regime had to be disposed of without hesitation. He had a considerable fighting force under his command as well as his *Einsatzgruppen* clearing up the undesirables behind the front lines.

He always supported Professor Carl Clauberg in his painful sterilization experiments, also that of Professor Klaus Schilling who used young Polish people for experimenting for a cure to malaria and other illnesses, by infecting them first. Perhaps the most notorious experiments were carried out by Dr Sigmund Rascher whose unpleasantness of character was his hallmark.* There were even some protests at the barbarity of these particular experiments which involved the question of lack of oxygen at high altitude, to which Himmler replied 'in these Christian medical circles the standpoint is being taken that a young German aviator should be allowed to risk his life, but the life of a criminal, who is not drafted into military service, is too sacred, and one should not stain oneself with guilt.'[47] Himmler saw such protests as pure narrow mindedness.

The reason behind Himmler's later appointment as Minister of the Interior was undoubtedly to strengthen internal security. Himmler reorganised his departments and used his new position to increase his powers for foreign espionage, and this increased his obsessive powers in the policies relating to ethnicity and looking for *lebensraum* in occupied areas. He left the main bulk of his work as Minister to his Under State Secretary Wilhelm Stuckart, and Himmler operated by sending orders from his various mobile HQs.

It cannot be argued he was just a cog in an evil machine, he was central to the concentration camp system, and for the indoctrination of the SS. However, the reality of war was watering down the racial ideals, but the war did not stop Himmler working frenetically on his General Plan East as he tried to organise who lived where in the appropriate race groupings, and he started to work out similar plans for the Baltic provinces. He spent time looking at those children who had been rounded up in anti-partisan actions, to check those who had racial leanings towards his Germanic ideal, and the rest were to go the concentration camps. The process of *Eindeutschung* (Germanization) was pressed remorselessly.

* Rascher's mistress had been a friend of Himmler's wife Marga. She claimed to have given birth to three children in later life and Himmler became a godfather. Later it was clear the children had been stolen from their parents. Rascher had left the Luftwaffe in order to continue with his experiments which were amongst the cruellest on record. They were eventually arrested for child abduction and Himmler gave the orders in 1945 for Rascher to be shot and the wife hanged.

Himmler was also trying to ensure that even working Jews in the armaments industry were despatched rapidly, and the ghettoes were emptied.

One thing is certain that while Himmler was ruminating on events Hitler suddenly appointed Himmler as Fromm's successor making him Chief of Army Armaments and Commander of the replacement Army. It was an inappropriate appointment since Himmler had no military experience of the front line, but Hitler by doing so gave 'Himmler responsibility for the indoctrination in Nazi ideals and control over military discipline…it was a significant inroad into the domain of the Wehrmacht'.[48] This was almost predictable as Fromm had been aware of the 20 July plot, and Hitler needed somebody he could always trust.

There is no question that Himmler was a major factor in the pure evil of the Nazi regime, and because of downright wicked policies, everyone was frightened of coming to the attention of his men. It was not safe to be an outspoken Christian, a Jehovah's Witness, a Gay, to be a trade unionist, to have an abortion, being Jewish meant death, and unsafe to come from another ethnic background unless one's children were blue-eyed and fair-haired in which case they were stolen. Even making a joke about any Nazi, passing on a rumour about the regime, being upset by their behaviour, criticising their actions, disagreeing with their policies could land any man, woman or even a teenager in a prison cell with all its consequences.

Goebbels had indoctrinated the German public in how and what to think, but Himmler's police state ensured that they never wavered. Out of personal safety for oneself and family, silence was the basic requirement even in family and amongst friends, and to guarantee safety it was sometimes considered safer to give the Hitler salute and show support. This was not a German illness but common to all human beings living in many countries which are under any form of totalitarian structure. A few years ago, this writer's chess club had to find a new venue, and the Conservative Club had a room available. It was mentioned that Labour and Liberal members should not mention their allegiance. It was a joke, but it would not have been under a totalitarian regime secured by its own police. It was, post-war, easy to deride all Germans as pro-Nazi, but fear played a leading role, and although statistics are not available, this type of political pressure should never be ignored, no more than those who had the unbelievable courage to resist at one level or another.

Fear on the Streets and in Workplaces

In 1932 nearly 40 per cent of the electorate voted for Hitler, encouraged by hopes of a promised better future and later endorsed by Goebbels' propaganda machine. Apart from the fact that 60 per cent either did not vote for him or did not bother leaves accurate analysis difficult to confirm. His early popularity was not as extensive among the public as is often portrayed, often helped by the archival films showing thousands of adoring adherents in massive rallies, but just before he was made Chancellor, he 'suffered his first serious setback at the polls, losing over two million votes'.[49] It was clear that many of the German voters had serious doubts. That a democratic state like the failed Weimar Republic suddenly became a dictatorship explains why so many Germans were not keen on a return to that form of democracy, but the risks of a populist politician making promises of change is always a danger in any democracy. The key to electoral success and the right to govern depend on the votes of the public, and when elections take place, most politicians know they have to make an appeal to the masses, which in most countries are best described as 'the workers'. Many people today will recall political cartoons of important ministers of state, prior to a general election, walking around working-class areas admiring babies in prams and pretending to be one of the masses. The need to have the support of workers was not plainly important for political support, but the working class was the key to industrial and agricultural productivity.

During the Weimar Republic workers had mainly given their support to the KPD and the SPD parties, and Hitler, like any other politician knew he needed the masses on side. He knew that the NSDAP had to appeal for their votes with promises of better conditions living in a revitalised country. By eliminating the traditional left-wing parties and the KPD the Nazi regime had virtually left the working masses politically rudderless. He also believed they had to be controlled, and in a 1930 speech said, 'a people must be taught to march through thick and thin with its government, it must instantly be susceptible to every psychological factor, able to be whipped into a frenzy, and be inspired and roused'.[50] It was a cynical view which expressed the reality of his thinking, knowing he needed the workers' support but at the same staying in control. The trade unions of many varieties were prior to 1933 a series of powerful organisations which, as seen in the General Strike in Britain in May 1926, lasted some nine days and brought the country to a standstill. In Germany, the KPD and SPD had called for a general Strike in February 1933, but it received little attention. However, this was a form of potential people power, of which Hitler would have to be in control by making the trade unions illegal. It would mean brute force to accomplish such a control, but the KPD thought the position could be mastered because the fascists would be powerless. According to a KPD official called Wilhelm Beyes, ' if the entire working-class rebels against the present system' it will collapse.[51] There may have been some daydreaming in this for two reasons. The first was that despite its popularity in some areas, the KPD did not have control over all workers, many of whom were deeply suspicious of communism. The second was not foreseeing the determined force the new regime would apply against opponents. The German workers would have been accustomed to seeing or being involved in street violence between the extreme right and left wings, but not the concentration camps and the Gestapo organised by the state government. Nevertheless, the KPD called for mass rallies on the streets, but the regime promptly banned all their publications, and in reality, the KPD did not have the grip on the workers as they hoped, as many workers belonged to the SPD, and others had turned towards the NSDAP. The Nazi regime soon initiated police raids on the leaders or any known communists. They sealed off working class areas with police and fire brigade units while premises and homes were searched on the grounds that communism (or any form of opposition to the regime) was declared illegal. The excuse first used was searching for weapons and thousands landed up in the hastily built concentration camps. It was clear that many were badly treated, and some died while in the custody of the SA, the *Sturmabteilung*, widely known as the Brown Shirts, the Nazi Party's paramilitary wing. It was not just the communists who suffered from this onslaught but also members of the SPD. A typical example of the brutality was an Adam Schaefer (Communist) who was purportedly shot by an SS guard in camp when Schaefer had, it was claimed, attacked him. In these early days, his coffin was allowed home, but his parents would not permit the coffin to be opened, as was the tradition. It was widely suspected the reason was because he had been beaten to death and the corpse would expose this feature. About 800 people attended the funeral, many came from a distance indicating that this was a form of protest.[52] It was during this early turmoil that the *Red Orchestra* sprang into existence with greater vehemence. It was an organisation of German communists, often supplying information to Moscow, but by 1942 most of its main elements had been tracked down and executed. Some were well known activists in previous days, some were often spotted by their unusual activities, and many denounced to the Gestapo or SA Intelligence ring. It was a genuine form of resistance to the Nazi regime.

The resistance or objections to the Nazi regime grew with some trade union leaders but how it was a feature for everyday members remains unclear. There was, for example, considerable unrest at the Middle German Steel Works, (Krupp) with complaints of inadequate work output, from its 6,000 strong workforce. Workers were often absent without reason, and there were vast numbers of men calling in sick.[53] It is impossible in the time distance from events to estimate how much of this was caused by political differences from the regime, or whether they were complaints about pay and living conditions. There is no doubt that the Nazi regime made various efforts to keep the workers in line, either by fear or encouragement. A metal worker called Willi Erbach claimed that 'you couldn't say anything because the shop steward was always standing behind you' and undoubtedly the Nazi regime had many adherents all too willing to denounce fellow workers.[54] Making anti-Nazi comments or jokes was just as dangerous in the workplace as it was in shops, bomb-shelters, drinking houses and across the garden fence. Sometime the denouncer was a Party member, sometimes for more personal reasons, but it was a major characteristic of the Nazi regime period. The Nazis also tried encouragement, they established the German Labour Front and the KdF, *Kraft durch Freude* (Strength through Joy) part of the German Labour Front to win over workers with many promises. This writer along with many readers drives a Volkswagen car, a firm founded in 1937 by the German Labour Front to mass-produce a low-priced people's car. After the war it became a global brand, but in the 1930s it was a Nazi promise to the workers, which mainly failed. The KdF offered subsidised cruises and holidays to workers, though much of this consisted of trips to German resorts, but the cruises made it appear as if the Nazi regime was offering paradise.

It was a Nazi way of ensuring support from the masses, but where it failed either by political discontent or often justified cynicism the control was maintained by fear. Every worker and all civilians would have known that not only the KPD and SPD, but other neighbours who had disappeared into concentration camps were rarely seen again. As for those who did return, they had a deathly silence about them, having been warned to remain quiet or they would be sent back to the camps.

As mentioned, many times the clue was the denouncer who could be a family member or colleague. Helmuth James von Moltke, a prominent leader of a resistance group, held regular meetings and his wife Freya recalled in her memoirs that it was one of her two trusted assistants at preparing the meals who probably denounced them.[55] There are many examples of such betrayal at every level of German society, even a joke at the family table could be dangerous. As mentioned above denouncing was often motivated by pure revenge. A classical case was in a police report in September 1942 where a ship's stoker had reported a prostitute for giving him venereal disease. She happened to be an armaments worker who was so badly off she sold sex to cover the financial shortfall, and had no idea she had venereal disease, and was imprisoned.[56] There is little doubt that the angry stoker on finding he had venereal disease had used political denouncement as his means of gaining revenge. The Nazi regime had allowed the worse side of human nature to be used to gain its own ends which was based on fear and terror.

Even a sense of humour could be dangerous, though as the years of early success crumbled to the inevitable end of defeat and total destruction, they were not just a form of voiced criticism or a quiet form or resistance, but were often a survival mechanism, very much like the graveyard humour of soldiers. They were often known as 'whisper jokes' with one being a parody of the child's prayer, 'Dear God make me good, so I can go the heaven' changed to 'Dear God make me dumb, so I don't do to Dachau'. As Nazism crumbled the jokes increased, and there is no question that humour tells a truth and helped relieve the high degree of tension, even in the height of the bombing raids when it was asked 'whom do we have to thank for the night-fighters? Hermann Göring. For the whole air force? Herman Göring. Upon whose orders did Hermann Göring do all this? On the orders of the Führer! Where would we all be if it were not for Hermann Göring and the Leader? In our beds!'[57] The graveyard humour played its part as when the order was given for *Volkssturm* old men and children to be sent into battle, it was said they operated in pairs, with one throwing a stone at the enemy and the other shouting bang'. The humour was risky if the Gestapo or informants were present.

In the post-war years many followed A. J. P. Taylor's view that 'it was a tyranny imposed upon the German people by themselves', a form of corporate blame was placed on the entire German population.[58] This appeared to hold some credibility induced by the horrific discoveries of the barbarism in the concentration camps, but while it was true that 40 per cent voted for Hitler, not all that number had realised the ramifications. As early as 1933 thousands upon thousands of political opponents went into so-called protective custody in concentration camps. Even as Hitler's regime began to lose total power and it became apparent that the end of the war was approaching, fear, terror and dread still gripped the minds of the majority of the population. Majority, because only 40 per cent had voted in his favour, and many of these soon turned against him. Joe Bloggs and his wife could be denounced for not being a Nazi, or telling jokes about them, or being mildly critical. If one of their children were intellectually mentally handicapped or physically deformed there was danger, a relative who was a Jehovah's Witness, a friend who was a Romani, a relative who was ethnically different meant serious problems. If the same Joe Bloggs and his wife were ardent Christians of any denomination they knew it was safest to keep this as quiet as possible. The German Pastor Martin Niemöller who will be mentioned in a following chapter later wrote that:

> First, they came for the socialists, and I did not speak out because I was not a socialist.
>
> Then they came for the trade unionists, and I did not speak out because I was not a trade unionist.
>
> Then they came for the Jews, and I did not speak out because I was not a Jew.
>
> Then they came for me – and there was no one left to speak for me.

These reflective words spoke for many ordinary Germans reduced to silence by fear of the consequences of being critical. As the war years unfolded and Hitler's promises turned to devastation and the horrors of Nazi barbarity were becoming evident, even many of his supporters became critical having realised they had been fooled, and they lived in the same fear as those who had not voted for him. Promise of hope and a better future had induced many to offer their support, but for those who were critical or even dubious they had to tow the Party line or suffer grave consequences. It was not just a fine, or loss of a job or position, but for them, and probably their family, it meant imprisonment or even death. Any student of history must ask themselves what would have been their reaction if living under such a frightening regime. The ordinary citizen was all too aware even before the Second World War started that any form of political opposition would instantly mean being interned if not interred, and the slightest criticism or joke could bring on denouncement by any number of informants normally personally trusted, and silence was the only safety line they could grab. The next chapter will start looking at those who found the immense courage to speak out.

Chapter Three

From Survival to Opposition

Author's Notes: *This chapter starts by outlining the nature of the vocabulary of 'opposition and resistance' for the sake of mutual understanding, to note the differences between opposition and resistance and when and how the adjectives 'passive and active' should apply.*

This chapter continues the theme of public reaction to Nazism by first concentrating on the vexed issue of the persecution of the Jews. It explores what happened to German Jews and why, seemingly, it appeared so acceptable to much of the German public. It also raises the question of why the Jews appeared to be led to the slaughter like lambs in a processing plant. It explores popular Jewish reactions and their hope of staying alive, indicating, understandably, that survival was the prime mover, but there were moments of resistance. As noted in the previous chapter it is impossible to escape the factor of fear and terror initiated and maintained by Himmler, both on the Jews and on those Germans who felt the Jewish persecution was wrong. This proved to be a painful chapter to write as anti-Semitism is racial, the Nazi regime took it to a brutal and evil extreme, but racism, including anti-Semitism remains rife in today's world despite the lessons and regrets of history.

For the nature and reality of everyday life experienced on the streets during Nazi times, it seemed appropriate to explore two diarists, who committed their thoughts at the time and not post-war. First the secret diary of Victor Klemperer a Jewish academic, who in his daily writing of the times demonstrated not only his own feelings of contempt for the Nazi regime, but provides some interesting insights into the public reaction to Jews, some very surprising and hopeful. This is followed by a German diarist Friedrich Kellner who strongly objected to Nazism from its first appearance. As with Klemperer it is important to note that the diary was written as events unfolded and not post-war. Kellner was once threatened by having his past explored to find a Jewish element in his blood stream, it failed, but it was an effort to explain his cynical comments about what was happening under the regime, and to bring about his downfall. Just as with the Jewish population at large, both Klemperer and Kellner lived in fear and like others their personal survival was paramount, but in this chapter, there are signs of what can be best described as passive resistance. Kellner's diary relates the way the general population reacted to news, which like so many people, was thought dependable if it appeared in newspapers or was heard on a broadcast.

Meaning of Resistance and Opposition

This chapter raises the perplexing issue of defining the nature of the word Resistance. It will be raised again later in the text when dealing with specific examples of opposing the regime. Historians and many others have argued over the precise meaning as there are not only many nuances in the meaning of the word, but even more when various acts and diverse factors are involved when defining and understanding the word resistance. To cut short and simplify this academic problem the reader is asked in today's society to consider something which makes him or her 'to want to resist' and thereby understand the various shades of grey.

For example, at the time of writing (2022–2023) the proposal to send immigrants or refugees to Rwanda has caused a sense of rebellion amongst many. A passive act of opposition (or dissent) could be refusing to vote for the government at the next election and convincing friends and neighbours to agree, or even making jokes about those proposing the policy. Passive opposition therefore anticipates that we do not let the government try to persuade us and encourage friends to resist the pressure. To write to the newspapers could be described as active opposition (or protest) because one has gone wider than normal privacy, and especially if one's firm or boss supports the government. If the government is like the Nazi regime it could be called resistance because the ramifications could be life threatening. In other words, the nature of the word 'resistance' in this context depends on the circumstances of the day. In terms of protesting about the Rwanda plan and trying to stop it, the next step is resistance by organising public protests and taking the government to court to stop the policy, this could be described as 'active' resistance. It is an issue which divides the public and whether it is passive opposition or active resistance it demands determination and resilience, especially when living in a politically policed state.

For the sake of clarity, it is proposed to use these words as explained above. There is a cosmic difference between living under a British government in the 2020s to living under Nazi rule in the 1930 and early 1940s, and because of these circumstances what may be called passive opposition today may well verge on active opposition under the Nazi regime. These expressions therefore demand a degree of elasticity dependent on the circumstances of the day. Shouting abuse at a government minister today could fall under passive or active opposition, whereas shouting abuse at Hitler or one of his cohorts would be dangerous and could fall under the meaning of resistance. It is all a matter of historical common sense.

The Jewish issue in Nazi Germany is explored next, indicating that survival was understandably the key intention, but there was passive opposition, and elements of resistance, and active resistance.

Why the Jewish Persecution

Once Hitler grasped power the infamous and well-known onslaught of his anti-Semitic obsession grew exponentially, becoming the greatest blot on mankind's behaviour ever recorded in modern history. It started with the boycott on Jewish shops and legislation banning them from employment. This was followed by the Nuremberg Race Laws, then *Kristallnacht* (November 1938), their financial assets were taken, they became slave labour, moved East to concentration camps thinking they would be resettled in some sort of agricultural commune, but quickly discovered it was to suffer extermination. It was a catastrophic crime by the Nazi regime, which reflected in the shadows of many other European nations where anti-Semitism was rife to one degree or another, and where fleeing Jews were not always welcomed.

The question must be asked: how did all this arise in the first place? Some have blamed Charles Darwin for his naturalist theory of survival of the fittest and natural selection, but nothing could have been further from his mind, and his theory of nature was politicised by others. When the NSDAP had seized on this it had already been pursued in many countries and academic disciplines, but more out of intellectual curiosity. For the NSDAP it became part of the project for the new envisaged Germany, and the foundation of enforced sterilisation and the death camps.[1] Despite the fact that thousands of Jews had died fighting for Germany in the First World War, in 1916 the Ministry of War in Berlin had carried out a survey to see how German Jews were contributing, implying they were either busy making money or avoiding being involved in the fighting. This emerged again in the myth of the stab-in-the back by the Jews had brought about the German defeat. As early as this Jews were being pinpointed by the higher levels of German society as blameworthy, which had an impact on the masses. The NSDAP took hold of this social prejudice and turned anti-Semitism into a major issue, projecting them as enemies of the state and sub-human. They transformed the social claim that 'they are not one of us' into the theme they were a dangerous 'international breed'. It had a major appeal to many Germans, building a deep prejudice which for some even outlived the Second World War, but not for all. It should not be forgotten that as late as February 1943 there was a major protest about the deportation of Jewish men married to German wives. It amounted to some 2,000 wives supported by 4,000 others and the men were released two days later.[2] This incident clearly indicated that not every German citizen had been taken in by the anti-Semitic Nazi claims, and the morality of what was happening had been questioned, and releasing the men indicated the Nazi authority was aware of such feelings. It was no surprise that every effort was made by the regime to keep the massacre of Jews and the extermination camps as quiet as possible. Fear also played a major part in blocking protests by many Germans who felt the Nazi policy was immoral. One historian related a curious account of a young 16-year-old, who had to commute early to work and was accustomed to sitting next to other passengers and chatting with them. When in September 1941 he had to wear the yellow Star of David he was embarrassed but his fellow passengers smiled, telling him to ignore the rules and sit down with them, one giving him a cigarette and another lighting it for him. The next day his friends were all in different carriages, and he conjectured correctly they were frightened of being informed on for being friendly with a Jew.[3] For some Germans they had believed all the Nazis had claimed about Jews, and it is known that the Gestapo heavily relied on informants whose motives may have been politically driven or out of some jealousy or feud with a neighbouring Jew. Denouncing Jews or those who helped them was driven by many motives, including personal grudges, avoiding repaying a debt, but it was more helpful to the Gestapo than their infamous index card system.

There were noticeable changes in the public response to the persecution, and it has been noted that the major impact was between 1935 and 1938 with many greeting the Race Laws as a further means of causing problems for Jews, others hoping it would mean less violence on the streets. However, there was a growing disapproval of the extreme violence, starting with the pogrom of 9–10 November 1938 resulting in *Kritsallnacht* with much criticism. The Nazi policy regarding Jews was becoming less popular when its stark reality was seen firsthand on the streets. It was not the first time this type of barbarity had been experienced in Europe as with the Turkish persecution of the Armenians, and in Ukraine and Poland there had been ghastly attacks on the Jewish residents, all earlier in the twentieth century.

However, in Germany the persecution continued for over a decade. These attacks against Jews were losing favour with many, and as it was the Nazi regime and Nazi members who organised these events, it did not auger well, but they used fear to repress any criticism. Later the extermination camps were kept as secret as possible, and like the Jews many people were under the delusion they were being sent to more if not better living spaces in the east. The regime used expressions such as resettlement, evacuation, and encouraged the Jewish victims to bring their most expensive belongings. Some even managed to persuade them it was for a better life, but boarding the cattle trucks exposed the lies for those who had believed in the Nazi promises. An administrative report from Lower Bavaria stated that most of the population did not understand the pogroms and they were causing unnecessary sympathy for the Jews.[4] There is no question that many everyday Germans accrued doubts as to whether the treatment of the Jews was right, there is some evidence that some helped or hid Jews, but the figures are obscure, not helped by post-war years when even those who baited Jews pretended to have helped, especially as the extermination camps were revealed to public view and notice. The Nazis had persuaded many people that the Jews were an international enemy and therefore German-Jews were traitors, but those not taken in, or who had changed their minds after *Kristallnacht*, knew the regime well enough to keep silent out of fear. If any other German objected or opposed the Nazi regime, they could still lead uninterrupted lives if they either conformed to Nazi regulations or kept a low profile, but to be a Jew in Nazi Germany was a death sentence, on grounds not of faith but race, as being a Jew who had converted to the Christian faith made no difference. Even having a mixed background of having a Jewish grandparent could be dangerous. Most Jews conformed to Nazi demands, but it was a useless effort: as their race marked them out as enemies of the state, they had no possible defence.

German-Jewish Situation

There have been many photographs of helpless Jews queuing up in places like Babi Yar and concentration camps waiting their turn to be shot or gassed, and seemingly without protest. It does not take much imagination to understand why consoling mothers quietly led their children forward with grandparents and others following and complying with the orders to step forward to their deaths. To raise a protest would not stop the killing but could result in a yet more brutal death. Speculatively, the thought must have passed through their minds that by bullet or gas they would either be with their God or not exist, which was preferable to the suffering they were undergoing.

The question has often been asked why, when they were rounded up, they appeared to go so meekly to their deaths with few signs of corporate resistance, and why they seemingly complied with all the Nazi regulations and orders. Undoubtedly some thought it best to avoid any provocation which might make matters worse, others who had experienced the Russian pogroms and persecution in Poland hoped it would run its course, and life would return to normal. The diaspora of Jews across Europe had been a phenomenon spanning well over a thousand years, and in Germany, as in many other countries, many Jews had abandoned their Jewish faith and become either Christian or had no faith, and they considered themselves primarily as German born and bred. According to the historian Hilberg Jewish people had survived persecution by conforming to the demands and values of their host countries.[5]

There was a census conducted in 1933 Germany, stating there were approximately half a million people who called themselves Jewish which was about 0.8 per cent of the entire population. Most of them lived in the cities (33 per cent) such as Berlin and large towns but rarely in the agricultural landscape. Many were in the professions of law, medicine, education, and commerce, and regarded themselves as middleclass Germans through and through by being part of the German fabric. The vast majority (80 per cent) had family background stretching back centuries in Germany, while about 20 per cent were recent immigrants fleeing from the east. These late arrivals known as *Ostjuden* (Eastern Jews) tended to be poorer than the long-term German Jews, and they tended to be more derided, even by some of their own race and faith.

Some 12,000 German Jews had died fighting for Germany in the First World War, and the Organisation of Independent Orthodox Communities wrote to the Reich authorities asking again that they be allowed to fight for 'their' country. It was never answered, and no Jews were allowed in the military services. The government had a total stranglehold over the country as a whole, but it had iron chains around their Jewish citizens. How to react to this severest of oppressions must have been bewildering, and various Jewish organisations helped one another by emerging for a time. They were too few and too widely dispersed and tended to remain localised, and they were simply slowly being crushed by the Nazi regime. Jew baiting, shouting abuse at them, humiliating them by making them scrub pavements was common and shocked many visitors to the country. Anti-Semitism was embarrassingly rife across Europe, usually based on social snobbery but in Germany the propaganda machine was accusing them of being *Untermensch*, meaning inferior to the so-called Ayran race, implying they were sub-human. In Klemperer's diary, explored later in this text, it was clear that not all the German public felt the same way. However, by playing on the ridiculous notion that Jews had betrayed them (stab-in-the-back myth), owned too much German business, money, and property, and controlled the theatres and films, the regime turned social distaste into pure hatred for many of the more unthinking public.

The various complaints to the authority, the committees established to help one another did not amount to resistance, it was more matter of trying to survive. This was epitomised by the efforts made by many committees to help Jews leave the country, to escape while they had time.[6] Many departed to safer countries, but many more stayed hoping that the whole ghastly situation would blow over given time. It has been noted that the USA's immigration quote of 25,000 people per year from Germany was never filled.[7] Later, staggeringly with the benefit of hindsight, many chose to return, probably hoping life had improved. It was also expensive to leave the country becoming more so as the years passed and the regime harshly taxed them. In all, 130,000 German Jews, or almost 20 per cent of the 1933 population, left Germany between 1933 and

1937.[8] More left after *Kristallnacht*, of those left (approximately 164,000) 50 per cent were aged over 50, and 13 per cent under 18.

The diminishing group of such a small section of the population had no opportunity to resist, and the expression of them being led 'like lambs to the slaughter' is unfair. As a people wherever they had settled and given their skills, they were accustomed to persecution, they had always survived by conforming, accommodating to new rules, and this way had survived many potential disasters. No one apart from the most politically alert had any idea of how extreme Hitler's dominating evil nature was. When they forged papers, hid, sheltered others, they were simply trying understandably to survive; they did not have the space in their lives to oppose or resist.

When they were in many places moved into ghettos, which was the forerunner to be transported to extermination camps, the victims found themselves controlled by Nazi selected Jews known as the *Judenräte*. There is no doubt that there were moments when the *Judenräte* could be brutal for their own survival, but it has been sensibly argued that many times they used their given authority for the good of the community over which they had been placed in charge. It was a form of collective responsibility because one man showing resistance could lead to Nazi repercussions and the whole community in that ghetto could be wiped out, again, a matter of hoped-for survival.* There were occasions when the *Judenräte* were able, by sheer bribery to save some potential victims.

There were moments of Jewish resistance when it was realised death was the only other possibility. In the Treblinka concentration camp, when it became known they were to be closed down because of approaching enemy forces which meant death the next day, there was one remarkable fight back. Some 750 inmates fought back with a riot and escaped, and only 100 were recaptured. There was a similar event in the Sobibor camps where about 200 escaped. This was a form of fighting back, but not so much as resistance but, understandably, for sheer survival.

There was one outstanding moment of German-Jewish resistance when a group of some thirty young people, mainly of the communist persuasion fought back against the Nazi regime, not to save themselves from execution but as a matter of offering their lives as a protest. It was a dedicated group led by a young Jew called Herbert Baum. He had been born in 1912 in the Province of Posen, but his family moved to Berlin, where he became a professional electrician. In 1926 he became an active member of various left-wing and Jewish

* For more on this see: Trunk, I, *The Attitudes of the Judenrats to the Problems of Armed Resistance Against the Nazis*, in Yad Vashem, *Jewish Resistance During the Holocaust* (Jerusalem: Yad Vashem, 1971) p.205.

organisations. He was essentially left-wing, often described as a communist, but his political leanings were best described as to the Left. In 1940 he was caught up in slave labour at the electromotive works of Siemens, where he helped Jews to escape deportation to the concentration camps by hiding them in the Berlin underground. In 1942 Goebbels had organised an anti-Soviet exhibition *Das Soviet Paradis* (The Soviet Paradise) in the Lustgarten in Berlin. The remnants of the Red Orchestra group had already printed leaflets disclosing Goebbels' intentions, but Baum demanded more direct action wanting to set the exhibition on fire. Working where he did it was easy to steal the necessary gear for such an attack, and others provided explosives and inflammable material. A small group led by Baum visited the exhibition, discreetly set the materials in place and the exhibition caught fire. They escaped unharmed, and the fire-brigade put the fires out but much of the exhibition had been destroyed. It was naturally kept out of the papers to minimise its impact on public thinking. It did, however, achieve what Baum wanted: to publicize that Jewish activists were working against the regime. It was suspected a Nazi agent had entered the group because Baum and his helpers were soon picked up by the Gestapo. Although he was severely tortured, he refused to give names of uncaptured members, but Baum and those taken with him died at Plötzenseea – a place of many martyrs against Nazism.*

There had been other attempts by young Jews. In March 1937 a student called Helmut Hirsch contacted Otto Strasser and the Black Front in Prague. He was encouraged to return to Germany with a bomb to throw at the anti-Semitic Julius Streicher or at Hitler, but he was known to the Gestapo, was captured, interrogated, and executed. In April 1938 the Gestapo were busy searching for a suspected group of Jews whom they had been told were going to assassinate Hitler, an indicator that some Jews were prepared to be active resisters.[9] A David Frankfurter, another student was Yugoslavian, but his father was Jewish, and travelled to Germany to kill Hitler, but on failing to get close enough shot Wilhelm Gustloff (Nazi Representative in Switzerland) in Davos. Gustloff had a ship named after him which was eventually sunk in the Baltic Sea. There may well have been other Jewish resistance efforts, but as with Baum, they would have been kept quiet in the press, no Nazi official would want it known that sub-humans dared challenge them. The Jewish element in Germany was widely spread, and they were not bound together except by race which for most of them was irrelevant because they were German. There were Orthodox, Liberal, Christian, and non-faith Jews and they existed in mere family groups

* For more on this see: Mark, B., *The Herbert Baum Group. Jewish Resistance in Germany in the Years 1937–42*, in Suhl, Y., *They Fought Back: The Story of the Jewish Resistance in Nazi Europe* (London: MacGibbon and Kee, 1968)

scattered across the cities and towns of Germany. There were many who did not realise they had Jewish blood until Himmler had the records searched. There was simply no way that they could challenge the Nazi regime, which in their way they soon realised to be evil, but they were, through no fault of their own, facing a regime which can only be compared to terrified feathered harmless birds suddenly find themselves being shot at or trapped in cages. That there was some resistance was remarkable and their fate has been a lesson to the world.

Victor Klemperer's Diary

For everyday life experienced on the streets during Nazi times it seemed appropriate to explore two diarists who committed their thoughts at the time and not post-war. The first was an academic Jew who lived in Dresden and who survived. He was Victor Klemperer, and he successfully maintained a diary for many years which has provided some interesting insights into the everyday German. He was married to a non-Jew which helped his personal survival, he was forthright, stubborn, and often insisted on doing the shopping where he met neighbours and shopkeepers and observed their reactions. He used the expression *vox populi* to indicate what everyone was thinking about, how they were reacting, and the way they were influenced, especially by the thousands of rumours. Although anti-Semitism was rife Klemperer noted there were many who found it ridiculous. 'Some shopkeepers served him below the counter, and one would snap his scissors pretending to cut up coupons' and he often mentioned other helpful Aryans.[10] His interest was listening to friends and their views because news was limited. He gave a record of the German public mind with all the uncertainties, false rumours, and occasional insights. Klemperer recognised that everyone was dependent on the latest remark or rumour. As his diary unfolded, he soon discovered that his usual shopkeepers varied as some became frightened to serve him with the anti-Jewish restrictions, with a few cautious but amenable, while others took the risk serving him thereby indicating their sympathy. Those who were not anti-Semitic often had to pretend they were out of personal fear and being denounced to the Gestapo. On one occasion when he tried to buy a loaf without the tokens required for Jews 'the shopkeeper whispered: for God's sake never ask the girl [Assistant] for that' because, he was told, that she was a Nazi supporter.[11] Time and time again he managed to record the time when some of the shopkeepers showed a degree of kindness towards him despite the prohibitions being imposed on Jewish people.

The sense of fear of being denounced by a neighbour or colleagues pervaded all of German society and must remain a factor in trying to understand how the Nazi regime maintained its grip over its critics. On one occasion while travelling on a tram, being a Jew, he was not allowed a seat, and he had become of interest to a young Gestapo officer and soon found himself inside the Gestapo building. He was treated badly, questioned about his life, where he had been shopping, verbally insulted, and whether he was in that area because he knew the shopkeepers. He was eventually released but badly shaken, writing 'the business of their fabulous tyranny, brutality, mocking humiliation had taken hold of me far too much. Since then, I have no longer been able to get rid of thoughts of death'.[12] To be a Jew under the Nazi regime to this day remains an horrific memory, and this fear percolated through non-Jewish Germans who tried to assist their one-time neighbours.

Klemperer was no fool, he soon learnt whom to trust, but even those who treated him as a fellow human being and shared their feelings were often influenced by Goebbels' broadcasts, and when they were missing, they depended on rumour. He had a good friend in the local grocer called Vogel. Klemperer regarded him as a calm man and not a Nazi, and when Klemperer asked about his thoughts on Poland, Vogel replied, 'he'll probably bring it off again', with Klemperer concluding that this was all too typical of the *vox populi* rumours.[13] When writing this diary it was evident that he was trying to penetrate the minds of his German neighbours, writing 'who can judge the mood of 80 million people, with the press bound and everyone afraid of opening their mouth?'[14] It was a repressed society and Klemperer exposed this fact.

Once on the way to a local dairy some 'Hitler Youth cubs' ran after Klemperer shouting 'A Yid' and when he emerged from the shop they shouted again. A few hours later at a nursery an elderly worker called out 'You, mate, do you know Herrschmann? – No? – he's a Jew too, porter like me – I just wanted to say: it does not matter about the star, we are all human beings, and I know such good Jews'.[15]

His life like many Germans was totally overshadowed by the Nazi regime, and since it was criminal to listen to foreign broadcasts, and they were only fed what the propaganda ministry wanted them to hear their information was gleaned by gossip, sometimes reflecting the truth, at other times wildly off-mark. He heard from his neighbour Frau Voss of some rumours from a tram-driver that soldiers fresh from the Eastern Front 'didn't want to go on fighting there', but everything remained vague. He heard from another fellow resident Paul Kreidl that Jews had been shot at Riga, later Klemperer would hear of Auschwitz, but he had little idea of developing Nazi policies known as the Final Solution, which he did not mention until 1946. By mid-January they became aware that mass-transportations to the East were happening, writing in his notes *cras tibi* (old Latin term meaning 'your turn tomorrow') hoping his marriage to an Aryan might save him. The residents were distressed over these rumours, and Klemperer tried to comfort Frau Voss.[16] The rumours in this part of his diary were correct, and there is no doubt that many Germans were aware of some atrocities, but many like Klemperer had probably not realised about the Final Solution and the sheer brutality of the camps. This and other pieces of information such as the persistent English bombing caused Klemperer to ruminate, writing that 'very little of this may be true…but gives much more credence to rumour or grapevine than to the newspaper, which lies and withholds information'.[17] Like many others the facts were so unbelievable he could hardly believe them.

It would be impossible to find an accurate statistical view of popular German thinking in a society controlled by the Gestapo, but Klemperer's diaries offered many insights into everyday life on German streets and in the shops. Klemperer had every reason to fear and hate the Nazi regime, he knew that it had many supporters but to this day his diaries provide some valuable insights, and although the vast majority of his neighbours were cowed by fear many Germans were brave enough to support the detested Jew designated by the state as the enemy.

Friedrich Kellner's Diary

The second diary amounts to a survey by a passive resister who kept a massive diary outlining his thoughts about Nazism. There are many endnotes in case the reader wants to read the passages from the translation. This diary which opens the complex issue of public thought was written by a mid-level German civil servant working as an administrator in the court system in the small town of Laubach in the Gießen region of Hesse. His name was Friedrich Kellner (1885–1970), who had fought in the First World War and had been a determined opponent of the Nazis from its earliest emergence to its final destruction. He wrote a diary of short essays with his views and those of others.[18] It was by Nazi standards an act of treachery, but demanded much bravery as his views, if known, would have led to his immediate execution. His diary brings to light many invaluable insights about the public reaction to the Nazi regime, not just those who were critical, but also his anger with fellow Germans who were entrapped by the Nazi promises. Although the 'resistance' element is not strongly represented, apart from his views, it is an important diary to understand why so many normal Germans stood by the Nazi regime until its final destruction. In his writings he reflects what he has overheard or gleaned from others about public reaction. Many times, he deploys a cynical and bitter language, mainly because he was aware of the barbaric treatment of the Jews, PoWs, and others who suffered from their treatment by the Nazis; he was in short, a highly moral person. His righteous anger against some of his countrymen was well-founded with the benefit of hindsight, but it raises the painful question of how easily a cunning political system can induce so many people into immoral behaviour. Kellner's observations and comments help today's generation understand why resistance to the Nazi regime was not as widespread as it may have been, while at the same time indicating the courage of those who did resist.

Kellner's experience of the First World War meant he hated jingoism, and his father had influenced his views, instructing him to read Hitler's *Mein Kampf* to foresee the dangers of Hitler's thinking processes. Although Hitler's book was monotonous and repetitive, it was a shame that it was not read more widely both in Germany and other countries because the warning bells are evident. When Kellner's own son indicated signs of being influenced by the Nazi indoctrination, he packed him off to relatives in America, such was Kellner's fear of the future.

Kellner was personally brave (along with his wife Pauline) as he often made his views known to friends and colleagues. At one time he was warned, mainly because of the way he challenged the immoral way the Jews were treated, that he and Pauline would be investigated for Jewish ancestry of which there was no proof. He was fully aware that he was being watched, especially when he offered passive resistance such as refusing to billet a German soldier. He once stumbled upon a note in the office, which read 'Kellner's attitude exerts a bad influence on the rest of the population, and in our view, he should be made to disappear from Laubach'.[19] Even his hired typist spied on him, and a Judge Bishoff kept probing him for defeatist remarks, causing Kellner to describe himself as a 'preacher in the wilderness'.[20] In June 1942 the former Mayor Julius Johann Boehm shouted 'Heil Hitler' at him, with Kellner noting that 'apparently I had answered his greeting too weakly'.[21] He was open with his criticisms, explaining how when he told some acquaintances that America and England will soon attack Germany 'I always meet with incredulity'.[22] When he spoke to Judge Bischoff explaining the Allied landings in North Africa had to be taken seriously, Bischoff replied it was a mistake because the Allied supply lines were too long. It was a dangerous conversation in Nazi Germany, and his friend Delp (to be mentioned later) told Kellner to be careful as Bischoff was an old Party member.[23] Later Bischoff told Kellner he blamed the Jews for everything, accusing them of profiting out of war, which, given that a Judge should have some education and intelligence, was astonishing. When Kellner replied pointing out that the firm Krupp-Essen also made money, Bischoff warned him he had a strange mental attitude he had noticed before.[24] The following year, in October 1943, Kellner was called into the Regional Court President Jacobi's office and warned to set a good example.[25] As an individual in what he regarded as an estranged or alien society Kellner exhibited unbelievable courage.

On Hitler

Had his diaries ever become known it would have meant the People's Court followed by immediate execution. The prosecution need only have looked at his cynical descriptions of Hitler for the guillotine to be oiled. In early 1940 he referred to Hitler as 'this unemployed immigrant from Austria who wants to control the world'.[26] He wrote foreigners may wonder why he is not overturned, but they do not see 'the jumble of interconnections that make up the Nazi Party's organisation, its federations and associations at ground level…have total command and grind down the people'.[27] He later wrote that 'A neutral observer can see the German dictator will endure no other god besides himself.'[28] He never held back on his forthright views, writing in the same year1942 'Who will be able to tell our progeny about this rat-catching pied piper, Adolf Hitler, with his absolute terribleness – he, the sole culprit in the mass murder which began in 1939? A great number of helpers share the guilt: stirrup holders, bootlickers, and fellow travellers without conscience and character'.[29] As the war turned against Germany (in 1943 for the more astute) Kellner wanted Hitler to live, otherwise people will say 'if only Hitler had lived' … 'with Hitler into the abyss, that is what I wish for the German nation', confirming this again when he heard of the 20 July Plot and Hitler's survival.[30] In 1943 he added to his diary that 'I almost forgot the Führer's speech of 10 September, It took the collapse of Italy to open his mouth'.[31]

He used the same vitriol on Italy, when hearing the Greeks had the better of the would-be Italian occupiers. He wrote 'Dear Duce! You are a complete Dunce' and later…'This Duce is for me a bandit. History will also treat him as such.'[32] He then added that the king of Italy will place his rusty Abyssinian crown in the junkyard of history.[33] In a society where the Gestapo's tentacles reach into every home and office it was amazing that he was clever enough to hide his writings, and brave enough to speak to colleagues even some of his more reserved thoughts. As with the man in the crowd who did not salute, Kellner stands alone but was noticed, shaping his own form of personal opposition.

Views on Conduct of War

He made immense notes on the conduct of the war, expressing his opinions in the privacy of his study. He may have been a Great War soldier, but he was no military strategist. In 1943 as the Allies were invading Italy, he wrote that on 'looking at the map Italy is hardly a country more difficult to defend' and later blamed the Allies for taking their time.[34] Military historians may agree with his criticism of Allied leadership, but with its terrain of valleys, rivers, mountains Italy was an ideal country for defence. He was much happier when Italy changed sides, noting the public response: 'Primarily considerable surprise, the hesitance, dark premonitions, shaking the head, and attempts to grasp at another straw' and cynically noting that Mussolini wanted a 1,000-year empire and had 20 years, Hitler the same but only ten so far.[35] He had a depressive attitude about the slowness of Allied reaction, noting in May 1940 that 'it is almost impossible to believe how the French and English committed so many tremendous errors these past years' and then listed them.[36] When he heard the King of Belgium had ordered his troops to lay down weapons he wrote 'only a madman could do that'.[37] Later in June he suggested matters would have been different if the French had attacked in September 1939, which may have held some possible veracity.[38]

He returned to his views on *Mein Kampf* writing that 'Only a single man among the opponents, in my opinion, recognised the danger, and that was Churchill', and opponents should have read *Mein Kampf* where Hitler defined France as the hereditary enemy.[39] When in November he heard Chamberlain had died, and German papers had branded him a firebrand, Kellner was more critical for him trying to establish peace.[40] Later he added that Chamberlain was the man who said 'peace at any price' and 'he should have been a parson in a small village.'[41] Again there would have been many who may have thought the same even in Britain. In 1942 when Britain was suffering from the U-boat attacks in the North Atlantic, it was curious that Kellner noted the English blockade is being felt increasingly, and he rightly understood that since the British Royal Navy had cut off German imports, he felt Hitler would turn east against Russia for resources.[42]

His Moral views

However, Kellner's diary is of interest, not solely because of his observations on the conduct of the war, but because he was a man who resisted the Nazi regime on moral grounds. He disliked the Nazi attempt to occupy other countries, the way they treated PoWs, the attacks on Polish citizens, but especially the way, as he had seen early in the regime's existence, their brutal attitude towards the Jewish people. Anyone living in Germany as the Nazis asserted their power would have been aware of the brutal anti-Semitism taking place in the streets. Many, as in other European nations were embedded with this racial attitude. Some may have rejoiced in the humiliation of their neighbours for financial jealously, many would have been hoodwinked by the nonsense of the 'stab-in-the-back' myth, others like sheep followed the crowd or kept quiet behind closed doors for personal safety reasons. In 1939 Kellner had noticed that in the grocer's store he used, the usual assistant had been called up for military service, so the owner came in and refused to serve a Jew, prompting Kellner to ask himself 'why have we become so cruel a people?'[43] In November Kellner mentioned Göring's special plans for Jews within employment regulations and listed the seven instructions. Kellner promptly wrote that it would have been easier simply to say 'Jews are not people but slaves'.[44] He later heard that Jews were being transported east, noting that 'they treat the Jews worse than animals'.[45] At this stage, he and many others would not know until May 1945 that his comment that treating Jews worse than animals was so pertinent as animals are not generally physically and mentally tortured on the way to the abattoir. In 1942 he noted that 'this so-called *clearing* of Europe of Jews will remain a dark chapter in the history of mankind', a comment true to this day.[46] He also noted other forms of Nazi oppression, in 1941 writing that there were more deaths in the mental care facility at Hadamar, a place for incurables, and they are building a crematorium.[47] In 1943, he noted the 'District leader wants a list of people who have withdrawn from their church', adding that 'yesterday the Area Farm Leader Metzger from Röthges had me notarise his declaration of withdrawal from the Church'.[48] From Jews, the mentally and physically sick, to Church attenders and many others, the Nazi regime imposed its evil laws by sheer force and brutality. It was so gross the question has to be asked why there was not a general uprising of protest.

Oppression and Propaganda

In April 1944 Kellner wrote that the Party big shot, Dr Otto Thierack [Nazi jurist and politician] had opened his campaign against alarmists and defeatists, demanding these people need to be exterminated.[49] The very word 'exterminate' should have sent a cold shudder through any person hearing or reading this speech, the sense of fear would have grown among many.

Kellner offers many answers, but not directly. He never stated that 'for this or that reason' people agreed, or kept quiet, possibly because he could not understand it himself, as he was opposed to the regime, but he could achieve little, other than passive resistance in his own way. Throughout his diaries he mentions the power of propaganda and the almost mesmeric effect Hitler had over the masses. For many, especially amongst the military critics, there was silence after Hitler's success in Czechoslovakia, Poland, the Low Countries and France, but even when the tide turned against Germany between the Eastern Front and the Western Allies, Kellner noted a few changes in attitudes, but still many continued to believe in Hitler and the Party. There were two components which Kellner noted in his diary: the element of persuasive propaganda and the fear of the guillotine, both of which influenced the public at large.

Kellner was acutely aware of how Goebbels' propaganda machine manipulated people's opinions and bolstered the belief in Nazism. He wrote about how the sinking of the *Royal Oak* [in Scapa Flow by U-boat attack] had created a frenzy along with the news of air attacks and victories, noting that these Nazi successes 'brought the majority of the people to believe in an omnipotent Adolf Hitler'.[50] When, in December, it was reported that the *Graf Spee* had been forced to scuttle itself, it was countered by reports of the number of RAF planes shot down, with Kellner recording he had a different story from the British, asking 'the prize question: which is the truth?'[51] These early successes were of prime importance to the German public, too accustomed to post-1918 and being treated as a pariah state, and now Hitler was fulfilling his promises of making Germany Great Again. In March 1940 Kellner heard about the supposed destruction of the entire English fleet, yet he noted that we conceal the fact that England has crippled our overseas trade, no overseas markets.[52] Kellner reported that the propaganda was ceaseless with news full of heroic acts by pilots, U-boat crews and reconnaissance troops, each article painting pictures of heroic young military men. It was not just radio broadcasts and newspapers, but the Party had various travelling speakers moving from community to community. Kellner was summoned to Solmser Hof Inn to listen to such a person, the 'babbler', who was on about money collections, said 'maybe after the war the soldiers who fought at the front will be shown lists, and those who did not give enough will have their faces smashed'.[53] Kellner added that 'after France's extraordinary collapse, the broad mass of Germans do not in the slightest resent the total imposition upon them by Nazi propaganda', and 'I have hardly met a German who believes we might possibly fail in our attack against England'.[54] In 1941 he was bemused that the Japanese Ambassador was given such a warm welcome, but Kellner worked out that it had all been organised by Goebbels' machinery.[55] He noted that the German people had been led to believe that all the English cities had been destroyed, but asked why, therefore, a second attack on Coventry was made.[56]

These propaganda themes were taken on board by many of the public, and in 1943 while in a waiting room Kellner found it 'torturous' to listen to two men saying the loss of English pilots would soon become too burdensome' for them to continue the fight.[57] Despite the military setbacks the propaganda wing started to praise 'defence' as a demonstration of success, and he listed a number of newspaper headlines which announced success after success.[58]

It was not just Goebbels' teams who influenced the public but Hitler's speeches, and on 1 January 1944 Kellner mentioned Hitlers' speech in which he stated 'Our one prayer to the Lord God should not be that He presents us with a victory, but that He weighs us justly according to our boldness, our bravery, our diligence, and also our sacrifices'. Prompting Kellner to write that 'The Lord God cursed by every National Socialist is beseeched in their great distress'.[59] As the war turned against Germany it still seemed strange that the anti-Church dictator appeared to be appealing to the Divine. Even to the end the propaganda continued. Kellner noted that the word retreat, which was happening on all fronts was never used, being replaced by the expression the 'shortening of our front'.[60]

In June 1944, the propaganda produced massive headlines such as 'MASSIVE DESTRUCTIVE FIRE ON LONDON' as V-1s, the wonder weapons were used.[61] The papers and broadcasts were offering hope, even though it was the same time that the Russians pushed towards Germany's borders and the Western Allies shattered German cities and towns with ceaseless bombing raids. The main bolstering news was about the production of special weapons (V-1s and V-2s) with hints of more to come. Kellner noted that 'the Party uses lies up to the last moment as a cover-up. Thus, it intimidates the political opponents and provides its Party comrades with sedatives'.[62] He accused the Nazis of being 'the greatest cover-up artists', writing that 'ever since Stalingrad they have been writing up all their defeats as successes and know the German people can be fooled into believing them'.[63]

Kellner's diary throughout its lengthy text underlines the power of propaganda and the way it managed to convince the German public of a final success even as enemy troops moved towards Berlin. Many modern readers may lack any sympathy for the way many of the German public reacted so positively to this propaganda, but this tends to rest on the benefit of hindsight, knowing the so-called wonder-weapons were only directed at Britain which although causing considerable damage, never hindered the defeat of Germany. There is in any national community those who are more gullible than others, and to this day the statement that 'it is in the newspapers' or 'it was on the TV or radio news' is sufficient for many to believe it must therefore be true. This is especially true when it appears that a potential disaster will be thwarted. Imagine if the news appeared that 'Climate Change can be Halted in a Month with a new Scientific Discovery'. There would be considerable rejoicing as a glimmer of hope was offered, for some they would want to know more details, others would be highly sceptical. Some would question the raison d'être for planting such unlikely news, but many others would accept it at face value as it appeared to offer hope in the context of an impending disaster. Kellner always managed a balanced view and others many have thought the same way, but to this day it is probably the case that most people would believe such headlines and propaganda as it offered hope.

Observations on German Public

Perhaps the most informative insights into the German public under Nazi rule comes from Kellner's observations of what Klemperer (the other explored diarist) called the *vox populi*, what the man next door or on the Clapham omnibus was thinking. Kellner often writes about what he overheard, sometimes his personal conversations with others, and information he had gleaned from various sources. His writing often exposes his sheer anger and frustration at the responses to his own anti-Nazi views, or declarations by others who had fallen under the spell of the regime and its promises. When it came to many of his friends and neighbours being hoodwinked by Nazi propaganda his cynical anger knew no bounds.

Probably because of the years leading up to the war Kellner had lost trust in the German public, having seen their adulation of Hitler, and indulging in violent anti-Semitism he had hoped they would come to their senses if a major war erupted. However, he dampened this hope by writing that 'unfortunately, the few Germans with sense and understanding will have to suffer through it, but such is fate'.[64] Kellner had been furious when Goebbels had stated 'insolently that Peace had been preserved only by Hitler's peaceful demeanour', and the Germans believed this, 'against stupidity the gods themselves contend in vain'.[65] When war broke out in September 1939, Kellner wrote 'the foolish people are intoxicated by the German Army's exaggerated initial success in Poland. Tales of atrocities of the worst kind are buzzing in the air and inside the heads of the armchair warriors and food ration cards measures introduced at home…many think the Axis alliance will work, but forget Italy changed sides in 1915'.[66] The Germans had allowed themselves to become slaves, 'a harassed tormented, intimidated, and extremely subjugated people are supposed to let themselves be shot dead for a tyrant', which was sadly prophetic given this entry was September 1939.[67] The one thing which gave Kellner some pleasure was noting in his daily work in the courts that the most notable offences of petty theft appearing in court were committed by NSDAP members.[68] Like others he was bemused by Rudolf Hess' unexpected arrival in Britain hoping it would help 'the scales fall from the blind German people's eyes!' At the very least he hoped it was 'the worm in the apple'.[69] He simply could not believe or understand why 'professional intellectual leaders with professors at the front shoved aside previous principles and stood by the Party'.[70] He later added that 'there are men among the German people who could bring about change, but nobody moves therefore everyone must be held to account'.[71]

As the years passed, he would hear of many executions among defeatists and opponents, and like many other people, Kellner wished to stay in post, so it was essential to be either a Party member or keep quiet. The Nazi control was extremely repressive and personal safety was and is often at the forefront of most people's minds. Kellner knew that he was being watched carefully with colleagues trying to rein him in, trying to get him to 'lie down'…'and among like-minded acquaintances I pull out all the stops.'[72] There were others who shared his views, but he was careful and selective, adding that 'not a single convinced Nazi remains in my circle'.

He once noted that 'when you glance at a stranger, your first glance is not anywhere in the face but at the heroic breast to ascertain what kind of spiritual offspring he is', as this would indicate whether the person wore a member badge or Nazi decoration.[73] He had a particular distaste for a Lutheran Pastor Goldman whom he called 'the fantasy endowed barstool strategist', who was always singing the Führer's praises, and Kellner often commented on the lack of direct opposition by the Church.[74] He also mentioned a Pastor Ferdinand Scriba whom he described as a convinced Hitlerist, preaching one day on 'thou shalt not kill', and next day followed by the blessing of weapons.[75]

Kellner was equally distraught the way children were indoctrinated in the Nazi dreams of adulation and war. He wrote that on the Führer 's birthday it was established as time for 'youth commitment for boys and girls aged 10. They get a uniform and feel the breath of militarism'.[76] Several times he heard young boys singing 'today Germany belongs to us, and tomorrow the whole world', and was told that kindergarten children were taught the following:

> Fold your hands; let your head sink,
> And always on the Führer think.[77]

It was as if the Nazi machine were trying to replace the worship of God by the figurehead of Adolf Hitler.

As soon as there were preparations for war, money was spent. Initially it was welcomed as much labour was required in the factories, industrial sites, and the building of new motorways. They were constructed more for the purpose of military transport than family cars, and by the war years Kellner noted that the 'Highways are quiet, ... no more motorised Germany as there is no fuel', and Kellner suggested they would be best guides for enemy aircraft.[78] It did not take long for the public to feel the lack of food and purchase power, and soon the papers were full of condemnations for the rise of the black market. Nevertheless, the propaganda machinery made rapid use of the situation blaming it on Jews and claiming England was suffering the same issue and therefore also hated the Jews for the same reason. Kellner wondered why the 'sideswipe at the Jews', providing no thoughts on the matter, but it may have been the propaganda's intention to indicate Germany had good reason to be anti-Semitic.[79] On the domestic front he heard his wife's sister had waited two hours at the butchers' for meat. Raising the question of how 'folks like us find themselves constantly asking the question of how it was possible a cultured people like the Germans could have handed absolute authority to a single man?'[80] Kellner observed that where he lived there were no signs or even sounds of war, but they were feeling the economic impact. Much later Kellner was obliged to collect for the winter war effort, noting 'I received 13.20 RM from 18 donators. I did not notice any joyous givers'.[81] Despite the desperate situation of food shortages and lack of spendable currency people were still buoyed up by the propaganda. He heard the wife of a farm leader in Münster declare 'we will have everything again in huge amounts after the war' and later a soldier's wife was convinced every fighter will be given a cottage on conquered land.[82]

Kellner was, however, more interested in listening to how the *vox populi* watched the war's progress. As early as 1939 chatting with a Major Goldman who opined that the 'War will be over in six days', made Kellner even more cynical. A Josef Hessler 'claimed French soldiers had set up signs along the Western Front with the words '*we will not shoot*'. Meanwhile the internal repression grew with an SS officer Wolf asking a man called Heck whether his supervisor Kellner greeted him in the morning with Heil Hitler? Frau Anna Steller Jochem said 'This is really a great and glorious time!' Weisel, the gardener, claimed that 'Mussolini was going after the Suz Can, Tunis and Corsica'.[83] A few days later Kellner commented on the depressed mood as 'the war measures are burdening people's minds…the blackouts greatly discomfort everyone…and shortage of labour' as conscription increased, with Kellner adding the rhetorical question 'who carries the blame?' and answering with 'the people without a brain!'[84] Kellner held strong opinions and in October 1939 felt safe to share them. He spoke to his senior clerk Becker who believed German troops would land in England supported by submarines and 30,000 aircraft but, Kellner noted, 'my few objections bounce off without success', ... 'success in Poland has deranged the majority of the people. At the least, it has strongly impaired their power to comprehend'.[85] It appeared to Kellner that what he was hearing was that after Poland everyone thought Hitler would continue to be successful. A Frau Monfang said, 'Adolf needs only to press on the button and then everything is finished', later a Karl Klein said, 'In four to five weeks we will be finished with the English', his wife adding that 'then everything will be available again'.[86]

After victory in France and initial successes against a surprised Soviet Union [whose leader Joseph Stalin refused to believe his partner Hitler in occupying Poland, would turn the tanks on him], the public on the whole believed Hitler would succeed. Kellner recorded that a young 18-year-old Helga Elbe said that 'it is completely fine with me that they attacked Russia, otherwise they would have attacked us'. On the other hand, Judge Dr Hornef was 'depressed about the war spreading', and a court Bailiff Ludwig Brunner told Kellner that 'we will not have an easy task with Russia and the war will no longer be ended this year', Kellner noting that Brunner had become a sceptic.[87]

Optimism was always in the air at the start of Operation *Barbarossa*, with Kellner picking up the vibes from a doctor's waiting room that most would be pleased with 'more conquests' in Russia, and Otto Schneidt claiming the 'Russian armies will be captured in eight days'.[88] One of Kellner's friends, Helga Elbe had visited a relative in a field hospital, and when asked how she had found the mood, replied patients and doctors thought they would be finished with Russia this year, then over to England.[89] A senior magistrate thought it had to be a German victory because he did not think Russians were intelligent enough to win.[90] He met a teacher on a train journey who expressed loudly 'that the British Empire will be completely destroyed within four months', a lady from Dortmund who 'is hoping the English will soon starve to death' and Frau Dietz who said 'Hitler has been sent to us by God'.[91] He heard from a Frau Doll the headmaster's wife, that she could not understand 'why other nations are against us since we only want to bring about good things. Such idiocy, [Kellner noted] is much more widespread than one would assume'.[92] Hilde Conrad claimed the 'Führer of course is infallible and untouchable', and Kellner mentioned so many similar views it would be absurd to list them all.[93]

Signs of Opposition

Much of Kellner's diary reflected his anger at fellow Germans, those who were Party members, and those who had allowed themselves to be indoctrinated to believe in Nazi propaganda and news results. However, throughout the diary occur snatches that there were others like Kellner who despised and did not trust the regime. He read about Oskar Uebel who was sentenced to 10 years for listening to a foreign broadcast, but on appeal that was not considered enough for the senior Reich prosecutor who ordered the death sentence.[94] Later he heard of 52-year-old Councillor Theodor Korselt from Rostock who was executed by the People's Court for 'aiding the enemy by his defeatist talk' and soon after the same happened to a pianist called Kaarl Robert Kreiten.[95] Even as late as 1945 Kellner reported Ferdinand Lang from Salzburg who had listened to enemy broadcasts, spread his hostility, and was executed by the People's Court.[96] Kellner recorded the time Josef Axinger had found leaflets dropped by Allied planes and distributed them, and for this was executed'.[97] When Frau Desch, an innkeeper's wife, denounced Captain Menz for insulting Hitler the officer was given 3 years in prison. Anyone could denounce anyone else and such denouncements were at times rife. The punishment was swift and often death, so it is not surprising that people kept quiet, but Kellner carefully noted the number of people who opposed and paid with their lives.

Although Kellner had at first refused to have a soldier billeted in his home he later accepted one, probably in case he was denounced. He knew the soldier staying with him was quizzed as to whether he was happy with Kellner. He mentioned his guest, Corporal Ehlert, describing him as a decent man who never spoke one word too many. He 'did not seem one hundred per cent convinced about National Socialism, but on the other hand he believed German weapons would be victorious'.[98] For safety reasons Kellner did not seem to push the questions, probably fearful of any ramifications, but he was evidently pleased to find a soldier who did not appear to be a full-blooded Nazi. When at the Giest Inn in Altenhain a soldier home on leave said, according to Kellner 'in front of everyone he believed all the stories about the attacks against England were lies, and he would not believe anything unless he personally could see it. Now there is a rare bird! It is encouraging that despite everything, small rays of light are visible'.[99] It was pleasing for Kellner not only to find people who questioned the regime but were prepared to speak out; it was potentially dangerous, and Kellner was right to call him a 'rare bird'. When the local teacher's son came home and was asked why he was depressed, he replied that it was because he was to become a paratrooper 'and it would be terrible until he got accustomed to murdering women and children…they were to kill everyone who got in their way.'[100] Later Kellner heard another soldier mention that he had seen the most terrible atrocities in occupied Poland, obviously marking a man of conscience who disliked what was happening.[101]

Not everyone agreed with Kellner's views and when he told some colleagues that the USA entry will achieve great things, he noted that 'I am met with disbelieving faces…it easier to storm a bunker'.[102] He found people's attitudes difficult to fathom, despite years of indoctrination and promises of success the growing disaster of bombing, and the number of wounded soldiers many people still held firm. When he took a brief vacation in Freudenstadt Kellner noted many sick and wounded armed forces personnel. Major hotels had been converted into field hospitals; business life was languishing, and he could not have been the only person to see this growing misery.[103] Some people were accumulating doubts by late 1944, and in the waiting room Kellner noticed in the chatter old Party members who were becoming pessimistic because of bombing raids, noting that 'so even the oldest Party comrades begin to lose their faith'.[104] Judge Boländer on leave from Crimea, who had once been critical of Kellner's views, told him that he had been right, and a day later another personal critic Judge Bischoff agreed. The lack of victories being announced made many understand Germany could not win, but Kellner noticed that many Party members remained optimistic.[105] Even as late as 1944 with the V-1s and V-2s were being utilised, with Kellner already noting they were used only against England, he overheard the conversation which maintained that 'if England collapses the war is over in six months'.[106] He took some pleasure when he related how 'one joker said 'V'

Adoring Hitler, 1939; the crowds became fewer during 1942–3. (*Public domain*)

The formidable building of terror in Berlin – Prinz Albrecht Straße Secret State Police Main Office. (*Bundesarchiv, Bild 183-R97512*)

Repression by terror – Gestapo torture instruments, 1946. (*Photographer unknown, Bulgarian Archives State Agency*)

A bathroom becomes a place of terror. Gestapo torture room. (*Photographer unknown, Wikimedia*)

The man who would not salute, June 1936. (*arastiralim.net, public domain*)

Dietrich Bonhoeffer. (*Photographer unknown, Bundesarchiv, Bild 146-1987-047-16*)

The place of execution today. (*Author's photograph*)

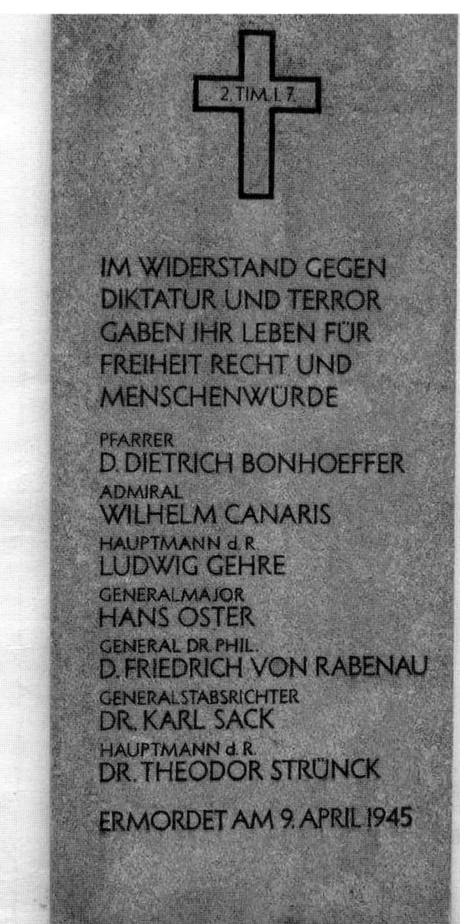

Flossenbürg concentration camp memorial. The plaque reads: 'In resistance to dictatorship and terror, they gave their lives for freedom, rights and human dignity'. (*Author's photograph*)

Bishop Augustinus von Galen. (*Photographer Gustav Albers, Bildersammlung des Bistumarchivs Münster*)

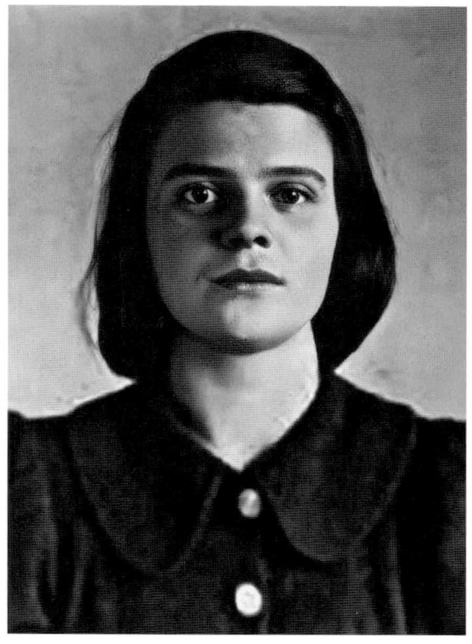

Sophie Scholl from Gestapo records. (*Author Madelgarius*)

Carl Goerdeler. (*Photographer unknown, Bundesarchiv, Bild 146-1993-069-06/CC-BY-SA 3.0*)

Schulenburg in People's Court. Note his disdainful look at Freisler. (*The Estate of Fritz-Dietlof von der Schulenburg*)

General Ludwig Beck. (*Photographer unknown, Bundesarchiv, Bild, 146-1980-033-04/CC-BY-SA 3.0*)

General Hans Oster. (*Photographer unknown, Bundesarchiv, Bild 146-2004-0007*)

Moltke in People's Court. (*Photographer unknown, BPK, Photo Agency of Art, Culture and History*)

Claus Schenk Graf von Stauffenberg. (*Wikimedia*)

General Henning von Tresckow. (*Photographer unknown, Bundesarchiv, Bild 146-1976-130-53/ CC-BY-SA 3.0*)

Mussolini and Hitler at Hitler's damaged headquarters after von Stauffenberg's failed assassination attempt. (*Photographer unknown, Bundesarchiv, Bild 146-1969-071A-03*)

A session of the People's Court, with Roland Freisler, President of the Court, in the centre. (*Photographer unknown, Bundesarchiv, Bild 151-39-23*)

Berlin Holocaust Memorial. (*Photographer Mike Peel, permission CC-BY-SA-4.0*)

in V-1 stands for *Verzweiflung* [desperation]. Not bad. Another took the saying, "Lies have short legs" and turned it into "The liar Goebbels has a short leg"'.[107]

Friedrich Kellner could not be described as an active resister but more as a passive opponent. Even this took courage not only in maintaining a diary but even expressing his views as he frequently did with colleagues. There would have been many more like him who despised the barbarities of the Nazi regime for taking Germany into a major destructive war. When the successful Allies insisted on 'collective guilt' it may have held some truth for the vast numbers of the public enthralled by the Nazi promises and initial successes, but not everyone. Naturally, Kellner was worried for his country in the post-war years, not just because once again Germany was a pariah state, but with the Nazi atrocities, Germany was hated by many other nations. He noted that 'the germs of this sickness are so deep it will take many years to form a new human type – of which other countries will say: "the German is a decent person"'.[108] Much later he added that 'Hopefully there are at least amongst the emigrants who left Germany some courageous and determined men because only they will be in a position at the end of the war to bring some order into this pigsty'.[109]

On 7 May when the war concluded he made a pertinent note amongst his final entries, that 'Allied broadcasts are reporting about what happened in concentration camps, some want to put the blame on the whole German people...'I would like to insert a caveat against such an unfair evaluation in which every German who offered active or passive resistance is being condemned likewise guilty, that is not logic on the accusers' part'.[110] He then added 'If this kind of blanket justice were applied against the decent people in the USA when negroes were lynched there, it would be most abhorrent', picking up the relevant point that what was being condemned was not just a German problem but a human issue with a long history, globally widespread, and with ongoing examples to this day.[111]

A couple of weeks after he had finished his diary, he pasted a pastoral letter written by the Archbishop of Canterbury, Dr G. F. Fisher from London on 31 May 1945 expressing his own feelings about the German people. It read:

> We may not forget there are Germans who opposed national Socialism and had been put in concentration camps to suffer. These Germans were ashamed of their own people and are deeply humiliated …we may not ignore the fact that there were also Germans who did fight against the evil…directly on these few lives rests our hope for the German people's rehabilitation and moral uplifting.[112]

The letter must have rung many bells for Kellner and many other repressed Germans who had not supported the regime, but they could do next to nothing to overturn the disgraceful and evil machinery which controlled their lives.

Chapter Four

Passive Opposition to Resistance

***Author's Notes:** This chapter outlines the different forms of resistance which occurred in Germany during the Nazi rule. The shape of the resistance falls under all the definitions related in the previous chapter, ranging from passive to active opposition, then on to the various shades from resistance to active resistance indicating a direct attack. This chapter starts by looking at several known individuals who objected to the Nazi regime and made their attitudes clear, ranging from passive opposition to active resistance. It then explores groups of people united in their conviction that the Nazi regime was criminal and immoral. This includes the little-known resistance by teenagers who, having refused to join the Hitler Youth, formed their own groups which eventuated in active resistance, often known as 'the pirates'. This is followed by rebellious university students, known as the White Rose group, who moved from active opposition to resistance under the circumstance of the day, and paid the price of martyrdom.*

Under the same pattern of opposition and resistance many church leaders of both the Lutheran and Catholic Churches are explored, again ranging from protests which was a form of opposition and at time resistance, with one Lutheran pastor involved in active resistance, namely assisting in the planned death of Hitler. This is followed by what can be best described as the elite conservative resister groups, studying key individuals, and examining two of the major groups which were in mutual contact but not always in agreement. The group led by Goerdeler falls under the nature of resistance to active resistance, the second led by von Moltke were resisters but were not united on active resistance. This was vastly different from the military resistance, which was often divided both in motive and intention, but which transpired to be active resistance, demanding the death of Hitler and a total revamping of the German government. In this chapter some of the main figures are given special attention. The section ends with the early resistance by the military and some civilians to try and stop Hitler starting a major war.

Introduction

Often overlooked in popular history of this period is that although the Nazi regime was regarded by many as necessary if not sound, there were many thousands of Germans who resented it and some who tried to oppose. A developing opposition was present in the early 1930s long before failure in Operation *Barbarossa* which made others change their minds as to where they stood on the matter of the Nazi regime. As noted in the previous chapter the Nazi regime ruled through fear and controlling public information. The political parties were repressed, many rounded up and sent into protective custody, a strange term for repression and torture of the interned. Only the communists survived as a loose form of organisation, often disregarded by other resisters because of the fear that their arrival would only replace Hitler with an equally repellent system. They may have been wrong in this criticism as many of the communist resisters had the simple aim of destroying the Nazi regime.[1] Nevertheless, the fear of Bolshevism tended to penetrate the various resistance groups, especially the elite conservative figures formed into groupings which had made contact. In their discussions it was eventually recognised that much of central Europe was populated by millions of proletarianised workers, ergo, an authoritarian government was required by the conservative resisters, having blamed the Weimar Republic for the rise of Hitler. Such was the fear that when Hitler and Stalin had agreed on the protocol over Poland there had been talk of overthrowing Hitler at that point. Some of these resisters, like the Nazis themselves later considered, considered encouraging conflict between the West and the Soviets, especially Goerdeler. For Moltke and the Kreisau Circle they regarded it as a European problem and talked about a European community. The distinct groups had often debated a name for themselves, one possibility had been the *German Freedom Movement*, but when the Soviets started their planned resistance with German communist immigrants and PoWs, they called it *Free Germany* which took the steam out of the idea. The Kreisau Circle, those involved with Goerdeler, even military met and knew of one another, but it was amongst the elitist conservatives that major and often conflicting views of how to prepare the future were discussed. They were far reaching discussions, ranging from re-establishing a German monarchy to a European economic community, maintaining the large agricultural estates in which most of the participants had a vested interest, how to deal with changes in a mass society of workers which put them off any form of democracy, and Goerdeler even raised the possibility of the two-party political system as in England. The discussions were wide-ranging and protracted, they often involved internal conflict, but by 1943 the removal of Hitler had not occurred, and by which date the war was turning to such an extent that his removal would not have major consequences. However, despite the odds being stacked against any real success they courageously battled on, and it must not be forgotten that 'they were fighting for the dignity and Christian destiny of mankind'.[2]

It was courageous, because throughout the Nazi era, as noted above, the Gestapo were always on the outlook for any dissenters, and whether it was remotely possible to overthrow Hitler was unlikely and could only be done by the military and needing much more than a small military clique. The Gestapo searched for critics at every level of society, from shopkeepers, postmen, students, to diplomats and top civil servants. As early as February 1942 the anti-Nazi diplomat Ulrich von Hassell discovered that he and friends from the Abwehr and others who were trying to find ways of overturning the regime were being watched by the SD (*Sicherheitsdienst*, Intelligence agency of the SS) yet all they had accomplished at this stage was to talk privately.[3] Everyone was aware of the Gestapo and the SD and the way they always used torture of an extreme nature, striking a sense of fear if not dread into everyone's minds.

As historians have looked back at the opponents of Nazism there has accumulated various views and interpretations many of which remain something of an enigma. 'In the first decade following the end of the Second World War, the resistance in Germany against Hitler's regime was preferably characterized as an *insurrection of conscience*', but other categories have since emerged. [4] The tradition is to classify them into groups which was a step in the right direction. They appear in groups which existed as identifiable entities, but often the necessity of the times brought them together. There have been efforts made to try and understand the various motives and the way some of these groupings of opposition tried to work together. A thread which has often been passed over too quickly is the moral quality of these groups, as to what drove and motivated them, and how, given their frequently different views, they clashed. There were, for example, many in the military who objected to the brutal expectations and outcomes of the Nazi wish for total dominance. Other military men were more concerned initially about waging a major war in the first place on the grounds they could not win, and after the defeat of France this group was mollified, but it rose again following the catastrophe of Operation *Barbarossa*. By this stage there were some in the military who still retained a sense of opposition because of the moral conduct demanded by the regime, but others who felt Hitler's military weakness was losing the war and he had to be replaced; it was, naturally, a mixed bag of opposition even within the same category of military command.

Outside of the military but often with contact with doubting commanders were the power elites, people who had at first thought Hitler was good for a transformed Germany but then changed their minds. Some changed their minds because they did not want a major war, but wanted the Versailles Treaty reversed, so they had worked for the Nazis, but with their various perceptions decided they need to supplant the regime either with a monarchical system or a military dictatorship, democracy was rarely mentioned after their perceived failure of the Weimar Republic. They constituted a form of bourgeois or national conservative opposition, and their ranks could be described as servants of the state seeking a revolt, but not to restore democracy.

They were opposed to Nazism but tended to be anti-liberal whilst looking for the rule of justified law and a state free from corruption. However, the vast majority of the public were now entrenched and indoctrinated by the Nazi regime, or terrified into silence, so any substantive effort had to be 'mobilised through religious and ultimately utopian thinking', and the tendency was to look towards a monarchical system.[5] The would-be resisters needed a political perspective because they needed to replace the Nazi political system with another. Some opponents thought they could tame the Nazis, some in the military looked to a martial law, others the monarchy, but the Weimar Republic was seen as a failure and there is little or no evidence indicating that democracy was ever discussed. The ironical twist was that the Weimar Republic had never been formally abolished. The Nazi grip on Germany and the chances of bringing down the regime were negligible, and later when unconditional surrender was announced it narrowed the psychological scope of the opposition, because once the Allies were in France a military effort to stabilise the situation was a hopeless pipedream. Nevertheless, despite the German public and the elite remaining silent or in support of the regime, the resisters persisted against what they mainly regarded as an inhumane form of government.

Therefore, the question is sometime raised as to how far the moral conscience was a component in this grouping. There is no doubt that both some military and members of the power elite group found the Nazi racism and treatment of prisoners downright evil, but they varied in their attitudes. There were exceptions to this over-generalisation, with one of the resistant leaders refusing the possibility of becoming a judge because it meant working for an immoral government.

In the category of Church leaders' protests there was a higher degree of protest at the immoral persecution of the Jews, but the church members were just as divided or terrified of being seen as opposition as the mass of the population. In terms of the 'people in general' this constitutes a fourth element in this study. It is an overly complex area but worth some analysis to function as a reminder of previous chapters in understanding public reactions, including why Nazism was so popular for a time.

It has been noted by a leading German historian, Hans Mommsen on the subject of German resistance, that in the post-war years the outside world was somewhat cynical about German opposition and resistance, seeing it as 'too little too late and for the wrong reasons' and there was too much discussion about the future and not acting fast enough to eliminate the Nazi leadership.[6] It was one thing not liking Nazism, another opposing it, and yet another resisting.

For many of those who did resist there were many who were uncertain about resistance to Hitler without compromising Germany's long-term future, which meant there were no real attempts until 1943–44 when it was obvious to most the war was lost.

One of the main obstacles in opposing any regime is that it is often considered that the government of the day has the right to govern and cannot be challenged. To make this point Hans Mommsen relates the time that Carl von Ossietzky, the pacifist editor of the weekly newspaper *Die Weltbühne* criticised the secret rearmament of Germany. For exposing this violation of the treaty on pacifist grounds he was found guilty and jailed for a brief time in 1933. As soon as Hitler came to power he was warned to flee by his friends after the Reichstag fire, refused and later died of illness in Oranienburg concentration camp in 1938. He had not been opposing Hiter, but as a pacifist he objected to military enlargement, and he was charged with treason.

It had long been a tradition in many countries that one could not challenge the power of the state, many regarding the state as having total supremacy, almost a sanctity in decision making, and feeling it was a moral duty to adhere to its directions. In democratic Britain Parliament makes the laws, and breaking them can result in punishment, making government directives legal and seemingly moral, which must be obeyed. There is often the assumption in a place like Britain that legal laws are always based on a moral foundation, and this has created some debate over the years. In the eighteenth century, in Britain, a jury found a man not guilty of stealing sheep, not because they were convinced of his innocence but because they believed the subsequent punishment of execution was morally wrong. It remains a complex jurisprudential issue to this day, as seen by the former Conservative government's wish to deport immigrants to Rwanda.

The Weimar Republic had assumed that as a constitutional state it could not be unlawful, and this became much more strongly presumed by the Nazi regime. There have been many incidents in most countries, when protests about government directives have resulted in protests which have been violently suppressed. There have been and still remain question marks over the legality of a government's direction, some protesting, others believing the government to have the rights of national direction. In Germany during the 1930s, even some 'leading Protestant theologians made it emphatically clear that a Christian had no right to oppose the established authority', based on Christ's statement 'to render unto Caesar what is Caesar's and unto God what is God's' and this was very much held by the older generation.[7] It remains an issue in Britain where peaceful protest is acceptable even against government directives, though there was a degree of violent reaction against the coalminers during Margaret Thatcher's time in office, protests about Tony Blair taking Britain to war against

Iraq which were large and numerous but considered legitimate protests. Today climate protestors although peaceful have taken to blocking roads for which they can be arrested, but in some countries any form of protest about the government is considered illegal and can have severe consequences for those involved.

The outlined issue of protest against one's government is globally universal, but by the time the Nazis were in power any form of open protest was immediately subjected to scrutiny by the Gestapo whose tentacles spread deep and wide. There were even rumours of Hitler Youth reporting on their parents and neighbours who were critical of Nazism. An arrest for even murmuring criticisms could result in public humiliation, beatings, imprisonment, and even death. The only question the present generation can ask is how we would have reacted. When a career or profession is suddenly removed, or one's life is at stake, one's family is in danger, it would take a gigantic amount of courage because Nazi imprisonment meant total sacrifice as with martyrs. This leaves a major issue in understanding German public reaction, because much of it was kept secret for reasons of personal safety. When open opposition was expressed in public or personal protests were heard it was known to be virtually suicidal, and challenging the regime in a form of revolt or putsch would need a major organisation such as the army, but it would need support.

There were many diverse groups of resisters some probably unknown about to this day, and it would take many volumes to give them space for study. The rarely mentioned Solf Circle formed to assist the persecuted, another the Stürmer group, and those led by Beppo Römer, who is briefly mentioned later. Luftwaffe Lieutenant Harro Schulze-Boysen with others formed the Red Orchestra, but in this study the areas of major importance will be explored, starting with individuals.

Individual Resisters

The Man who would not salute

Many people would have experienced the social pressure and fear of being denounced for not raising their arm in the Nazi salute, indicating they were possibly critical of the regime, many others would have felt happy to oblige for the sake of personal safety. In the famous picture of a group of workers raising their right arms one man was not saluting, with his arms folded determined not to join in. In close examination of the picture a few people look determined in their salute, the vast majority look grim which can be read either way, and quite a few appear bored. In the outlined circle it is possible to see behind the man not saluting, a younger man talking to his neighbour, possibly pointing out the malefactor, and within the top of the circle one man is looking at the man as a possible culprit. There is no doubt that here stood a member of the masses who was determined not to show any support, a brave act in itself, a form of passive opposition which he must have known could result in trouble.

As to who he was and why there has been some debate. One family have identified him as Gustav Wegert (1890–1959) a metal worker who always refused to salute on religious grounds. Another was August Landmesser who had a Jewish wife, he was imprisoned and later placed in a penal battalion where he was killed in action in October 1944.

In terms of this study his precise identity is not that important, but his reaction was, because it indicates that despite the popularity of Hitler and the fear of being denounced there were members of the public who were courageous enough to object to the Nazis, and many more probably felt the same, but who but kept their objections to themselves for safety.

One little known individual called Maurice Bavaud who was a Swiss theological student attempted to assassinate Hitler in 1938. He was not part of a German resistance, but he had the foresight to see the dangers of Hitler if only from the church perspective. Because of the Nazi attacks upon the Catholic Church Bavaud had decided that Hitler was the anti-Christ or an incarnation of Satan, and he decided he had a duty to kill him. He stalked Hitler awaiting the moment, hoping it had arrived when there was a Hitler procession through Munich on 9 November celebrating the Beer Hall Putsch. He arranged himself on a platformed grandstand, and as the figure of Hitler emerged the crowd stood up to give the Hitler salute which stopped any opportunity of aiming the pistol. It was a misplaced tactic for a theological student to think that even if he had a clear aim, shooting accurately with a pistol over some distance would require considerable skill and experience. It also took considerable courage, because if the crowd had even seen the pistol, there would have been no need for execution. Having extricated himself from the potential personal disaster he tried to make his way back to Switzerland, was picked up by the Gestapo for being a foreigner without a train ticket. They soon found his gun and maps, he confessed, and in May 1941 was guillotined in Berlin's Plötzensee prison. After the war, his father attempted in 1955 to challenge the death sentence but failed on the grounds that Hitler's life was protected by law as were all other lives. A year later in 1956 the court reversed the sentence and paid Bavaud' s family compensation. Had Hitler been killed before the outbreak of war most nations would have sent messages of condolence (though perhaps only for diplomatic reasons), had Hitler been killed after 3 September 1939 the assassin may have gone down as a hero and an active resister despite being of another nationality.

The facts of his motives are not entirely secure, one historian noting that Bavaud had belonged to a small group of Swiss students whose intention was to destroy communism. According to this account Bavaud had been sent to Germany to convince Hitler to attack the communists, and if he refused to kill him.[8] This sounds unlikely as even Swiss students would have realised that gaining an interview with Hitler carrying a gun would have been out of the question, and for a foreign student to influence the German leader was a nonsense even if it were a suicide mission. The former explanation of an incensed Catholic student carries more weight, and with the benefit of hindsight not only was it courageous but a shame it did not succeed.

Bavaud was a foreign resister, and the mystery man who stood alone in the crowd was a passive critic, and they both contrast with a more active resister. On 8 November 1939, Johann Georg Elser made a singular effort to assassinate Hitler with a carefully placed bomb in Munich's Bürgerbräukeller (large beer Hall in Munich opened in 1885), where Hitler planned to give his annual speech on his failed putsch in November 1923. Elser was not connected to any known resistance circles, but he had spent a brief time with a communist organisation, but this attempt to kill Hitler he made alone, which was probably the safest method. Elser was a carpenter by trade and found work in a quarry in order to steal dynamite for his bomb. His carpentry skills were useful as he hid the device within a pillar, working in such a cleverly planned way he was never spotted. It later transpired from his interrogation (known as the Berlin Interrogation Protocol) that he was a paid-up member of the KPD (German Communist Party) in his home of Konstanz, but he never held any specific post. It was natural therefore that he was an early opponent of Nazism. He claimed during his later interrogations that what had made him carry through this attack were the poor living standards for workers, and later added his objections to Hitler planning a major war. He claimed he wanted to eliminate all the leading Nazi figures to stop war.

Elser had the skills to make the bomb, conceal it cleverly, and set the fuse for the best time, which was not an easy task because Hitler chose when and where he would appear. This was not a problem for Elser who appeared indifferent 'to current political events and his lack of desire to inform himself', he simply waited for the right moment.[9] He set it and followed his plans to return to Konstanz and then make his way into Switzerland. The bomb exploded at the right time of 21.20 killing eight people and injuring nearly 60 more, but by this time Hitler had left unexpectedly, and Elser was arrested while escaping to Switzerland having raised suspicions at the border controls. He had not helped himself, because under his coat's lapel he had a badge of the Red Front

Fighters' league, and he was soon in Gestapo headquarters which was the start of a major investigation.

Under torture he soon confessed to placing the bomb, his wider family was instantly arrested, and he was interrogated for a long time, noted in the now well-known Berlin Interrogation Protocol mentioned above. The heads of security could not understand how one man could have devised not only the bomb, but also prepared the attack so efficiently, they were convinced there was a larger more professional organisation behind the incident. They did not think a carpenter by trade had the skills or knowledge to conduct such a task. They even made him rebuild the bomb to prove whether he was capable or not. The investigators under orders from Himmler used every available means to illicit the truth behind the scheme, torture, drugs, and even a psychiatrist.

Goebbels wanted to place the blame on the British Secret Service, and he had already announced this possibility in the press releases. He undoubtedly thought this essential as it would not look good to have a German workman trying to assassinate the Führer. There were efforts made to connect the attack with the capture of two British agents at the Dutch border, known as the Venlo incident. The Nazi newspaper the *Völkischer Beobachter* blamed British secret agents which the Venlo incident had made even more tempting to believe. It was an attempt to stir up a sense of war frenzy against the British, but this motive consequently led to the conspiracy theory that the Nazis planted the bomb to serve this purpose; this may seem incredulous, but it was an alternative view that will be explored later. Göbbels wrote in his diary that 'we launch swingeing attacks against London for the Munich assassination attempt. The moral guilt is clearly entirely theirs'.[10] The press also seized on communist connections, and conspiracies were invented around Otto Strasser (member of the Nazi Party Left-wing who had tried to split the Party and remove Hitler), that the situation in the German government could only be modified by the removal of the immediate leadership.[11]

Curiously Payne Best, one of those agents captured in the Venlo incident, would later meet Elser in a concentration camp. Quite why Elser was imprisoned and not executed immediately is an enigma, he was eventually killed at the end of the war. Martin Niemöller started the rumour that Elser was not what he seemed, but he was in fact an SS *Unterscharführer* (an SS paramilitary rank), and Payne Best claimed that Elser had told him he had been recruited while a prisoner in Dachau. He was, as far as these men were concerned a puppet of the regime. These rumours started a series of conspiracy theories which seemed impossible to resolve, around the rumour mentioned above that it was a Nazi machination. It should be noted that the anti-Nazi diarist Friedrich Kellner wrote about the bomb blast that it caused no great impression. People are worn out, 'the mentally nimble part of the population has its own thoughts and does not believe it was a real assassination attempt but rather another kind of Reichstag fire charade to enable the Nazis to pursue disagreeable elements among them'.[12]

It is frequently referenced that the trusted German Pastor Niemöller had met Elser in Dachau (Elser had a privileged cell with woodwork tools) and discovered he was an SS-*Unterscharführer*, and he had been directed by two men, whom Padfield assumed were Heydrich's men, to build a bomb into a wooden pillar. It has been noted by one historian that although Hitler was in a rush, when the news of the explosion was given to him on the train his secretary said his eyes 'flashed with excitement'.[13] Hitler decided it was providence looking after him. He had mentioned providence in his earlier speech, and Heydrich tried to motivate priests to claim God was protecting the Führer. It was also argued that when Elser was caught with a communist badge and a picture of the beer cellar with a red cross on the pillar, that it appeared an unlikely item on a man who had committed this incident. The historian Padfield argued that the timing of these two incidents was beyond a coincidence and both incidents arose from the same source. Himmler also dragged Otto Strasser's name into the affair presumably trying to kill two birds with one stone. The generals were unhappy about Hitler's projected attack on France in the autumn, but this stopped any protest or action on their part, and it provided further vitriol for an attack.

There is no concrete evidence for this claim, but such was the Machiavellian nature of Himmler and Heydrich many believe this was conceivable. It is often regarded as another conspiracy theory, and generally seems unlikely. According to the historian Longerich, Himmler personally interviewed Elser to find the 'men behind the scenes' and 'during the process he kicked him [Elser] brutally several times, abused him, and had him tortured…this is, in fact, the only example in his whole career of Himmler personally using physical force'.[14] Himmler's involvement may have occurred because there was good reason for his organisation of being accused of incompetence. However, these conspiracy speculations will undoubtedly always flourish, but if there were any truth in them, the so-called perpetrators would have Elser killed at once to stop any chance that he might disclose information, and if the effort were genuine, he was an active resister before others surfaced.

It was because of these various theories post-war that it took time for Elser's actions to be qualified as one man's effort to eliminate an evil dictator. Many gifted German historians have examined the Berlin Interrogation Protocol and the whole episode, and it took decades before Elser was eventually recognised as a genuine resistance fighter against the Nazi regime. Such resolute individuals are rare in a society which has been suppressed by fear, and whose propaganda machine has indoctrinated a mass of the population. There were many who undoubtedly wanted an end to the war and an end of Nazism, but Georg Elser stands out as a courageous martyr who stood against an embedded system. He has now been recognised in Germany with many roads and streets bearing his name, but for the rest of the world he remains little known apart from historians. This writer asked everyone he knew in family, friends, colleagues, and Elser's name rang no bells.

There were many other assassination attempts, and Hitler claimed there had been seven, but there were many others which were planned by individuals and small groups. It was realised by many that the only way to stop Nazism was by killing the man at the top, the Führer. Only the army could conduct a successful coup d'état, but motivated individuals could start the ball rolling by assassination. As early as 1933 there were planned attacks, one by a small group of communists led by Kurt Lutter but thwarted by police knowledge, and another by Dr Helmuth Mylius but nothing happened.[15] Another similar event occurred in 1938 when two men, known as Döpking and Kremin had set out to kill but were captured first and executed. In 1939 Hoffmann relates how the British Military Attaché offered to shoot Hitler from the balcony on his apartment, but the British remained too polite to be involved.[16] Hitler was all too aware that he was always a possible target, and lived in the unbelievable trance that Providence protected him, or rather he liked his followers to believe this connection with the deity.

Rebellious Teenagers

As noted in Chapter Two the Hitler Youth had been ruthlessly indoctrinated in Nazi policies and encouraged to join the military or serve the regime to the best of their ability. There is no question that the vast majority of German youngsters joined willingly, there were others who felt they had little choice, some who never enjoyed the experience (though some may have felt more inclined to express this sentiment post-war), but others who resented it, formed their own alliance, and possibly without realising it established a small corner of opposition and resistance. There was one distinctive group of young anti-Nazis in the Ruhr and Rheinland [Rhineland] areas who went under the name of the Edelweiss Pirates. It was not one organisation but consisted of many small groups with different names. The Gestapo had investigated a group called the Kittelbach Pirates, another the Navajos. There can be no certainty whether they were groups who were anti-Nazis or who simply rejected the repressive conditions under which they lived. Like the Hitler Youth they enjoyed rural camping and bonfires, but in their case, it was more a way of keeping themselves safe from any attention by the authorities. In the Hitler Youth the sexes were kept apart, albeit that the German Maidens were nicknamed the League of German mattresses. It was no surprise that the Nazi authorities were aware of these breakaway groups, resented them, and were soon in pursuit of them as potential enemies of the state.

One newspaper reported how the police had carried out and orchestrated a raid on a group of the Kittelbach Pirates (1936) describing their decadent (by Nazi standard) dress standards, claimed they were all drunk, and they had British and American nicknames.[17] Their trial was held in camera, and the two leaders were imprisoned for a few months, and the rest were given a 75 Mark fine. It was pointed out to these teenagers that had they been older, then they would have been tried under high treason and subject to the death penalty. An ominous threat given their age, but there is considerable evidence indicating they still met. There were even confrontational moments between these rebellious teenagers and the Hitler Youth. In the end years of the war some of these group members were joined by deserters and became bandits. In January 1945 'the authorities in Cologne were reporting twenty such groups up to 128 members strong. They stole food, terrorised local party officials and committed a number of murders'.[18] In these final months of the war some of them were hanged, and one was only 16 years old.

It could be argued from these young people that the Nazi control of society was not total as they expected and claimed, and their opposition to the regime was clear, and at their age highly courageous. Motivations may well have differed, some may have opposed the regime on political grounds, others, as mentioned above, may have resented an oppressed society. There may have been some determined not to fight and die for the Third Reich, others it may have even been a rebellious nature. While their motivations may have been vastly different, they clearly indicated that despite their youth they stood apart from the regime. They were never a united form of resistance, but their actions may be eschewed as their form, first of opposition and later active resistance, even from young rebellious teenagers.

Church Opposition

As noted above the NSDAP had promised a brighter economic future, a higher standard of living, employment, a German unity of class, and returning Germany to its so-called previous greatness, but a potential major war and genocide was never mentioned. To many people the early signals of the evil aspect of Nazism revealed itself openly in the 1930s (and before to the more astute) with its notably cruel attitude towards Jews, its over fondness of eugenics in pursuing the myth of a pure Aryan race, and the way their political opponents had been so cruelly treated by public humiliations, pursued by the Gestapo, and imprisoned. Many of the more intellectual critics came from the Church, and this section explores some of the more notable churchmen who criticised the regime, but there remains a serious question mark over the Church's corporate response. As with the industrial workers noted in Chapter Two the various congregations were equally divided as to where they stood on political affiliations. On 20 July 1933, the Pope had agreed a Concordat with Hitler in return for religious freedom and the bishops were expected to swear loyalty to the state. This agreement could be seen as a mistake later made by Chamberlain at Munich, because both leaders failed to understand Hitler's warped deceitful nature. One thing was clear about the Concordat, it was the Pope ensuring safety for the Church alone, and not over-worrying at that time what was happening to the persecuted minorities. Hitler's appeasing façade did not last long, because within months of the Concordat the Hitler Youth were ensuring that Catholic youth groups were to be integrated into their political organisation. In 1934 in a Good Friday march the usual procession in Cologne had many more participants than usual, and this was seen not only as support for their faith but a protest at the regime.[19] If so, it was a reaction to the way the regime was treating the Church. The Concordat meant little to minor Nazi officials, and when an attempt was made to remove crucifixes from schoolrooms, some locals broke into the schools to replace them. The following is a police report of one such event:

> The fact is that 30 to 40 villagers got into the unlocked school on the night of 6 January 1937 [Festival of the Epiphany celebrating the arrival of the three Wise Men] to hang the crucifix back in its old place...despite the advice of witness R that it was a government order...the accused BA hung the crucifix right up beside the picture of the Führer, which had been put in this newly assigned place.[20]

It was of little surprise that 'BA' received a custodial sentence, and the same event happened elsewhere across Germany. It did not take long for the anti-Church elements of Nazism to become obvious, and by 1937 Pope Pius XI was equally aware. He wrote an encyclical entitled *Mit Brennender Sorge* (With burning Anxiety), and it was sent to all clergy and German congregations. He expressed concern about the harassment the German Church, once enlightened by St Boniface, was now suffering, and pinpointing the immoral singling out of race and attitudes contrary to God's order of things. It was in spirit the same as a Lutheran document (to be noted later) known as the Barmen Declaration, challenging the views and attitudes of National Socialism. There were elements in both the Lutheran and Catholic Churches, which appreciated the Nazi promises and some who welcomed the regime. The Nazis, as was their purpose, made every effort to control the churches while aware of some of the public's religious sensitivities. A Concordat with Rome and appointing a Reich Bishop for the Lutherans had been mere side-shows to quieten criticism, by trying to keep the public onside in taking total control. In his diary Ulrich von Hassell (July 1941) mentioned Bishop Heckel, who had once been a willing collaborator with the Nazis to bridge the gap between the church and the new regime, but he had explained to Hassell he had found out that he had been wrong, and discovered evidence that the Party had every intention of destroying the Church which 'took its orders from an Asiatic (Jesus Christ) which was unsuitable for a German'.[21]

As noted in Chapter One there had been considerable hostility against Catholics in Germany after the Reformation, as had happened in Britain, but it lasted much longer within Germany. By tradition, the Protestants had tended to dominate, especially in Prussia and many were nationalistically inclined and had supported Hitler in his rise to power. Overall, it has been worked out that out of the 17,000 Lutheran pastors in Germany only some 50 received serious prison sentences.[22] Many more Catholic clergy were sent to concentration camps, and many were killed, more than a third of their number. The parish clergy only had to say something slightly against the regime and they could be reported. When Polish industrial slave labour appeared in his parish a Catholic priest, Chaplain Seitz, told the children not to be rude to these men, and his mother took the Poles home for a coffee.[23] They were placing their religion above politics and Gestapo interrogation followed, with even Himmler taking a personal interest and Father Seitz was placed in 'protective custody', which for many must have been a warning that German Christianity was in serious danger.

The Catholic hierarchy did not suffer the same consequences as their clergy, only one bishop was expelled from his diocese, and one sentenced to long imprisonment for opposing the regime.[24] The Catholic hierarchy could not have been unaware of the relentless persecution of the Jews and many others, but also against their own institution. Any state official or minor functionary whose children attended a Catholic school was officially warned to find a state school. In 1934, 65 per cent of children attended these schools, (which was not surprising given that in 1939, 95 per cent of Germans said they were Christian of either Protestant or Catholic persuasion) but three years later in 1937 only five per cent, and by 1939 all denominational schools had become a thing of the past.[25] Overall the Lutheran clergy tended to be quieter than the Catholics.

However, despite the bravery of individuals the corporate response of both the Protestant and Catholic Churches tended to be on the weak side, undoubtedly for the reason of self-preservation of their institutions, even though by 1936–7 they must have known the Nazi regime was as evil as the image of the projected

Satan. Men like Hitler, Himmler and many others were using their power to subjugate their own countrymen, eliminate others for a wide variety of non-sensical reasons, making Satan a mere myth or excuse for man's worse possible behaviour. The early successes of Hitler and the *Anschluss* had the same effect on Churchmen as it had on most Germans, the public acceptance that Germany was regaining what belonged to Germany. Even over the Sudeten crisis with its threat of war the Church leaders were silent. After the Munich crisis Hitler received letters of congratulations from leaders of both denominations. There were some Nazi actions which were so unbelievably evil and immoral it managed to bring forth direct protests, as with the Nazi policy of euthanasia for those considered unfit to be German stock. This will be mentioned later in this chapter when Bishop von Galen is explored. Bishop Hilfrich of Limburg wrote a letter of protest to the Reich Justice Minister Gürtner in 1941, stating what was happening to victims in his area, pointing out the public were well aware of what was going on, and 'all God-fearing people feel this extermination of the helpless is an almighty crime'.[26]

There were in the Christian faith some outstanding men who had sufficient courage to stand out by protesting or trying to resist the regime, but as corporate bodies the denominations did little, for a variety of possible reasons: the preservation of their institutions, self-preservation of their own lives, the understanding their flocks were politically mixed, or the knowledge that they never had the power to overthrow Hitler. For some it may have been a failure of belief in their faith or lack of depth, some may have been ordained for social more than religious motivations, and for some nationalism overrode their faith which was centred on the theme of 'love your neighbour as yourself', which was by nature contrary to nationalism. Only one senior churchman became involved in the 20 July plot to exterminate Hitler, and that was Dieterich Bonhoeffer, and before this chapter concludes it is important that three of the most outstanding and well-known resisters are explored.

Dietrich Bonhoeffer

Many had realised the Nazi Party's intentions much earlier and had recognised the moral depravity of the new regime. Dietrich Bonhoeffer a Protestant pastor and theologian was a well-known figure whose books, prayers, and views have been widely read in Germany and overseas during the post-war years, and he still remains a leading light to many. Bonhoeffer stands out because from the minute the Nazis became known, he openly and swiftly opposed them for their attempted control of the Church, but most especially because of the euthanasia programme and treatment of the Jews. He travelled during the 1930s to America and Britain in pursuit of his theological studies, became part of the Christian ecumenical movement, claimed by one writer to be the factor which led him to resist Hitler, but he probably did not need this element to recognise the dangers of Nazism.[27] He lectured in systematic theology at the University of Berlin, and in following his ecumenical leanings was appointed to promoting friendship between all churches at an international level.

The Nazi regime had promised all sorts of hopes to attract the masses, but Bonhoeffer saw through them, and without hesitation in a broadcast just a few days after the Nazis came to power, he warned, as Max Weber had once done in 1918, about the dangers of creating a cult around a political leader. The broadcast was cut short making many listeners query if this were the Nazi sympathisers taking early control. As early as 1933 Bonhoeffer openly opposed the Nazi behaviour towards Jews, stating that the Christian Church could not 'simply bandage the victims under the wheel, but jam a spoke in the wheel itself'.[28] In the meantime, Hitler aware of possible resistance from Christians introduced quite illegally, church elections, and despite Bonhoeffer's efforts it resulted in high positions going to Nazi supported German ministers, who readily accepted the Aryan policy and excluded Jews from various posts. Another well-known anti-Nazi pastor, Martin Niemöller founded the Pastors' Emergency League which formed the basis for the Confessing Church. Some Nationalist German Christians were busy demanding the removal of the Old Testament because it was Jewish. There was a sharp division in the German churches which made the Confessing Church demand that Christ was the head of the Church and not Hitler. Far less than half of the German pastors joined, but Bonhoeffer was one of the founding members. He then took a post in London at German Lutheran Churches, was criticised for leaving Germany, and he decided to return.

In 1938 he contacted what was dubbed the German Resistance via his brother-in-law Hans von Dohnányi within the Abwehr. Dohnányi, Hungarian by birth, was a German jurist who used his position in the Abwehr to help fleeing Jews. By 1938 Bonhoeffer soon heard of the possibility of war and as a resolute pacifist did not want to be conscripted or swear an oath to Adolf Hitler. He was concerned about the ramifications on the Confessing Church as he knew many nationalistic Christians thought his attitude misleading.[29] In June 1939 he went to the USA but felt he had to return to Germany after two weeks, despite friends imploring him to stay. On his return the Nazis were well aware of his views, and he was banned from public speaking and had to report his activities to the police. His brother-in-law Hans von Dohnányi persuaded him for safety reasons to join the Abwehr, on the grounds that his ecumenical contacts might be useful, and Bonhoeffer would have known about the anti-Nazi machinations within that organisation, which enabled him to function as a courier for the developing resistance.

In the published correspondence of the Bishop of Chichester George Bell, there are many letters between Bonhoeffer and Bell, indicating not only a very warm relationship, but also their joint opposition to the damage being caused by the Nazi regime.[30] Bonhoeffer travelled to London to meet and stay with Bell seeking his advice and support on the Nazi control of the Lutheran church, especially when Hitler had appointed Ludwig Müller as the Reich Bishop, naturally protesting at this, not least because the swastika had been attached to the Christian symbol of the cross.

Swastika attached to the cross of Christ.

During the early war years Bonhoeffer and Bishop Bell had met in Sweden, where Bonhoeffer acted as the courier passing on information about the hope of overthrowing Hitler, as well as the opportunities for a peace agreement with Britain. The news of an active resistance was hereby communicated to Bishop George Bell, a deep sympathiser of the Confessing Church, but when Bell went to see Anthony Eden, he soon discovered the British government had no interest. The letters continued being posted and received in Switzerland and reveal Bonhoeffer's determination to resist despite the dangers. He became an active fringe worker with behind the scenes help in the 20 July Plot.

Bonhoeffer also assisted von Dohnányi in helping Jews escape. By April 1943 they were both in Tegel Prison, where he wrote prayers and letters which sympathetic guards allowed him to do and smuggled them out for him. This singular act by uniformed guards was indicative that even those in uniforms bearing the swastika were not all committed Nazi followers.

Bonhoeffer was soon seen as a traitor once Canaris's desktop diary was discovered, and he was executed at Flossenbürg concentration camp on 9 April 1945, along with other resisters such as Oster and Canaris. Bonhoeffer had met a captured British agent called Payne Best at the prison camp, and just before he was hanged he asked him to convey a message to George Bell in Chichester with the following words: 'Tell him that for me this is the end but also the beginning – with him I believe in the principle of our Universal brotherhood which rises above all national interests, and that our victory is certain – tell him too that I have never forgotten his words at our last meeting', which was duly delivered personally.[31]

There was no chance that a kind and compassionate theologian could overthrow the Nazi regime, but he stands out as a Christian German individual who had the intellect to see through the evil fabric of the regime, and he had the courage to make his views known, even though he knew it would lead to his death. In Bonhoeffer there stood a singular example of a Nazi critic and an opponent. He made it clear that if he could have been a more physical resister he would have been, he did what he could, but like many Germans he was confronted by a regime which few but the international military enemies could destroy. Most normal people under these circumstances of the Third Reich, at first hijacked by promises, then failing to see the evil and the consequences, found it safer to stay quiet and submissive. Bonhoeffer like others was looking to avoid a major war, but later engrossed in trying to destroy the leadership once the war turned against them, Bonhoeffer opposed the Nazi regime on Christian and moral grounds.

Pastor Martin Niemöller

Another well-known opponent was Pastor Martin Niemöller but one hounded by his traditional conservative background. During the First World War he had fought in the U-boat warfare rising to command and awarded the Iron Cross First Class. He was a born German traditionalist and disliked the Weimar Republic, and in 1920 he commanded for a brief time a *Freikorps* unit. He decided to become a Lutheran minister and trained accordingly and was ordained in June 1924. He even authored an autobiographical book *From U-boat to Pulpit*, and some rare copies still pop up on Amazon but at a hefty price, and it was warmly received by the growing Nazi propaganda machine. However, during this initial period with his abhorrence of the Weimar Republic he welcomed the prospect of Hitler taking power, hoping like so many others for a national revival.

Nevertheless, he resisted the Nazi policy of objecting to Jews converting to Lutheranism, obviously failing to understand that for the Nazi their anti-Semitism was not based on faith belief, but racism, and in 1936 he signed a petition disapproving of their attitude. As early as 1933 Niemöller had founded an organisation of pastors against the rising tide of hatred about stopping Jews being converted to the Church, and the Nazification of Protestant Churches. This was the Emergency Association of Pastors which transformed into the Confessing Church, starting with 1,300 and within a year 6,000 clergy.[32] It stood in clear opposition to that section of the Lutheran Church which supported the NSDAP, in which a new Reich Bishop, Ludwig Müller, had been elected in an effort to unify the Lutheran Church, which raised the profile of racism within the Church.* Niemöller and a small group of clerics had met Hitler in 1934 in a brusque meeting interfered with by Göring. In a biography of Niemöller it was recorded that Hitler told them that 'they should confine their efforts to the Church, and I will take care of the German people', at which stage he declared the meeting closed.[33] Niemöller had the courage to stop and challenge Hitler arguing that the Church had a duty to the people entrusted by God, stating that 'neither you nor anyone in the world has the power to take it from us'. Hitler stared at him, turned his back, and left the room. Many historians believe that Hitler was at this stage unsure how to deal with the Church issue, but as the years passed, he soon regarded men like Niemöller as dangerous resisters, not because they could overthrow him, but damage his seeming popularity by influencing the many Germans who still sat in the congregational pews.

When the Emergency Association drew up what has been called the Barmen Declaration which, by using selected texts from the Bible, hammered home the points that the Church was of God, and therefore was not subject to any government control by the state and it accused the regime of false teaching. In 1934 Bishop Müller's assistant, August Jäger, drew up a document calling on all clergy to sign an oath of loyalty to Adolf Hitler as a result of the Barmen Declaration, and many protested and some were placed under house arrest. Such was the outcry that more senior clergy met Hitler and August Jäger lost his post. This was a sure indicator that the Nazi heads were all too aware of the Christian life amongst many people, and even they realised some sensitivity had to be used for a time.

It has been claimed that Niemöller remained critical of the Jewish faith but protected Jews who had become Lutheran Christians, and occasionally there are suggestions that Niemöller made anti-Semitic remarks. He appeared at times to be ambivalent in his attitudes and sometimes appears almost contradictory, only prepared to tackle the forces of the Nazi regime when they threatened the church. It was not long before he was arrested (1 July 1937), but he was fined and given

---

* Ludwig Müller was later asked to resign, but he refused. He committed suicide at the end of the war in Königsberg.

a short prison sentence (seven months), but Himmler found this too lenient, and he was interned at first in Sachsenhausen and later Dachau concentration camps. In 1939 he had even offered to command a U-boat but was rejected. It would seem that Niemöller was more opposed to the Nazi regime on the basis that it was an atheistic movement rather than on humanitarian grounds, so it was no surprise that post-war he was denied Nazi victim status despite many years in a concentration camp, but he never denied his own personal guilt. What made Niemöller stand out was not his opposition to the Nazi regime, but his courage in challenging them on some aspects of their conduct; he rose to fame more in the post-war period by admitting guilt and working for a repaired future.

Augustinus von Galen

Bonhoeffer and Niemöller were both Lutherans, but the third selected churchman was the Catholic Bishop of Münster, Clemens Augustinus von Galen who had been born into German aristocracy. The anti-Nazi diarist Friedrich Kellner, explored earlier in this study, had been shocked by the German Churches not taking a stand about the atrocities committed against the Jews, but nevertheless, referred to Galen as 'the shining star'.[34] Very much like Niemöller, Galen was traditionalist by background and disliked the Weimar Republic, having been a staunch monarchist, disliked the Treaty of Versailles, agreed with the 'stab-in-the back' myth, and feared atheistic Bolshevism. In the difficult post-1918 years he organised food and clothing for those suffering, but it has been suggested that it was more out of fear of the working classes embracing the hopes of communism which remained one of his main fears, which may sound cynical, but his motives can only remain speculative.

However, as early as 1934 he swiftly became critical of the Nazi policies. The first issue catching his attention regarded the Nazi educational policy, when 'the Münster council ordered that all schools should teach their pupils about the fundamental inferiority of the Jewish race...bellicose as ever, von Galen refused to allow any change to the curriculum, immediately sending out precisely the opposite message'.[35] Despite his high standing in the Catholic hierarchy this must be regarded as brave, as it was well-known that there were many clergy, especially Catholics already in the concentration camps. He was aware of this, later saying that 'many of my best priests died in concentration camps, and all because they distributed my sermons'.[36] He started early and persisted in attacking the Nazi theory of a pure race and attacked in published essays the work of Alfred Rosenberg who helped produce this ideology. He was visited by SS officers threatening him with reprisals if he did not stop his propaganda against the government. He explained to them that the Church would remain obedient to the state in all lawful matters. To men of the SS this may have sounded as if they had been successful because many people, as noted above, believe that what the state orders must be right. Galen was of the better understanding that the state is not necessarily a moral entity, and as with the Nazi regime was immoral and criminal in its so-called legislation.

The Church Catholic hierarchy had at first attempted to work with the Nazi government if only for a peaceful setting, but soon realised it simply was not possible. This resulted in Galen being summoned to Rome to assist Pope Pius XI with *Mit Brennender Sorge* (With Burning Concern) in which the rights of the Church were asserted, the Nazi racial policies were condemned, the Jewish culture and Old Testament were defended, referring to the Führer as 'a prophet of nothingness…at whom Heaven laughs'.[37] The document was secreted into Germany and distributed, causing the seizure of printing presses, clergy were arrested, with yet more laws to tighten the hold on the churches.

He attacked the arrest of Jesuits, church property being confiscated, but most importantly the *Aktion T4* which was the name given to the policy of euthanasia.* He never let this matter drop, always attacking the Nazi policy of trying to create a pure race by killing the intellectually handicapped, the mentally ill, and others who were incurably infirm. He also opposed the Nazis on the political front being critical of their totalitarian approach. Galen, it has been suggested, welcomed the attack on Russia because for him it was an atheistic state, but when the news of the extermination of Jews and others percolated through to the public, Galen and many others voiced strong objections, and he attacked the cruelty of the Gestapo against Church clergy and members, basically making a stand for human rights.

His sermons were immensely important because they were often printed and given a wide dispersal, which was technically illegal, and encouraged more opposition. The congregation would be full when he preached because it was widely known by many critics and opponents that Galen had the courage to oppose the Nazis, and for this reason there would also have been Gestapo agents in the pews. His sermons were so full of rage against the Nazi regime he was soon nicknamed the Lion of Münster. The Gestapo knew that somehow these sermons were percolating throughout German society.

The Nazis were by 1941 unsure how to deal with an aristocratic German Count who held an elevated position within a vast international organisation such as the Roman Catholic Church. There was no doubt that the Nazi powers intended to hang him at the successful conclusion of the war, and there were calls for his immediate execution, which was considered too risky by Goebbels in terms of worldwide publicity, along with the losses on the Eastern Front being

* *Aktion T4* referred to the address *Tiergartenstraße 4*, the administrative centre for this policy.

experienced at this time. Instead, he was placed under 24-hour surveillance, which amounted to virtual home imprisonment. His sister, a nun, was imprisoned by the Gestapo but was rescued and escaped, his brother was deported to a concentration camp but survived.

Many historians differ over Bishop von Galen, some claiming he was silent on the mass murder of the Jews, that his support for the War against Soviet Russia encouraged others, but the evidence, including that of many pro-Galen Jews after the war, his sermons are still in existence, and the many times it is known that he confronted Nazi policy making it no surprise that he was beatified on 9 October 2005. He was a Catholic Bishop who was not only critical of Nazi behaviour, not only opposed it, but was a courageous active resister.

Despite the bravery of a few leaders and many Catholic clergy it appears that the Churches failed to assert themselves against the regime. It was probably the same reason for the fear which as seen in Chapter Two which had gripped most of the population. They would have seen, as with their Catholic Father Seitz mentioned above, the threat of protective custody in a concentration camp, for even asking children to be polite to those suffering from slave labour. However, there was no coherent force to threaten the regime, only mild dissent. The Protestant Churches never condemned the war, and one researcher found that for the entire duration of the war 'out of the Catholic male population, which was 15.5 million strong, only seven individuals actually refused military service'.[38] Even the courageous Bishop von Galen offered his gratitude to the German soldiers fighting on the Eastern Front, but speculatively he may have been more worried about the dangers of alien communism than German fascism. Even in the euthanasia policy he may well have been aware that Catholic and Protestant nurses were part of that crime against humanity, but he used his only weapon and spoke out publicly.

In a resistance movement known as the Kreisau Circle, Frau Moltke mentioned later, referred in her memoirs to the facts that for generations since the Reformation Protestants and Catholics merely talked, but they became active and worked together with a major contribution from the Jesuit Father Delp. In short, there were some courageous Christians who were prepared to be martyrs for their faith, but the major Church institutions were weak in their opposition and spent many post-war years trying to mend their weakness by public apologies and acknowledgement of their inherent weakness. There were some outstanding Lutherans and Catholics whose opposition became resistance, the number of clerics who landed up in concentration camps makes this evident, these brave individuals must not be forgotten.

White Rose Students

Distinctive individuals met and formed a resistance group called the White Rose. They were young university students, many studying medicine, who had, as most undergraduates do, come together with like-minded people. Their common theme had been their disgust at the Nazi regime, and this was their entire motivation to work together to try and make the public see the truth of the evils of the regime. They were not straight out of school, and some of the men had experienced the war on both fronts, knowing that at any moment they could be called back for further service. Some of them had been obliged to work on and off in the labour services, and some of them had experienced life in the Hitler Youth. Those who had been at the front had seen the barbarous treatment of the Jews and Poles, others the harshness of the labour service. However, they were evidently intellectually gifted and had minds of their own, and even the Hitler Youth policies had failed to indoctrinate them. The Hitler regime had been especially clever in capturing the hearts and minds of the youth-generation, but this group of active resisters had not been entrapped, probably because they were above the intellectual level of many of their peers and could think for themselves. A French historian once told this author that the more active French resistance often came from a group of youngsters who previously had a bad social status by attending nightclubs and creating rumpus on the streets, acknowledging that the younger generation have a mind of their own and should not be judged too quickly. The Nazis may have thought they had taken on board the younger German generation, and they would have been 85–90 per cent correct, but not 100 per cent.

Central to this group were siblings, Sophie, and Hans Scholl. They and their friends produced pamphlets which were direct attacks on the Nazi regime, and on those of the public who had believed in the Nazi promises not foreseeing the impending disasters. It was a risky and dangerous enterprise of which they were well aware. They sent many through the post because they knew the Gestapo would have problems tracing them, but part of the Nazi law demanded such material should be handed into the Gestapo or other officials; this was done, and the security services were alert and wanting to find the perpetrators. On one occasion Sophie, in a moment of excitement, showered incoming students and staff with the leaflets from a high balcony, but she was spotted by a Nazi caretaker who arrested her. This led to her and her bother appearing in court and a few days later they were executed at the guillotine. There were other core members of the group such as Christoph Probst a 23-year-old father of three, a supporting Professor Kurt Huber and a Willi Graf, all suffering the same fate. When international judgements post-war occurred it usually focused on matters such as collective guilt, but the White Rose demonstrated that in the midst of this regime were brave attempts at resistance, and it should not be submerged in the detritus of a war which created so much hatred. They worked hard at resisting and died as a consequence. However, they remain a beacon of light as with many other Nazi opponents they demonstrated that there were many Germans who never succumbed to Nazi rule and had the courage to stand up against a regime which crushed criticism. Many of the records, writings and manoeuvres of the group remained unknown for a long time, not just because they were students but because they remained the other side of the Berlin wall until the early 1990s.

These were young people with good intellects, who often met and talked their way through the issues which they regarded as critical. They remained determined to the end, both as individuals, and as a group when they tried to challenge the general public to take a more careful look at the Nazi regime by challenging it as they were doing. In their meetings they discussed the best way to write their pamphlets, the nature of the content, how to make the appeal understandable while creating a sense of urgency. The pamphlets or leaflets were called *flugblätter*, what we might call today 'fliers' used for advertising.

They were not restricted by any ideology but bound together by pointing out the evil of the regime, with no punches pulled. They demanded the Nazi regime be demolished and thereby bring an end to the war. They knew as a group they could never achieve this, so their aim was to influence as many of the public as possible. Considerable thought went into the distribution of the pamphlets, including everyday workers, professionals such as doctors, academics, shopkeepers and anywhere they hoped they would be received and welcomed.

They became a community of thinkers, from a wide variety of academic disciplines, using their various intellects to try and achieve their goal. They knew as a group they could not bring about the downfall of Hitler, but they had a driving sense of urgency and did their best to influence the wider population. Nearly all their pamphlets started with a sense of challenge and telling the reader to look to the future which was growing increasingly dismal. This was especially true after the first 1,000-bomber raid over Cologne, followed by news of military defeats in North Africa and dismal news from the Eastern front. However, the pamphlets referred to the evil behaviour of the regime to the Jews, and their key word was 'freedom', which thinking Germans had not experienced for a long time. They wrote in this pamphlet that 'Nazism is a cancerous tumour on the German people' which was corrupting the whole nation, referring to the regime as *untermenschentum* (sub-humanity).[39] These were bold and forthright comments which were meant to stir people to think, but they knew it would be their death sentence if caught. They were intelligent and knew that individuals could do nothing to overthrow the regime, but constantly argued that 'acting together' might make it possible. They made a specific appeal on Christian grounds that it was essential to make a stand. They used the Bible and many other sources to base their arguments, casting their net of opinions as wide as possible, knowing all the time the dangers they were facing. As mentioned above, some of the young men in the group had seen action on the front and witnessed the cruelty, making a point of drawing the attention of this to the readers. They made nonsense of the Nazi claim that other people such as the Russians were somehow inferior to the so-called Aryan race of Germany.

As events turned against the Germans and at the Casablanca Conference 'unconditional surrender' was announced the group promptly used this threat to send their warnings. They alerted everyone that the war was ending, raised the persecution of the Jews, and challenged the public's apparent acceptance of this infamy. They raised the question, which many must have felt, that a form of retribution would fall upon Germans, and referred to the *untermenschen* (sub-human) as being the Nazis themselves. It was not only pamphlets, but they also applied graffiti with their views on public buildings, especially the university, demanding Hitler's downfall and calling for freedom. They argued that the failure at Stalingrad was entirely Hitler's fault, which must have rung bells with many senior military commanders.

After their arrests, the Gestapo tried without much success to work out who wrote what because it was a genuine combination of intellects. The investigators had been aware of the documents since they started in the summer of 1942 but had major problems tracking down their source. The investigators realised that the pamphlets were the product of educated and intellectual people. Once they were captured, Judge Roland Freisler was brought in to deal with the court cases as he was widely known as an ardent and fanatical supporter of the Nazi regime, and they were referred to as despicable criminals. They were interrogated in the usual fashion, and the Gestapo tried to find out from them information about another resistant group called the Red Orchestra (*Die Rote Kapelle*). This was a group of resisters which was similar in opposing the Nazi regime by pamphlets and helping fleeing Jews. Despite the name it was not Soviet directed, but another group of people demanding civil disobedience against the regime. It is important for the post-war generations to recall that there were many German people who despite being terrified were brave enough to resist the Nazi threats. The White Rose leaders were promptly executed and others on the sidelines imprisoned. Kurt Huber's widow even received a bill 'for wear and tear to the guillotine'.[40] The pamphlets, even after the trial, continued to flourish, not least because they found their way to the Allies who used the RAF to flutter them all over Germany. Moltke initiated this, who will be mentioned in the section dealing with elite doubters, and Thomas Mann the German novelist who had fled the country broadcast them in the Western world.

The pamphlets the White Rose had produced and distributed were powerfully expressed and always to the point. The first pamphlet started with the lines:

> Complicity with the governance of an irresponsible clique of rulers driven by their darkest urges, and complicity without resistance – nothing is more unworthy of a civilised people. Is it not so that in the present day every honourable German is ashamed of their government? And who among us can foresee the extent of the infamy that will be on us, and on all our children, when the veil is one day lifted from our eyes and the most horrific crimes, crimes beyond measure, come to light?[41]

This first pamphlet forecast the gloom of dishonour most Germans felt when the length, breadth, and depth of Nazi crimes became known, but its existence was a glimmer of light for many when the White Rose activities came back into public view. They may have been criticised for their impetuosity and the chances they took, with some asking whether it was worth the risk. They brought some light to those later who felt the guilt of accepting a corrupt government, by knowing that some had protested, but the question which must always be posed is whether we would personally have dared.

The second pamphlet started with some dry cynical humour, stating that:

> 'National Socialism cannot be confronted intellectually because it is not intellectual…even in its earliest form this movement was dependant on deceiving the German people; even though it was rotten to the very core and could only save itself through ceaseless deception…a cancerous tumour on the German people.[42]

They raised every issue which they hoped would not only prick the conscience of Nazi supporters but raise hopes of a better world. In their third pamphlet they argued about the right of people to have a viable government which ensured their freedom. They informed their readers that they understood no individual could do much against the regime, but they suggested massive passive resistance, and later suggested rallies and even sabotage of factories making arms and ammunition.

The fourth pamphlet reminded readers of the old adage given to children that 'those who will not listen must feel' but however clever a child, they often burn their fingers on a hot stove, but only once.[43] They had noted that with Hitler claiming success in Africa and Russia giving rise to optimism, when the losses had become known it was leading to pessimism and for many a sense of despair. The pamphlet capitalised on what many people may well have been thinking, cleverly encapsulating the voice of the people, the *vox populi*, hoping it would do more than ring bells; it was a stark warning against misplaced optimism, and warning that every word Hitler spoke was a lie. The Nazi authorities and their iron-grip on German society with a war raging against them may have not been overly disturbed by a group of young students, but there is no doubt they would have been furious. Even German generals threw their cigarettes away if Hitler were in sight, and to call him a liar no one would dare.

In another pamphlet they made an appeal to the people that the war was definitely lost and raised the following:

> But what are the Germans doing about it? They refuse to see, and they refuse to hear. Blindly they follow their corrupters into ruin. 'Victory at all costs!' they wrote on their banner. I will fight until the last man, Hitler says – meanwhile, the war is already lost.[44]

Many may have recalled these words when later they heard that Hitler had committed suicide, and the promised wonder-weapons which never materialised, but such was the psychotic grip Hitler held on so many that they trusted him to the end expecting a promised miracle. They wrote to their fellow students about the Stalingrad failure blaming it on 'the ingenious strategy of our Great War corporal', then reminding their readers of the number of lives lost in this battle. In their fifth pamphlet they appeared to indicate a common purpose with Moltke and the Kreisau Circle when they advocated a new European order.

These young people were clever, well-educated, had intellectual depth, but above all they had the courage to point out the reality of the Nazi world in which many had been indoctrinated by a pernicious political ideology, and were now mentally imprisoned by sheer fear of their own government and its policing. Even a reported comment could have one executed or at the best imprisoned. Hans Scholl's own father was arrested and sentenced to four months in prison for calling Hitler a 'scourge of God'.[45] He was denounced by his secretary, a person whose very role would indicate a sense of personal trust. As is well-known, even family members had been known to denounce one another. In these written pamphlets Hitler is referred to as our Great War corporal, called a liar, and the whole Nazi regime denounced as evil and misleading the country, resulting in a ruinous war whose only promise was one of despair and shame. There can be little doubt that while some thought their work was shameful, others would have first admired their courage and set many thinking. Such was the Nazi grip on its own people the pamphlets could only raise questions, but with no real hope of overturning the regime. After the war, the victors and other national bystanders were shocked by the exposure of the Nazi regime, the Nuremberg and subsequent trials of Nazi organisations and individual war criminals held the international headlines, and the German population could not but feel the weight of guilt pressed on them. Hitler had stirred up a sense of deadly hatred and this now confronted the post-war Germans with intense heat.

It took a few years for the rest of the world to realise there had been genuine opposition and resistance even in a thoroughly repressed German society, so the White Rose youngsters, may have failed in their time, but their success came after their death when they shone like a beacon of light that not all Germans took Nazi repression and hatred just sitting silently. As a group they could be described as active opposition, but given the risks they were all aware of, they must go down in history as a dedicated resistance group.

The individual and small groups of resisters who opposed the Nazi regime trying to influence the German public were faced by a public who knew it best to keep themselves to themselves for pure safety reasons. Speaking the slightest criticism of the regime could bring denouncement by a trusted friend or colleague and instant recrimination. For some it was a time when it was safer to salute the regime even if reluctantly, to keep one's feelings to oneself. Members of today's generation must always ask themselves if they would have dared to act otherwise. Many were so entranced by the regime's claims they even remained loyal during the bombing raids, the invasion of Germany and post-war still felt the same way. In seeking out the honest views of the public there are few sources. Ulrich von Hassell noted in his diary (25 February 1939) what he entitled 'a few expressions from the man in the street', which might raise a few eyebrows as Hassell was far from being a man who talked to people in everyday life, but then making sense when he added 'according to my somewhat talkative barber'.[46] He was told the people's spirits were sinking rapidly, high Party officials were being cursed, and when asked by Hassell about the principle complaints was told everything, especially about Goebbels who was the chief subject of public scorn along with other Party bosses. When he spoke with Prince Konstantin of Bavaria, he related that 'his stories about the Labour Service indicate that he has hardly discovered a single 100 per cent National Socialist. Everybody was either up in arms or bored by the methods of the Party rulers'.[47] Whether it was his barber or aristocratic friends there were complaints about the Nazi regime, but few by this stage would go public for fear of being denounced to the Gestapo. By July 1939 Hassell noted 'everybody is in fear of war. The same old story between Russia and the Western Powers', namely a repeat of the First World War.[48] It was of course Goebbels' staged events and Hitler's rhetoric which increased some fervour for the conflict and the state police which silenced the doubters.

From 1933 onwards the political opposition to the NSDAP had been silenced by prison camps and sheer fear. The Nazis had hoodwinked many everyday ordinary Germans with promises for a better future. and it is a challenging task to analyse precisely what the potentially opposing public thought and how they reacted. That there were critics is undoubtedly true from the moment the Nazi regime unleashed its reign of terror on Jews.

Elite Conservative Doubters

The would-be opponents of the elite class of objectors sometimes met and merged their thinking, raising issues of how to respond. Ulrich von Hassell's diaries clearly indicate many of these discussions took place over breakfasts, lunches, and dinners in their private residences, and they were not always of the same mind in how to make progress against the regime.

There was the Kreisau Circle which was headed by the jurist Helmuth James von Moltke who had been drafted into the Abwehr (later arrested for trying to save some Jewish people) combined with others to form an intellectual resistance, which included Church representatives, Jesuit priests like Augustin Rösch (who was arrested following the 20 July Plot but survived). Carl Goerdeler (conservative politician who opposed the treatment of the Jews) led another major group Circle with General Beck. There were others, including a group of army officers with names such as von Tresckow, Olbricht, von Stauffenberg, and others. These growing resistance groups knew about each other's existence, and they have often been criticised for spending too much time discussing the type of future after Hitler had gone, and not enough time working to unseat him. Many of those involved in the Goerdeler Circle had held posts under the Nazis, tended to be traditional right-wing, but quite how they could topple the growing strength of Nazism with its wide popular support raised many doubts. Many of these critics of the regime had been opposing it since its inception, but one Prussian aristocrat, Fritz-Dietlof von der Schulenburg had been a party member and served the regime both in the civil service and the army. He changed his mind for moral reasons and became an important key figure in the active resistance. As with those in the military opposition it seems appropriate to highlight some of the most significant characters involved as in this study individuals had to lead the way.

Carl Goerdeler

Carl Goerdeler was a traditional German conservative politician, a monarchist by breeding, who rose through the civil service ranks because of his economic professionalism. His father had been a judge, with a strict moral background, somewhat judgmental as he did not appreciate divorced people, and he tended to be somewhat dictatorial in his views. Like his father Goerdeler was always certain that his views and opinions were correct and was able to persuade others to accept his views.[49] During the Great War he rose to the rank of captain, and afterwards worked for the German military in Minsk. Like most Germans he was angry with the Versailles Treaty and early on argued for controlling Poland to stop further losses on the eastern borders. His rise was meteoric and Chanceller Brüning made him the Reich Price Commissioner for combatting the oncoming inflation, which post convinced Goerdeler that the Weimar Republic was a failure. By 1932 he was even considered a possible Chancellor, but Franz von Papen was eventually selected. Goerdeler refused to work with von Papen and resigned as Price Commissioner.

Initially, and like many others, Goerdeler thought Hitler was a hope for a better German future which he later confessed was a mistake which he regretted. The first hiccup came in April 1933 after the Nazis ordered a national boycott on Jewish businesses which as Mayor of Leipzig, Goerdeler ordered the SA not to enforce in his area, arranging for some Jews to be released from custody. Nevertheless, he sent Hitler suggestions of a better economic policy and rules for municipal government, but he always refused to join the NSDAP.[50] He disagreed with Hitler's peace pact with Poland in 1934, pointing out to Hitler the economic ramifications stating that 'the German people must fight for the security of their existence'.[51] He was reappointed under Nazi suggestion as Price Commissioner again, although he was having serious doubts about Nazi policies. There were matters which worried him, not least the removal of the Mendelssohn statue in Leipzig while Goerdeler was away in Finland.* Goerdeler resigned as mayor when he proved unable to rectify this incident (March 1937).

It was after this issue that Goerdeler started to involve himself with those wishing for the downfall of the Nazi regime, mainly collaborating with civil servants and businessmen, but this would soon enlarge because Goerdeler was always totally committed to following what he perceived to be the right course. He was determined to bring about the downfall of the regime, at first not supportive of assassinating Hitler, but as times became more desperate, he realised this was a necessity. He travelled widely on a global basis always making a point of meeting senior people in various countries, and ensuring they heard his views on the dangers that Hitler was presenting. This was a significant move of active resistance, and he became part of General Beck's clandestine intelligence movement. This support by Beck encouraged him to try and

* Removed by a senior Leipzig city official called Rudolph Haake because the musician was Jewish. They wanted a statue of Wagner instead.

influence his military contacts to overthrow Hitler. He informed his British contact (Sir Robert Vansittart) that the resistance, which he often implied he was leading, sought better relationships with Britain, and that many Germans were seeking to replace Hitler with a military dictatorship, which only wanted the return of German lands from Czechoslovakia and Poland, and later he also suggested a return to the monarchy. He was taken seriously by some countries because he offered hope that the dictator was being actively opposed, and he even met Churchill. The only chance of a coup happening at this stage was by the military, but there were too few in the army who would back this to make it a realistic possibility. He was enthusiastic and determined because of the nature of his strong assertive personality, but appeared, at times, out of touch with the sheer support for Hitler and the military sense of obedience. Nevertheless, he joined with Oster and others in a plot in 1938 to start a *putsch* against Hitler over his plans for occupying Czechoslovakia as, he feared it would lead Germany into a major war. As such he felt let down by the Munich conference because its success for Hitler put the potential *putsch* on the shelf.

Goerdeler continued to bring potential opponents of the regime together for discussions on how to deal with the future, by which time Hitler was becoming aware of his critics and Goerdeler in particular, but such was Hitler's popularity he tended to dismiss them as a group of intellectual nobodies. Goerdeler, through his links, told the British that Hitler was coaxing Italy into his plans, and considering an attack on France and also Britain, doing his best to alert the outside world to the potential dangers. In May 1939 he told the British that the Germans and Soviet Russians had started to talk possibly with the idea of dividing Eastern Europe, insisting the German resistance was gathering force. This was far from the truth and was probably based on his personality's self-assurance that he was right, and others would therefore follow. The resistance, what there was of it at this time, certainly hardened following the news of the brutal behaviour of the SS during the Polish campaign. Goerdeler remained persistent and even drafted a possible peace treaty with Britain after the fall of Hitler, proposing to keep the once German portions of Poland, the Sudetenland and Austria. It was a pipe dream because by 1939 Hitler appeared to be fulfilling his promises of overturning the Versailles Treaty, and after the victory over France any hope of dissidence amongst the military was rapidly dwindling. Even though Britain was hard pressed and in danger, there was no way that Churchill and his stalwarts would accept the offer Goerdeler was making, as the proposal had every intention of retaining the occupied territories. Men like Goerdeler and Beck had initially supported Hitler, but they had seen only what they wanted to see. It had been a good sign for Beck when the Kaiser's son, Prince August Wilhelm had joined the Party. For some historical critics it raised the question as to how long this type of resistance would have lasted had Hitler been successful.

Operation *Barbarossa* brought some hope of resistance, with Ulrich von Hassell noting in his diary of 15 June 1941, that there were 'a series of conferences with Popitz, Goerdeler and Oster to consider whether certain orders which the Army Commanders have received (but which they have as yet not issued) might suffice to open the eyes of the military leaders to the nature of the regime for which they are fighting…Brauchitsch and Halder have already agreed to Hitler's tactics'.[52] It would need a near total disaster for enough military commanders to think along the same lines as men like Goerdeler and Oster, so these men in opposition spent available secret time discussing the possibilities of the future, mainly discussing plans such as if the monarchy were restored who would be the right candidate. For some critics this all amounted to a group of dissidents grumbling in secret but being unable to change what was happening. On the other hand, at least they were in opposition to a regime they all found morally repugnant and potentially dangerous.

The news of Jews being deported East to be exterminated or worked to death caused revulsion to the growing opposition. Goerdeler wrote to the government suggesting German Jews whose families had lived in Germany before 1870 should be seen as Germans, and others as Jews of a state yet to be established somewhere else in the world. This has since raised a debate as to how far Goerdeler was anti-Semitic. It has been argued that at least his memo to the government was a better alternative than the Holocaust, others that he suffered from entrenched anti-Semitism, and his views remain a confusing and complex web of debate. The accumulated evidence tends to favour that Goerdeler was a morally upright man who was undeniably against the treatment the Jews received from the Nazi regime. Although von Hassell in his diary could be critical of Goerdeler, accusing him of being imprudent and under close surveillance, he wrote 'I find it a relief, though, to speak with a man prepared to act rather than grumble'.[53]

As early as late 1942, Goerdeler made an illegal trip with forged papers provided by Oster to meet up with the generals Günther von Kluge and Henning von Tresckow whom, it was known, had little time for Hitler's regime. Some of the generals he met constituted the third rather nebulous group of military officers, their motives were mixed like their civilian counterparts, torn between the fear of German military defeat, and concerned about the barbarities they had been instructed to order. Hitler never trusted his generals, and after any promotion or victory he always awarded them with huge sums of money to either function as a bribe or confirm they stood with the regime. Keitel later wrote in his memoirs that Hitler had 'a pathological delusion that his generals were conspiring against him, trying to sabotage his orders on what were in his view pretty shabby pretexts'.[54] The bribery helped keep many on side, and it has been stated that von Kluge eventually fell to this form of persuasion. Goerdeler, given the circumstance under which he lived in a policed state was best described as hyper-active, remaining in touch with the Wallenberg family in Sweden which provided him some form of contact with the Western Allies. At times he was dangerously over-enthusiastic even suggesting he should meet Hitler and persuade him to resign. This was in 1943 when the war was turning against Germany, but victory was still anticipated, opponents were met with brutality, often the same treatment was meted out to their families, and his friends at last managed to dissuade him from such a dangerous proposal.

At the same time Goerdeler met Claus von Stauffenberg where at first there was a feeling of mutual animosity, but this led to the one significant chance of eliminating Hitler in the 20 July Plot. This led to Goerdeler's execution with the failure of the plot and will be explored in a later chapter. At this point, it is necessary to at least see Goerdeler who was active from the start of the Nazi regime, not just a critic and opponent, but an initiative-taking resister, seen by some as a figurehead of the resistance from 1937, even at times if he were somewhat unrealistic.

Helmuth James von Moltke, the Kreisau Circle

Some of the opponents against Nazism were stirred by a multitudinous number of reasons and motives, and some by pure conscience. Bonhoeffer was such an example, but the layman Helmuth James von Moltke stands alongside him within this category of the morally motivated, and for this writer was one of the most dedicated resisters. He was related to Helmuth von Moltke (the Elder) who was awarded the estate as a signal of Prussian gratitude for the battle he won against the Austrians near Königgrätz in Bohemia (July 1866), thus the emergence of the name Kreisau, the name of the estate. Helmuth James von Moltke was the inheritor after his father died in 1939. Curiously, in 1941 it was the 50th anniversary of the field marshal's death, a major service was held, and the Nazis wanted to build in place of the small wooden family chapel a magnificent mausoleum, but Moltke changed their minds, arguing the case that it was a matter of respect for the field marshal's lifestyle being honoured.

His resistance movement is always referred to as the Kreisau Circle, but Moltke, according to his wife Freya never knew this expression, and only heard of this title when Moltke was in prison near his end-days. A member of the group known as Haubach had later been interrogated by the SD (SS Security Office) and the term was used from this time.[55] There were three weekend conferences at Kreisau, which was deep in rural Silesia, with members arriving by different trains under the pretext of a gathering of co-workers, covered by a mixture of social meals and walks when serious discussions about the future were the point of meeting. Many more meetings took place at Peter Yorck's home in Hoternsienstrasse in Berlin, some in Munich and others in Stuttgart. In many ways Yorck, who was an attorney and civil servant, was with Moltke a co-founder of the Kreisau Circle. Yorck's cousin was Claus Stauffenberg, but more pertinently Yorck and Moltke had been united by their shared objection to the Nazi treatment of Jewish people and other moral considerations.

Moltke was a talented lawyer who turned down the opportunity to become a judge to avoid having to join the NSDAP in 1935, and he specialised in International Law having trained in Germany and London. In his early legal practice, he had helped Jews to escape from Germany and later during his military service he tried to gain a better treatment for PoWs.[56] He was a man of conscience and could easily detect when normal codes of morality were breached. He often tried, through his post and occupation, to persuade the military to a more moral and measured approach as outlined in international law. When Moltke was on his travels, he wrote to his wife Freya about the scenes he had witnessed: 'In one part of Serbia two villages have been reduced to ashes, 1,700 men and 240 women of the inhabitants have been executed. That is the punishment for an attack on three German soldiers. In Greece 240 men and were shot in one village'.[57] He, like any person with any sense of morality was shocked by what he saw and heard about. His wife explained how, unlike her, he had bothered to read Hitler's book *Mein Kampf* and foresaw the dangers of Nazism.[58] He had been preparing for law examinations in London when he became concerned about the way the European political scene appeared to be reshaping, with Hitler and Mussolini as dictators, Franco was rapidly emerging in Spain, and with a rampant Oswald Mosley causing Moltke to wonder if Britan might turn fascist.

When war started in 1939, he was ordered into the Abwehr as an expert in international law. He travelled much, and when seeing some abusive situations in occupied territories, and as mentioned above he tried to insist the Germans should take heed of the Geneva convention. He attempted to argue the case based on what the outside world could construe about Germany, but he was ignored. He was an astute observer of unfolding events from what was happening on the streets to what was emerging from the corridors of power. Moltke stopped enjoying Berlin because it was 'an agonising mixture of knowledge about what was going on and the direction in which it was developing'.[59]

He was also remained deeply disturbed at the way the Jews were being rounded up, and he found support for his views from Oster but little elsewhere. He drafted a paper on the necessity of following international law, the Geneva and Hague Conventions, but it was rebuffed by Hitler's nominal head of the OKW Field Marshal Wilhelm Keitel, who was well-known for always obeying and reflecting Hitler's views. One of his most outstanding achievements was warning the Danish opposition of Nazi plans to sweep up all Danish Jews. The Danish opposition response was instant, and they promptly organised a fleet of fishing boats to transport their Jews to the safety of Sweden. This single act must mark him out as a courageous man of deep integrity and with a sound sense of morality. After December 1938 he was not officially allowed to help Jews seeking help, but according to his wife Freya he never stopped making these efforts.

By this stage Moltke's disgust of Nazism and its bellicose attitudes was deeply embedded, and he managed to persuade a visiting Brazilian to return home and influence the President of Brazil to stop contemplating some form of alliance with Germany. He went on an official visit to Turkey but with the quiet intention of starting a widespread opposition to Nazi rule. While there, the resisters met as a group in the relative safety of Turkey and managed to send a message to Roosevelt, who doubted its credibility. One of the problems Moltke faced was that his uncle was the German Ambassador in Spain, so when he let many in the outside world know about the concentration camps and promised to find opposition, the British and Americans remained sceptical. However, it should be noted that whereas Goerdeler and later Stauffenberg had in their peace overtures wanted to retain Germany's gains, Moltke, when in Turkey, sought only collaboration, noting that 'the group is convinced of the justification of the Allied demand for unconditional surrender, and realises the untimeliness of any discussion of peace terms before this surrender had been accomplished', which the Allies must have felt more realistic.[60] This was all very different from Goerdeler and Stauffenberg who would not have wanted Germany's defeat, and it was probably the case that Moltke never wanted a Russian victory and occupation, but no one in the anti-Nazi German camp seemed to have realised how tightly bound the Western Allies and Soviets had become to destroy the Nazi danger.

Moltke travelled a great deal in his military post (Brussels, Paris, The Hague, Oslo, Stockholm, Copenhagen, and Istanbul) but also as a resister. He attempted to contact foreign resistance groups, with some success in the Netherlands and Norway but not in France. He had sound intelligence and knowledge of the world. When the war had started, and despite its initial successes for the Nazi regime, Moltke was totally convinced it could not win. He argued that even if the Nazis occupied Britain, the leaders and monarchy would go to the colonies and fight from there, and they would never give up.[61] Even before the war had started, he had begun conversations with trusted friends, people who distrusted Hitler's regime even with the early military successes. It had to be accomplished with the greatest care and according to his wife Freya he would often ask her what she thought of the proposed resisters he wanted to enlist. She recalled he once asked her about Konrad Adenauer, but she thought he was too old, causing her to reflect that it reminded her of how young they then were.[62] He was eventually successful in finding a substantial number of contacts who soon recruited others.

A group of students in Munich known as the White Rose, already mentioned in this chapter, had produced their pamphlets attacking the regime. It was very much a localised protest by young resisters, but Moltke had one of their protest pamphlets from a visit to Munich, took it to Berlin and then to Norway where it was copied and used by their resistance. It eventually went to Sweden and on to England, where millions of copies were made and dropped over Germany by the RAF.[63] Moltke had managed to elevate a protest at a German university to an international level. Moltke, who belonged to the conservative elitist resisters, was one who wanted the resistance not to be always associated with his social cast, but to include all elements within the German class system, as can be seen by his support of the student protestors and later contacting once prominent members of the Social Democratic Party.

Moltke wanted not just the demolition of the Nazi regime but a complete change in Germany's political and social life, he would often refer to this as Day X.[64] He wanted to resurrect a sense of humanity in every German, as in the heart of a religious upbringing, and regarded social reforms as essential. It has been noted that 'central to Kreisau Circle was people's religious security'.[65] He wrote that 'a mass [of people] without faith can be corrupted by any statesman, but a solid rank of believers cannot'.[66] His Kreisau Circle wanted a change in German history, as Hans Schlange-Schöningen wrote 'We must build a new state, not in order to repeat the vicious circle of German history, but to begin a new history'.[67] Many in Moltke's group disliked the way the democratic Weimar Republic had failed, but they also recognised the dangers of German history, but finding a solution in the hope of overturning Hitler took time and, at times, appeared fruitless.

Moltke was deeply religious, claiming frustration for not being believed when he said that only by believing in God could one be a total opponent of the Nazis.[68] Without wishing to be cynical there was probably some truth in this view, as any opposition to the Nazi regime often meant torture and death, so those who believed in life after death were probably more likely to be prepared to become martyrs. His wife Freya was thrilled when Father Augustin Rösch, the Provincial of the Jesuits, the highest official of the southern German province, attended the group. When they met on the Kreisau estate she noted how they would walk together and go to their own churches, that no political discussion was allowed during meals. She observed since the great divide of the Reformation, how now both Catholics and Protestants were prepared to sit down together and seek a solution.[69] It was the Jesuit Provincial who introduced Father Alfred Delp to the group. According to Freya he was full of life and ideas in the discussions, and like Bonhoeffer had left his book of prayers and reflections while awaiting execution.[70]

These discussions were a major characteristic of the Kreisau Circle, and a selected member would be given a remit on which they had to report and encourage discussion in what were study sessions. They were wide in their outlook, ranging from issues such as why the Weimar Republic had failed, whether democracy could work within the German tradition, and as Moltke's wife recalled there was seldom total agreement, which can be anticipated in discussions which are free. 'They were also convinced that the sovereign European nation-state was coming to its end in this Second World War; securing world peace required "the creation of an order that comprised the individual states"'.[71] Many of their discussions in the Kreisau estate tended to centre on how Germany would recover when defeated, and they emerged with what was termed a pan-European concept which eventually eventuated decades later in the European Union. They also considered how Germany as a country would face the anticipated global assault on the crimes committed by the Nazi regime. He was opposed to Hitler's assassination for fear it would make the tyrant a martyr, a view projected by the diarist Fredrich Kellner, explored in the previous chapter. Sometimes he was accused of putting the brakes on the plans as he and his Kreisau group wanted the result of Hitler's downfall to be successfully followed by a better system. They tended to ignore what was called the 'German way' and from early on (1941) had discussed ways of demobilising Europe and establishing a large economic unified Europe with people of like-minds joining forces. They arrived at many major resolutions, especially 'the abolition of all discrimination on the basis of race and religion'.[72] They agreed that Germany was to be organised by regional commissioners on Day X, and if necessary, they were to explain to the occupiers that there had always been a resistance. He had done his best to keep notes and memoranda which have often revealed some interesting insights. Most of the circle wanted the restoration of the Christian way of life, and they anticipated a United States of Europe, so for some they have been seen as too futuristic while for others outmoded, but above all, they represented those who never succumbed to the lure of dictatorships. Moltke always argued in favour of bringing in other resisters apart from the traditional elite conservative class, probably on the grounds that any form of resistance against an unlawful regime could only be viable with a large cross section of the previous political divides. In the next chapter it is noted how he was somewhat successful with the SPD and trade union leaders, but the essential component that they had to be people who were highly competent.

The notes were typed by Moltke's trusted secretary, kept secret, and hidden by Moltke's wife with him not wanting to know where, for obvious reasons of possible interrogation. She hid them in the attic of their farmhouse on the estate where they remained undisturbed until the Russians arrived in May 1945. They used coded expressions at times, with Moltke referring to Carlo Mierendorff as uncle and Julis Leber as 'substitute uncle'. Moltke was arrested but on the grounds that he had recently warned a colleague who was about to be arrested. Freya was allowed to visit him, and it did not seem too serious to her, until the 20 July Plot. He appeared before the People's Court lorded over by Roland Freisler, but they could not find evidence that he participated in the plot. Freisler used a new law, similar to one deployed by the English Tudor King Henry VIII, that even to 'think' against the monarch was treason. This led to Moltke writing to his wife telling he was to be executed for his ideas which for him was matter of pride.

Moltke was a man with a sense of morality and conscience who, recognizing its inherent evil, opposed the Nazi regime. He had been well aware that to criticise or oppose the regime would end in his death, but he persisted in sowing the seeds of opposition and did his best to keep the Western Allies in touch as he was a determined resister.

Ulrich von Hassell

Ulrich von Hassell was from the German upper-class and a steadfast nationalist like most of his generation. He was wounded in the First World War at the First Battle of the Marne and later worked as Admiral Alfred von Tirpitz's secretary, later wrote Tirpitz's biography, and married his daughter. His well-known relationship with the Tirpitz family probably did not encourage the British to take him seriously, with Lord Halifax dismissing him out of hand. He was by breeding and nature a conservative, and post-war he joined the German Nationalist People's Party (DNVP) and in 1933 the NSDAP. He worked for the Foreign Office in Rome, Barcelona, Copenhagen, and Belgrade, and in 1932 was made Ambassador to Italy. Although a member of the NSDAP he was never happy with their policies, and he was against the Anti-Comintern Pact which had included Germany, Italy, and Japan (1937). He had been all too typical of the conservative elite, only seeing in Hitler what he wanted to see, and thinking the dictator could be controlled.

While in Italy he had much to do with Ciano, Mussolini's Foreign Minister, and son-in-law, both suspicious of Hitler but not part of their mutual conversations. 'Ciano was pleased to say farewell to Hassell, in a "cold, hostile and rapid meeting", concluding that Hassell belonged to the Junker class and was not supporting the Nazis', who Ciano's master Mussolini needed.[73] There is no question that despite his suspicions of Ciano, Hassell maintained a good relationship with Mussolini.

Following the Blomberg and Fritsch dismissals, Hassell was recalled (or dismissed) from Italy and led a German delegation to some of the northern European states to put their minds at rest, namely that Germany's incursion into Poland should not worry them. He was bitterly opposed to the regime but being a traditional right-wing German from the Junker class, he always hoped the Western Allies would regard Germany as an important central power, be allowed to keep the union with Austria and other territorial gains. He anticipated that this would find support because of the communist threat, a view shared by many resisters of the conservative family, many of whom also wanted a monarchical state. His views of a united Europe were not as important as was his determined effort to stand up against the criminal regime, the dictator Hitler, and his cohorts to restore his version of a trusted Germany.

He had a private breakfast with the British Ambassador Nevile Henderson in September 1938, and learnt more about Ribbentrop being the cause of problems between Britain and Germany with the possibility that it could lead to war. Henderson asked Hassell to pass these views on to Keitel whom he was meeting later the same day. He mentioned this to Weizsäcker, who explained that Keitel was 'simply too stupid to understand such things'.[74] It was clear that Hassell was testing the waters of a possible resistance meeting and talking with people who might be of the same opinion in the hope they could form a viable opposition. The same afternoon he visited Schacht whom he knew was worried about financial and economic matters in Germany. He made contacts with military men like Beck, with the Abwehr, civil servants and the financial administrators. Hassell became almost hyper-active trying to find groups of resisters who would be prepared to overthrow the Nazi regime. He focused on people like Goerdeler, Ludwig Beck and the Kreisau Circle, mainly concerned as to how Germany should be governed post-war. He was an active resister as he could see that the Nazi regime for him was just a group of gangsters who had hoodwinked their way to power.

In November 1938 following *Kristallnacht*, he referred to this pogrom as 'under the crushing emotions evoked by the vile persecution of the Jews…not since the World War have we lost so much credit in the world'.[75] He added later that 'the Bruckmanns and Karl Alexander were here for tea. Their horror at the shameless persecution of the Jew is as great as that of all respectable people'.[76] Hassell may have been worried about Germany's international reputation, but it is abundantly clear from many of his diary notes that he was against the Nazi attitudes towards Jewish people and found them abhorrent.

There were few aspects of Nazi behaviour which escaped his attention. When Pope Pius XI died (10 February 1939), he noted the press comments were decent, but he wrote in his diary these articles were 'apparently [written] under instruction', then adding that 'the Catholic Theology Faculty in Munich is to be closed because of a dispute about a professorial chair' and 'the public is permitted to hear only one side'.[77] In noting this he highlighted the ignorance of most of the population caused by Goebbels' control of the press. Later, when he drafted an article on what was happening in Spain, he 'noted the fear of German editors in the blue-pencilling 'as if Goebbels were its managing editor'.[78] It was clear to Hassell that all potential print for the public came under the scrutiny and guidelines of Goebbels' office.

When Hitler ignored the Munich Agreement and occupied the rest of Czechoslovakia he noted (March 1939) that it came to 'the utter astonishment of the world, which looks on aghast…this is the first incident of manifest depravity, exceeding all limits, including those of decency'.[79] Hassell was no mere critic in family circles, he was an outright opponent who became an active resister. He was arrested nine days after the 20 July Plot, faced the People's court, had a two-day trial between 8–9 September, and he was executed within an hour of the verdict at Plötzensee prison in Berlin.

Ernst von Weizsäcker

Ernst von Weizsäcker has often been portrayed as one of the high rankers who opposed Hitler. However, in Weizsäcker's case this was somewhat borderline, because compared to many others it has been claimed he was possibly a more lukewarm critic, having, it has been thought, none of the willpower of Hassell. During the First World War he became a naval officer but afterwards he was a politician and served as a diplomat, joining the Foreign Service in 1920, serving in Basel, Copenhagen, Geneva, Oslo, and Bern with a variety of posts. In 1937 he was made Director of the Policy Department in the Foreign Office and a year later appointed State Secretary second only to the Foreign Minister. He was working for the Nazi regime and on advice to better his future he joined the NSDAP in 1938 and was awarded an honorary rank in the SS. He had no issues about the recovery of the Sudetenland but was concerned that it might lead to a major war, and he had what is best described as some mild contact with members of the opposition. It was only post-war at his trial he claimed to have been in the resistance and had worked to overthrow the Nazi regime. He even wrote to Ribbentrop (Foreign Minister) warning that Czechoslovakia should wait until Britain lost interest for fear of starting a major war, but never sent the memo.[80] In this effort he was not opposing the Nazi regime, just concerned about their tactics, not the overall strategy. The resisters hoped the attack might lead to Hitler's overthrow.

Weizsäcker was subsequently promoted SS-*Brigadeführer* (January 1942) but after battle of Stalingrad fiasco he resigned and was appointed as Ambassador to the Holy See (Vatican) for the rest of the war. It remains questionable that had Stalingrad been a victory whether he would have resigned, and by appointing him to Rome the Nazis were only putting a potential critic in a safe place where he could do insignificant damage. In his diaries von Hassell heard that 'Weizsäcker is pressing for action [opposition] with the utmost vigour. That is easy to do from the Vatican! Before that he certainly did not get that involved'.[81]

The Vatican was a strange appointment because when the Pope had protested against the brutality meted out in Poland, Weizsäcker had refused its acceptance.[82] It has been claimed that Weizsäcker did little to help Jews when Rome was occupied by the Germans, though it was later argued that he was under the mistaken belief they would be safer in the eastern deportations than staying in the west. It is known that he attempted to help the Pope's (Pius XII) reputation and also to avoid anti-German feelings growing in Italy. The main thrust of his thinking was to paint the picture of the dangers of communism which he had always feared. When the war finished, he stayed protected in the Vatican for a time, but in 1946 he returned to Germany and was soon arrested and put on trial in the Nuremberg series of Ministries Trials. Many came to his defence stating he had been a member of the anti-Nazi resistance, but it was claimed he had helped deport Jews to Auschwitz from France. He was sentenced to seven years in prison, later reduced to five but released in October 1950. He later published his memoirs in which he claimed an active role in the resistance. There seems little doubt that at the absolute best Weizsäcker was known by other resisters, may have agreed with some of them, but despite the post-war rumours was more a silent critic and had been grateful to have found sanctuary in the Vatican. He represented many others who had supported the regime, had become critical, but during the post-war period possibly elevated their opposition to stand in a better light.

Curiously, his son Richard, who was the sixth President of the German Federal Republic, defended him in court. His son, who studied at Balliol College, Oxford and joined the Wehrmacht, was more of a resistant man than his father, as he and many of his colleagues engaged in a plot to kill Hitler and was on the edges of the 20 July Plot. Weizsäcker is raised here because he underlined that a high-ranking person, as he was, remained critical of the regime.

Fritz-Dietlof von der Schulenburg

Unlike many of the elite members noted in this chapter Fritz-Dietlof von der Schulenburg (1902–1944) was a relatively late-comer to the German resistance, but he was important. He had been born in London, as his father was the German Empire's military attaché, and he was born into a highly traditional Prussian family and educated in the same format. He was by training a typical Prussian civil servant and when Hitler rose to power, he used the opportunity to gain position by his support of the Nazi movement. He was not an ardent fanatic but like many Germans wanted Germany to restore its old status, and believed Hitler's promises, with the more elite believing that they would be able to influence the dictator. By inclination bred from his background he was a dependable selfless servant of the people in the civil service, seeing the rulers of a country as coming from the soil and blood of the history of Prussia, where the country was best described as a civil service state, which largely corresponded with the thinking of Goerdeler.

It has been suggested he joined the Party, because he wrote in 1932 that 'he wanted to play an active role in the political battle'.[83] His belief was that the Nazi Party was the only body which could rally the people, a form of people's movement. The end days of the Weimar Republic had not impressed him, and he had felt a deep distrust of the Papen cabinet and its rule. One of the major factors which this study has explored earlier, and one which may be difficult for the modern reader to comprehend, was the almost psychological grip that the Nazi regime portrayed of a 'national renaissance' which Nazi propaganda exploited nonstop.[84] It was a myth by today's views but very real for the inhabitants of a pariah nation, many who believed it to the bitter end, while others like Schulenburg, had been prepared to give it the benefit of the doubt for a time, but soon changed their minds. This phenomena of wanting to believe promises made by politicians touched upon every aspect of German life, from the intelligentsia in the corridors of universities, even some clergy, prepared to overlook the weaknesses of a Party leader promising a better future. He probably saw the Nazi power more as an interim step to a restructuring of Germany based on the Prussian ideal, which Hitler had often promised when in the company of people of this tradition for political tactical reasons. As a typical Prussian, and like many other Germans, Schulenburg saw in Hitler's claims to restore Germany, all that he considered to be sound.

It remains a prevalent feature of today's political life, with the current writer thinking of many examples, across the world, in America, and elsewhere, where populist movements are placing a strain on constitutional democracy and the rule of law, and the rhetorical strategies of Hitler are still reflected in some of today's leading so-called popular politicians, of whom most readers are aware. When history is ignored the same patterns of Nazi Germany could arise again.

Schulenburg was appointed as advisor to the now infamous Gauleiter Erich Koch of East Prussia.* Koch's 'Byzantine intrigue, corruption, and almost feudal airs and graces' immediately drew Schulenburg's criticisms within a year or so of becoming a Party member.[85] Schulenburg was a Prussian aristocrat who always expected high standards of conduct, and it was hardly surprising he found a man like Koch distasteful. It is equally true that he never remained silent on the matter, letting his views on Koch's behaviour and corruption be widely known. It is known that he found even the top men such as Göring and Röhm far from his liking.** His association with the NSDAP was founded more on his relationship with Gregor Strasser (the original founder) who was murdered in the Night of the Long Knives, but Schulenburg continued to work within the government's administration in Königsberg where he grew in influence. His main task was implementing *Gleichschaltung* (forced coordination of social, economic, and political groupings to enable total control) but he remained in conflict with Koch. However, in 1937 he was promoted by the German Interior Ministry by being posted to Berlin as vice-president of police, then in 1939 he became *Oberpräsident* of Upper and Lower Silesia although he was gathering some critics who doubted his political trustworthiness.

When war broke out, he volunteered to serve as a lieutenant in the reserve battalion of Infantry Regiment 9 in Potsdam, saw action in the Russian campaign and was awarded the Iron Cross, first class. On seeing the conduct of this war based on Nazi orders he became extremely critical of the way the war was being waged, he did not oppose its aims, but was angry about the barbaric orders. It appeared that he did not disagree with Hitler's aggressive wars or have any issues over the *lebensraum* policy, seeing it as the liberation of the East, and his political views may be suspect to the modern world, but his morality and sense of fairness to the conquered started to change his support of Nazism to one of opposition and active resistance. He objected to the way civilians in occupied areas were treated, having believed they had a right to follow their own traditional customs with their own cultural and political leanings. It is difficult in the twenty-first century to come to grips with the thought processes of a man like Schulenburg, deeply influenced by their past and with a deep fear of Bolshevism. It is difficult to understand why a man of Schulenburg's breeding and background one minute could fall to Hitler's mesmeric hold and suddenly

* Koch was sentenced to death for war crimes in Poland, but it was commuted to life imprisonment where he died.

** Schulenburg had serious objections to Röhm and his grandiose plans for a militia.

change his mind so dramatically. It could be paralleled to a young man growing up and suddenly faced by reality, but in Schulenburg's case it was seeing for himself the evil barbarity of Nazi behaviour.

He returned to his Potsdam unit, and it was probably from this point onwards that he became actively opposed to the regime. He had been shocked at the way enemy civilians had been treated, and for a man of his class this was uncivilised, and was soon discussing this with fellow Prussian aristocrats, and by 1942 was participating in some of the Kreisau Circle discussions. Because of his high-society connections he was soon an invaluable recruiter of people who were also critical of the regime. His social standing was such that he was able to move between the various groups of opposition. Already considered part of the Kreisau Circle, he knew army critics, Goerdeler, the socialist opposition and many others. In 1943 he spent a night in prison because of his activities, but his social status and connections enured it was only one night. He soon became a major figure in the 20 July Plot, and it was intended that in the event of a successful outcome he would head the Interior Ministry.

He was a thorough Prussian in the better understanding of tradition, with strong principles 'deeply with Protestant ethic…never allowed himself to become corrupted even in minor matters…a personality firmly grounded in deep religious commitment' and always distanced himself from the politics of personal enhancement.[86] He had much in common with Goerdeler in terms of long term national plans post-Hitler, but his main strength for the resisters was his continuous need to activate matters for a better future, and he had a natural inbuilt authority when dealing with others, and his ideals tended to evolve from his sense of a Prussian utopia.[87] He attempted to help create a list of personnel who would create the new restructuring of a new Germany. All his ideas were based on the initial premise it would happen at the end of the war. It was when he realised that the war would end with Germany in the abyss of failure and destruction that he placed all his efforts into the 20 July plot.

During his trial under Freisler he exemplified courage and Prussian disdain, he often put the dreaded Freisler in his place, who sentenced him to death, and he was executed the same day at Plötzensee on 10 August 1944. He may not have been an early doubter or critic of Nazism, but once he saw with his own eyes the evil nature of the regime his sense of morality was stirred, the better side of his Prussian aristocracy came to the fore, and he will always be remembered for his active resistance.

Military Doubters

General Beck

Within the military command, known for its Prussian background of obedience and loyalty and pretence of having no interest in politics, a few still resisted, but many of the up-and-coming officers came from the Hitler Youth where they had been thoroughly indoctrinated in the policies of Nazism and the adoration of the Führer. Nevertheless, there were some outstanding figures who emerged, not least General Ludwig Beck who eventually was part of the 20 July 1944 plot to be explored later. During the 1930s, he had initially been attracted to Hitler because of their shared hatred of the Versailles Treaty, but he was a German traditionalist who was averse to swearing the too personal allegiance to Adolf Hitler. As Chief of Staff to the German Army (1935–1938) he soon became uncertain about the totalitarian nature of Nazism and especially the growing importance of Himmler's SS. However, his background influenced him to support Hitler in remilitarising the Rhineland, whereas Blomberg had feared the French might react.[88] In the early days he had ignored the regime's many crimes even though he found them distasteful, and as such 'he had contributed to the process whereby Hitler had been able to increase his strength and consolidate his control over Germany and her Wehrmacht'.[89] It took the fear of a major war caused by possible occupation of Sudetenland and possible defeat to turn Beck against his one-time hope in Hitler, which will be explored in the next section of this chapter. Interestingly he used civilians as part of his own intelligence network, one being Carl Goerdeler, the German conservative politician who opposed the Nazi regime and its anti-Semitic policies. Beck was uncertain about the *Anschluss* in case it provoked war, as he was over Czechoslovakia.

Beck was more concerned about the Nazi stronghold than he was about Hitler, and deeply aggravated by the growing power of Himmler's SS, and as such during the Blomberg and Fritsch crisis in 1938 he saw it as an opportunity to assert army influence against the SS, but it never worked.[90] There was no doubt that Beck's moral standards were part of his rebellion. After the attack on Poland in 1939 Beck had heard and then reported to other Nazi opponents that 'the SS had taken 1,500 Jews, including many women and children, and shuttled them back and forth in open freight cars until they were all dead. Then about 200 peasants were forced to dig immense graves, and afterwards all those who had taken part in the work were massacred'.[91]

Beck's main military concern was the size and power of the French Army which Hitler tended to denigrate. It was Beck's belief that the fault was not necessarily Hitler but the poor advice he was being given, blaming it on Keitel, which was unlikely. Beck was beginning to think that certain elements in the

Nazi Party were starting to control Hitler, which with the benefit of hindsight was nonsense, but he felt they were having a controlling effect if not deeply influencing Hitler.[92] Beck suddenly found himself as not so much anti-Hitler but part of the anti-war group, meeting others of the same mind such as Admiral Canaris (Head of *Abwehr*) and the Secretary of State for the Foreign Office, Baron Ernst von Weizsäcker, and the diplomat von Hassell who were all opponents to war. Hitler recognised that Beck had a mind of his own and, knowing he could not win, Beck resigned on 18 August 1938, going on the retirement list and being replaced by General Franz Halder.

At this stage Beck could hardly be described as anti-Hitler but he was deeply suspicious of the Nazi powerhouse, namely the cabal surrounding Hitler. Being a traditionalist wanting the Versailles Treaty turned inside out he stood with Hitler but opposed policies which he thought might start a major war. At this stage Beck might be regarded as an opponent, but he was a man in waiting and soon became a resister. Slowly but surely by the start of the war he was regarded by civilian resisters as a potential leader because of his influence over military men. Ulrich von Hassell, a dedicated resister wrote that he always found Beck 'very intelligent and calm, but he sees no way out at the moment'.[93] As the months passed Hassell recorded in his diary that Beck's main problem was 'that he is very theoretical. As Johannes Popitz says, [Johannes Popitz a Prussian lawyer and dedicated to resisting the Nazi Regime] a man of tactics but little will power', but the civilians recognised him as a potential leader of their group of dissidents.[94]

General Hans Oster

Beck was only one of a small military espionage group. General Olbricht, General Henning von Tresckow, and others were unhappy about the regime, probably from early on, but they would need to see the major war develop and see or hear of the atrocities before they reacted and could claim the status of being a Nazi resister. However, General Hans Oster was one of the first to try and confront the regime. He was Canaris's deputy in the Abwehr, and he knew Hans Bernd Gisevius (Intelligence Officer and Diplomat) and Arthur Nebe, who although working for the SD and Gestapo became a co-conspirator working with Oster against the Nazi rule. Oster like many had at first regarded the Nazis as an opportunity for Germany to find its feet after a decade of turmoil, but in Oster's case it was the Night of the Long Knives which cast his views into doubt, but this time on moral grounds. His name is associated with what has been called the Oster Conspiracy of 1938 when he and Gisevius and Hjalmar Schacht attempted to persuade Beck and Halder to try and bring Hitler down, even contacting the British. Beck and Halder were more concerned about avoiding a war than a coup, and when the Munich Conference concluded it brought a significant pause to these plans. It now appeared that a military conflict with the West was unlikely, but following the defeat of Poland and France their hopes were further weakened. For the military it would have to wait until the disasters they suffered in Russia for their hopes of a coup were re-ignited. Oster was a keen activator and agreed with a few friends 'that they would kill Hitler even without the agreement of the other conspirators'.[95] Time and time again Oster was always looking for an opportunity to throw a bomb, but even seeking out such a weapon or explosives was not easy and could raise Gestapo interest because of their many informants.

Oster objected to Nazi behaviour, especially their behaviour towards the Jews, but the military tended to focus on the question of first avoiding war, then later avoiding defeat. Oster was initiative-taking in his opposition to the Nazis, and he could be regarded as the first dedicated resister of Nazi plans. He sent numerous warnings to a Dutch friend, Lieutenant-General Bert Sas (Dutch Military attaché) in Berlin about the proposed invasion of the Netherlands, but the Dutch thought it was a clever ruse to activate them thereby giving Germany an excuse to invade.

Following the German success in Poland and the West it was virtually impossible to build any resistance against the successful Hitler, but Oster persisted. When the organised annihilation of Jews was seen after Operation *Barbarossa* had started, it provided Oster with more impetus to react. He contacted Generals Henning von Tresckow and Friedrich Olbricht about using a British devised bomb explosive to kill Hitler, but it failed to work as hoped. They also tried to help some persecuted Jews, but the Gestapo became suspicious, and Oster was dismissed. Oster, with the help of Hans von Dohnányi and his brother-in-law the famous Protestant theologian Dietrich Bonhoeffer, they had tried to help a group of Jews to flee into Switzerland disguised as Abwehr agents. Oster is raised at this stage because he was one sound example of an individual who became an active opponent and resister to the Nazi regime on moral grounds.

Admiral Wilhelm Canaris

Oster's chief was Admiral Wilhelm Canaris, who in the popular understanding of this era is often seen as an opponent of Hitler, and probably one of the most referred to because of his status of being head of the Abwehr (Military Intelligence Agency). In reality he was in fact a supporter of the regime during most of the interbellum years. He remains of interest because even during this period he showed signs of a better humanity than many others. He was a strong traditionalist and after the First World War had organised some *Freikorps* units to subjugate the Communists. He was part of the court system trying left-wing revolutionaries (Rosa Luxemburg *et al*) for their part in the Spartacist revolt and made sure some were acquitted and even helped one escape (for which he was imprisoned for a few days). This indicated he was no extremist himself and had a compassion not shared by others. He was part of the clandestine build-up of the German military, even being sent to Japan looking for submarine improvements. He was no lover of the Weimar Republic, so like other traditionalists he tended to look to the NSDAP as providing a form of firm leadership prepared to overturn the Versailles Treaty. It was, with such support, that Canaris was made Abwehr head. Admiral Raeder first opposed the idea, but he gave in when it was proposed to select an army officer instead.[96] Canaris appeared to work well with Reinhard Heydrich (top-ranking SS/SD/ Police) also an ex-naval man, but they were more like rivals, as Canaris considered Heydrich as brutal, while Heydrich often referred to Canaris as a 'wily old fox' with which one had to be careful.[97] However, at this stage Canaris was very much pro-Nazi with its views on re-establishing Germany as a major power, and it has been suggested that it was Canaris who proposed or supported the use of the Star of David to identify Jews to increase their sense of alienation and isolation within the community.[98] However, Canaris was spending time with Hans Oster, and must have been listening to his views or asides, and like him at this stage wanted to avoid a major European war, especially by Hitler's plans to seize Czechoslovakia which brought him in touch with others who thought the same way. Again, it should be noted that they were more concerned about Hitler's cohorts than the dictator himself. At one stage there were suggestions to unseat Hitler and the Nazis to avoid the war in Czechoslovakia, but the Munich diplomacy overrode such ideas. Canaris wanted to influence Britain to move away from appeasement by warning them that Hitler intended to take the Netherlands to create bomber sites to attack Britain. It was not entirely successful but stirred Chamberlain enough to commit Britain to France.

When War started in September 1939 Canaris witness Warsaw bombed to ruins, he objected to the atrocities, but Keitel tried to warn him off several times, but by this time Canaris was rapidly becoming an opponent and resister to the Nazi regime. Like so many other military traditionalists it took time even for a civilised man to start to understand that the Nazi regime was evil and could not be persuaded otherwise, and like other traditional German conservative-minded figures, it was discovered that Hitler could not be controlled.

It is noteworthy in this brief sketch of these three well known military men that they all started as pro-NSDAP seeking the restoration of Germany by a firm leader. There is no doubt that at various stages they stopped being mere critics, and it took the war's barbarity to turn them into opponents of the regime, and as a last resort they became active resisters. The one exception was Oster who was actively resistant before the others, there are hints that Canaris was deeply disturbed by his governmental masters, but as with Beck it took the barbarity of Nazism to make them into active resisters. Whether many of the later military were resisting losing the war, or anti-Nazism is like a mixed luggage rack and will be explored in the next chapter.

Early Military Resistance 1937–1940

It is known that from the late 1930s, that there was some critical concern in top military circles as to what was beginning to happen. Hitler had in the early days avoided announcing his military plans, though his ambitions for expansion could be found in *Mein Kampf* in his demand for *lebensraum*. In a meeting on 5 November 1937, he met in the Reich Chancellery senior Wehrmacht officers and opened up some of his projected plans which were not met with the eagerness he would have wanted. The mention of Czechoslovakia and Austria aroused in the military listeners a fear of a war with France and even Britain. A Colonel Hossbach who kept the minutes noted the sharp differences of opinions between Göring against Blomberg and Fritsch. The Chief of Army Staff General Ludwig Beck was also deeply worried about Hitler's possible policies, causing his later resignation and making him an active resister, not that the term was used at this time. Only the army had the power to challenge Hitler, but the dictator took control with his henchmen plotting the downfall of those who had questioned Hitler's ideas. This resulted in the well-known incidents of dismissing General Blomberg because of rumours about his new wife's past sexual activities, and General Fritsch on trumped up charges of homosexuality, replacing him with the servile von Brauchitsch. Hitler never trusted his army commanders, and he later took over the command of the entire Wehrmacht and promoted Keitel to Field Marshal and Chief of the OKW because he knew he would never disagree with the Führer. Hitler ensured he had men whom he presumed would follow orders, and he applied the same tactics in the Foreign Office. Many have seen this military crisis as an act of resistance, but it hardly qualified at this stage, more like active opposition, as it amounted to no more than a quiet protest indicated by trying to dissuade Hitler.

There were many in the upper reaches of society who may have developed mix feelings about the regime, but they tended to follow his foreign policy, especially the *Anschluss* and the apparent bloodless regaining of Sudetenland, but not knowing that soon they would be involved in a total war involving crimes and genocide. The pre-Munich months produced many oppositional moves, many unknown, made by influential Germans trying to make the British and

French aware of Hitler's dangerous brinkmanship. There were even, in some elevated circles such as Goerdeler and Beck discussions of a possible coup d'état to avoid a major war, which felt more like resistance. Goerdeler had even argued with Hitler, which gave himself and others the wrong impression that Hitler could be controlled. Goerdeler and others of the same persuasion had meetings with British and French politicians and men of influence, attempting to describe the dangerous policies being concocted by the Nazi regime. In Britain Sir Robert Vansittart, a senior British diplomat and early anti-Nazi was an excellent contact, but he was not a member of the British Cabinet, and although he personally trusted Goerdeler he was not a major political figure, and nor was, the British concluded, Goerdeler. There have been some who criticised the British government for lack of response, but Chamberlain did not understand Hitler until it was too late, and many of the mentioned opponents to the regime were at the time working for the German leadership. It was not that Chamberlain was a soft-hearted pacifist, but after the Great War disaster prudence, understandably, was his policy, and 'appeasement' has since become a maligned term, unfairly. Even journalists belonged to various camps, and at this time were still able to move freely across Europe, and they were used or acted themselves to send out warnings. Internal efforts within the military were made to ask General von Brauchitsch to influence Hitler, but this general had been selected by Hitler because he knew him to be weak, though he did try several times, but to no avail.

The dangers of Hitler starting a major war became more evident and concern grew. The Great War of 1914–18 had witnessed more deaths than countries could bear, and to the more astute another war would be even more destructive with modern technology, not least airpower. It has been estimated that more than 2.8 million Germans (soldiers and civilians) died between 1939 and the 20 July Plot in 1944, and another 4.8 million between that date and the end of the war. There was understandable concern about more war as the end result was to prove.[99] As such there were a few characters beginning to try and activate a resistance which would demand Hitler's downfall. Amongst the military Beck was possibly the greatest activator, supported by Hans Oster (who after the Night of the Long Knives became a resolute opponent) and others, while on the civilian front it was mainly Goerdeler. Using the benefit of hindsight main pillars of the emerging resistance were Goerdeler and Oster at this time.

Beck's main objective was to prevent war as it was believed that the French army was the largest in Europe and Britain would stand alongside France. Initially Beck had thought he might be able to influence Hitler, but his superior Brauchitsch disagreed. The idea of some sort of general strike by generals was mooted, but it seemed unlikely, and it was doubtful that Hitler could be coerced in this fashion. This needed a realistic assessment, not least because it had to be accepted that at this period in time the regime was still popular. If a strike could not work Beck suggested a united front by all the generals, this too was unlikely to succeed. Many of the generals held to the Prussian tradition of obedience, and not all thought Hitler was wrong. Beck wrote memos on the problem of starting a war and complained it was all being done by Hitler who had not consulted his military. Brauchitsch never disagreed with Beck, but he did nothing. Beck even organised a war game to show how Hitler's policy would fail. It did not take long for Beck to be in an open struggle with Hitler, as Beck appeared to be on the verge of starting a coup d'état, not that Hitler knew this. Beck realised there was little he could do and asked to be relieved from his post which Hitler promptly accepted, and when offered another post he asked to retire, which was also readily agreed. As this study will unfold it will be seen that although retired Beck, he stayed as an active resister.

General Franz Halder replaced Beck who at the time and since has been viewed as anti-Hitler, but the tradition of obedience and keeping his position dominated. However, it should be noted that in 1938 he remained in cooperation over the proposed coup d'état, but he was a no action-man, and soon indicated he was less resolute in the matter. Many knew of the plan to topple Hitler but the need for a person prepared to activate the plot was lacking, although some plans for action were established. There was also concern that even if the coup were successful the follow up on how to proceed remained haplessly vague, apart from a military state of emergency, along with the problem of how to deal with other senior Nazis. Another question was what to do with Hitler, put him on trial for criminal behaviour, but as previously when Hitler stood trial, he was more than able to defend himself in the popularity contest. Another suggestion was to send him to a psychologist, and finally simply kill him. They tended to meet on Oster's private quarters with military and civilians desperately seeking a plan which would or could be successful.

There were some generals and senior officers prepared to move at once, but not only was time running out but there was a degree of uncertainty about other generals who might disagree. Some younger men such as Major Friedrich Wilhelm Heinz developed an assassination plan, and when he heard of this it may have had a few approvals, but not from everyone. Amongst the civilian doubters there were debates about the future government which would dominate the strands of resistance to the bitter end as will be noted in later chapters. It was also known that, at last, the British were rapidly mobilising their military which created for many a sense of deep concern. The coup remained in place awaiting some form of go-ahead, but then came the Munich meeting. This international conference was supposedly conducted by Mussolini, with Hitler meeting Édouard Daladier the French prime minister, and Britain's Neville Chamberlain. It concluded with Hitler appearing to have gained his territory without bloodshed. To those who were about to pounce on Hitler, they must have felt as if the Western allies had betrayed them.

For the general public there was a general ignorance of what was going on apart from the propaganda's trumpet call of Hitler's success, which must have dampened the spirits of those who opposed Nazism and those in the military trying to stop a major war. The fact that Hitler intended to take the whole of Czechoslovakia was known by many military commanders who remained concerned about a major war. As Hitler manipulated his way through his plans many of those who had been involved in the potential coup or knew about its possibility, found themselves moved around in preparation for further territorial incursions, and with Hitler's seeming success for many the possibility of a coup faded. It would take time for those in opposition to the regime to reform with any sense of dedication. Hitler, who appeared to have an uncanny sense of the opposition sent out an executive order denying the military of holding or having any political judgements, as this was the business of the governing regime. This would have made sense to many who always believed the military simply obeyed the country's leaders, with many pretending they had no political allegiance as soldiers.

On the civilian side of the resistance men like Goerdeler, Hjalmar Schacht the economist and banker, Moltke, the diplomats Adam von Trott zu Solz, von Hassell, and Erich Kordt with many others made desperate efforts to warn the outside world of Hitler's intentions, his madness, and therefore his danger to peace. They passed on inside information from men like General Beck, and although the possibility of a coup was fading the outside world remained uncertain. The British and French were aware these men passing on the information and warnings may have been important people, but they were not high German government figures. Nevertheless, their warnings were heard, sometimes with doubt, but there were serious concerns and mobilising their forces had been deemed necessary. The invasion of the rest of Czechoslovakia found a degree of public opposition. To prepare the public for this move Hitler organised a show of military might through the streets and avenues of Berlin. 'Hitler noted with annoyance the solemnity of the passersby and the glacial silence with which they observed the troops before turning away … William Shirer the journalist observed that this was the most striking antiwar demonstration that he had ever seen'.[100] This observation alone was indicative that not all the German public were happy with the regime's policies.

The nascent resisters continued to try and dissuade the move for military action being prepared against Poland. Hans Oster, the deputy to Canaris in the

Abwehr tried to influence Major General Georg Thomas chief of 'Economics and Supplies' to warn the Nazi power elite that Germany was ill-prepared for war. Schact helped him prepare a memo on these grounds to present to Keitel, Chief of the OKW. Keitel, on hearing his views dismissed it out of hand, telling Thomas that Hitler would not want to see it, ordering him to produce a more hopeful report. He was guilty of blind obedience to the Führer, expressing his doubts only later in his own self-defence at the Nuremberg Trials. Efforts were discussed to persuade Halder but like many others, Hitler's recent successes had caused him to waver. Hitler was sure of his policy and convinced that France and Britain would avoid war, expressing the opinion that 'our opponents are little worms. I saw them at Munich', and all he wanted to do was avoid some mediation plan.[101]

There had been hopes up to the last moment that Hitler would not move against Poland but despite the efforts of many and armed with Soviet support the almost inevitable happened in September 1939. The German public was told that the Poles had started the war which was manipulated by the Germans creating an incident at a border post. The Polish war was swift and successful which increased Hitler's popularity for some, while causing further doubts amongst others about facing a war with the Western Allies. There had been some appalling news about the way Jews and Poles were treated by the SS during the Polish occupation which raised questions in many minds, not least reports of disgust expressed by General Johannes Blaskowitz. There were many reports of the shocking details, and it could be justifiably claimed that for many the popular side of the regime started to evaporate from this moment and gave more numbers to the opposition and resistance. However, the fact is that most of this early military resistance was based on the fear they may be entering a war which they could not win. Several generals such as Bock sought interviews with Hitler to dissuade him, and even Brauchitsch tried again, but like many had failed to see they had a dictator who always believed in himself and no one else. They had discovered, like the conservative resisters, that the belief that Hitler could be controlled was pure nonsense.

There were many junior officers who were concerned about the direction Hitler was taking, and the theory that the generally right-wing military supported Hitler was far from any truth. Major Groscurth acting as a liaison officer helped form a link between the various resisters and his work was known about by Halder and Brauchitsch; there were many other involved such as General Fritz Fellgiebel, Colonel Eduard Wagner, and General Henning von Tresckow. Even Captain Liedig, a naval officer, reflecting a group of possible naval resisters, sent a memo over the Soviet-Finnish conflict, pointing out Hitler was betraying his own aims as by allowing Stalin into Poland the threat of Soviet western expansion was even closer, Russia being the number one enemy. It was apparent that Liedig was also looking towards some form of coup. It was known that Halder continued to follow the plan to topple the Nazi regime even if it meant killing Hitler. The German historian Hoffman described in his account how Halder would always carry a loaded pistol with him on the grounds that if the right opportunity arose, he would assassinate the Führer.[102] He never did because he did not want to be an assassin, and it also underlined his main problem of inconsistency towards the possible coup. Hans Oster had drawn up a secret list of those involved and what their duties would be once the coup was successful, including what would happen to the lead Nazis such as Göring, Himmler, Ribbentrop, and Goebbels. Many of the younger officers mentioned above were keen on action, but both Halder and Bauchitsch remained uncertain if not nervous about the developing situation. This undoubtedly arose for a variety of reasons, ranging from Hitler's growing popularity, questioning themselves as to whether they would have the support of the lower ranks, their tradition as obedient German officers, unsure about total support from colleagues, the rumour the Western Allies might take advantage by invading, and none of this was helped when Hitler awarded Bauchitsch and Halder and others with the esteemed Knight's Cross. Halder a few days later made another effort to cause Hitler to think, but it was a waste of time.

Oster had provided a key codeword for action, and rumours circulated that Hitler was going to be arrested in early November 1939, but it is easy to gain the impression from the more detailed accounts that the plot was running out of steam, enthusiasm was fading at the senior level of Halder and Brauchitsch, and maybe even a sense of panic. This loss of nerve may have been because Hitler often let it be known that 'he would annihilate anyone who was against him… an internal revolution against his regime was as unthinkable as capitulation to the enemy'.[103] If there were to be a coup it could only be done by the army which would require orders from the highest level, which was losing heart for the task. Beck remained persistent, always arguing that Germany could not win a major war, but although respected he was now retired. There is no doubt that Halder recognised the Nazi regime as illegal if not immoral, but he lacked the strength required by the would-be martyr and like Brauchitsch lost confidence.

In this section of the early resistance to Hitler's demand for war between 1938–1940 there was some cooperation between leading civilian resisters and the army as a coup d'état was being planned with the assassination of Hitler being proposed. The main focus was on the military who were the only ones capable of carrying out the proposal with any hope of success. This section clearly demonstrates that many leading figures opposed the Hitler regime, but the main focus of the military was avoiding a war they thought they would never win. It was not just opposition, but resistance, failing to become active resistance because the final orders never came. When the French and British were swiftly and unexpectedly defeated it put the ball back into Hitler's court making him all too popular in Germany. The military would reactivate themselves later when facing defeat because of Hitler's often insane orders, but there would also be that moral element of disgust at his orders and the brutality of Himmler's SS.

Overall, there were undoubtedly many Germans of noted intellect who doubted the Nazi Party and would have been devastated as its evil unrolled to the public view. Many 'everyday Germans' were also highly educated, politically astute, with high moral standards, from shopkeepers to university professors, but it was the men at the top who were potentially influential. It would need men with the status of being a senior general to activate resistance, it would need Church leaders to influence the pews and general public, and amongst other civilians they would need to hold high positions in the world of diplomacy, the Civil Service, and finance which explains the necessity of this chapter exploring such individuals. Above all, from the military point of view they needed a leader to amalgamate their efforts and one determined enough to act while there was time.

Chapter Five

A Divided Resistance

Author's Notes: *This chapter explores the people and nascent resistance groups in Nazi Germany, how they sometimes worked together with their various intentions and motives often at variance, but with the fundamental agreement that the Nazi regime had to go. There were many discussions on how to replace the dictatorship, ranging from a restored monarchy, a military leadership with martial law, a Bismarckian state with local elections and a chancellor, and even some form of European union. A return to democracy was not widely discussed as it brought back memories that the system had failed to prevent the rise of Hitler. It was a wide-ranging discussion often causing the criticism that they were mere talking shops. As much as their intentions about the post-Hitler future varied, so did their motives for Hitler's downfall. There were those, especially in the military, who wanted to avoid military defeat and keep the territories gained in the war, some had not wanted war in the first place but had accepted the early victories, and many changed their minds one way or another depending on the military circumstances of the day. It was the devastating Eastern Front which caused many military leaders to turn against Hitler's leadership.*

After the Unconditional Surrender by the Allies some hoped for a union with the West to destroy Bolshevism, others for a peace treaty, and a few accepted that defeat was necessary to rebuild Germany. The moral arguments played a part but not as major as many of the political motives. The greatest moral dilemma the Nazi regime had produced was the treatment of prisoners, the massacres, and above all the Holocaust. Therefore, space is given in this study to the attitude towards the Jews by those who resisted, which tends to indicate that moral motives were not a top motivational priority. The main thrust of active resistance came from the conservative elite and the military, but Moltke ensured that members of the old Social Democratic Party became part of the resistance, as well as trade union leaders, mainly in order that a revolution should involve a wider mixture of German society. The most conservative branch of active resistance arose from the military sector, where there had been a couple of failed assassination attempts on Hitler. The military were mainly focused on military objectives with the intention of a military government as an interim situation, while seeking some advice from selected civilian resisters. It was not just the death of Hitler but a coup d'état on the Nazi regime that was necessary. As such, it was widely accepted that only the army had the possible means to kill Hitler and bring down the Nazi superstructure, making them the only possible active resisters.

Introduction

The previous chapter outlined some of the main characters from the various resisting groups, including those in the Church and the military, across a wide range of different professions and personalities. In this chapter more figures will be introduced as the efforts of the resistance unfold. German resistance differed vastly from that in other countries where open violence was frequently deployed to rid themselves of the occupiers. German resistance looked only to one moment of violence, namely the removal of Adolf Hitler, and not all elements of German resistance agreed with this viewpoint. Because of their proximity to the leadership, they were vulnerable to closer scrutiny by the Gestapo, but the main problems which evolved demonstrated a mixture of motives and intentions amongst the conspirators. Some groups were in touch with one another, sometimes closely, and more often by a few personally linked personalities, with some groups being more isolated. There were many groups, often called 'circles', but for simplification purposes only the major elements are explored. Each group had different strands of thinking, varying plans, not only in how to deal with the Nazi regime but many arguments on how to replace it in political governmental plans, leading some post-war critics to deride them as mere 'talking shops'. The resistance is important to German history, but there is no question that it was too often divided in motive and intention.

The Mixture of Motives

As mentioned earlier many critics have accused the resistant groups of being mere talking shops, and much of this arose because a critical issue was how to govern Germany after the downfall of Nazism and the anticipated death of Hitler. The main task was agreeing on some form of constitutional draft and how to deal with the interim period following Hitler's death. The latter was simple for the military, the only ones capable of conducting the coup, would take control for the time being until there was victory or peace. Oster prompted the earliest draft in 1937, using plans by Professor Friedrich Alfred SchmidNoerr, which focused on the German concept of the 'community of the people'. This was linked to its Christian ethos and the concept of peaceful existence with other nations, and a safety guarantee for other ethnic groups. How to govern was the vexed question which caused the most problems, as SchmidNoerr suggested a form of what the British called the House of Lords with a possible monarch. Hassell had similar ideas as did Goerdeler, Popitz and Beck, but they at least were seeking some form of a just society. They knew there was a need for new laws, and there was considerable discussion between the various groups, especially between Goerdeler and Hassell (connected with the Freiburg Circle) and Moltke with his ideas over some form of European union. Within Moltke's Kreisau Circle there were differences of opinions, they produced several drafts, and they tended to put them on hold as did the other groups. In his major work on German Resistance, Peter Hoffman spends many pages outlining the numerous ideas of the various proposed heads of the government's ministries, which, even with his clarity of thought and expression, can sometimes feel confusing in their complexity.[1] For some critics these various efforts looked like a series of pipe dreams because nothing could happen until Hitler was dead, the Nazi regime overthrown, and international stability regained. However, they are important to indicate the thinking processes of those who were resisters. The very confusion of the ideas with proposals ranging from a restored or new monarchy to Bismarckian ideals revealed only one thing in common, the need for some authoritarian ideal. The purported failure of democracy in the Weimar Republic was seen by nearly all as ruling out what may be termed a more liberal approach, and some might claim it revealed a degree of political ineptitude. In the first chapter of this study the background of the German nation was shown to be always under an authoritarian regime, and from 1870 until the Great War they could be described as idyllic in the eyes of the upper crust of German society, but somewhat distant from reality.

Most of these main resisters came from the upper echelons of German Society, but Moltke and his group had, as noted previously, invited or had been contacted by others such as trade union leaders and members of the SPD. It would appear that the socialists such as Julius Leber and the others were not overly involved in these political discussions, probably because as a party, they had formed the Republic which had been obliged to sign the Versailles Treaty, and they were seen by many on the right-wing, quite unfairly as traitors to Germany, and under them the Republic had failed, thus bringing Hitler onto the central stage. Nevertheless, Leber remained committed to a socialist way forward while struggling to retain solidarity with the other more traditional resisters, which demanded some compromises. Later he would come close to Stauffenberg who was more inclined to what can be best described as more free movement in the political and social scenes of the future.

There were some tensions between the Christian elements where there was a mutual suspicion with the Marxist inclined trade unionists, despite the fact that true Marxism declared itself tolerant of religious and racial differences. These were generally smoothed over or put on the shelf, because it was realised that first and foremost the Nazi regime had to be collapsed.

Morality and Nationalistic Divides

Throughout this chapter it will surface that there was often a divide between the emphasis on moral resistance because the regime was basically evil, and on the other hand, nationalistic resistance to save Germany from the abyss of failure. The latter camp was concerned that Germany survived militarily and retain its territorial gains. Those based on moral grounds recognised the regime as evil and had to be brought down at all costs. It was not a simple divide as many in the nationalistic camp also recognised the inherent evil of the regime.

Men like Pastor Bonhoeffer and other Church leaders, the Abwehr officer Hans Oster, and Moltke objected to Hitler on moral grounds. After the Allied declaration of Unconditional Surrender, along with the Soviet pressure epitomised by the fall of Stalingrad because of Hitler's ridiculous battle directions, there were those like Claus von Stauffenberg and Goerdeler who wanted to save Germany from the nationalistic point of view. Stauffenberg, now regarded in the post-war era as a hero, had nevertheless supported the regime much longer than Beck. While in Poland he had written to his wife that the Polish population 'is an unbelievable rabble, there are a lot of Jews and a lot of crossbreeds'.[2] Undoubtedly Stauffenberg later developed a more critical approach to Nazi behaviour. His main motive was the preservation of the German military and nation, but having become disgusted at Nazi behaviour, he also wanted the world to know that being a Nazi was not the same as being a German. They were more concerned that the Wehrmacht remained intact, that previous territorial gains were preserved, and possibly guided by a military dictatorship. Before he was shot, Stauffenberg's final words were 'long live sacred Germany'. Men like Moltke, Oster, Bonhoeffer were more concerned that Germany rebuilt its moral structure, even if it meant defeat.

Some of the more conservative-inclined such as Goerdeler, Hassell, and Beck continued to hold to a belief that Germany as a state should always be built on military power, and that the upturned Versailles Treaty should be maintained, basing their hopes on a preserved and still powerful Germany, although it should be recalled that Goerdeler also had strong moral objections. However, their resistance was mainly founded on national hopes. They were living in their own dream world after the Unconditional Surrender demand, and this may well have moderated some of their nationalistic hopes. Goerdeler had used his connections in Sweden to try and bring the Western Allies to take the German resistance seriously, but it had never transpired, and unconditional surrender had put paid to such anticipative hopes except for men like Moltke. On the other hand, the Allied demand did not stop the drive to topple Hitler. However, there was simply no way the West would offer any concessions to a non-Nazi

German government. Goerdeler had hoped the Allies would not take military advantage from the fall of Hitler, but no such assurances were ever offered.

On the other hand, and very different from Goerdeler's nationalistic approach, Moltke as previously noted, remained inclined more to a whole European solution, a form of prophetic forecast of the European Union. This viewpoint of which Goerdeler was suspicious as to its value, meant Moltke and his Kreisau Circle were more inclined to the view that Germany could not win such a massive and protracted war, and his hope was that peace would materialise because of exhaustion by both sides, but as the war turned against Germany on both fronts, he believed that Germany would have to be defeated if his wish for a European resolution were to work. Mainly with the benefit of hindsight, both these conflicting themes amounted to nothing more than pipedreams. Goerdeler's nationalistic approach meant he still had visions of Germany being in charge and even talked of a European army, but he had the moral sense of humanity to warn that Germany should not humiliate the smaller nations.[3] Such were the devastating results of Hitler's aggression and conduct meant that there could be no such possibility as far as the Allies were concerned, whose anger and revenge were more than evident. By the same token, Moltke's hope for a joint European economy all based on a Christian renewal would have been met with the same derision. This was to a degree understandable, with France occupied, Russia attacked, many smaller states totally repressed, and all marked with unbelievable barbarity meant the Allies intended to crush Germany, and by the end of 1942 and especially by mid-1943 this all seemed highly likely.

However, this is not meant to denigrate the efforts of the resistance, since they were looking for an end to Nazism and a better world. The sadness was the division of opinions, with perhaps understandably, their inability to have an understanding as to how many in the outside world were already condemning Germany, and who would never make promises to the enemy. A further problem was the resisters' belief that they could still hold back the Soviet forces. As the Eastern front became more alarming for the Nazi regime, the propaganda started to project the image of 'defending Europe' from the dangers of Bolshevism, some with the hopeless attitude the West would co-operate, and this was also in the mind of some of the resisters, especially a few military men.

The main groups of resisters can be divided into broad groups: the Kreisau Circle, the Goerdeler and Beck configuration, and others, with the military and its various groupings. Each cluster had its own views and internal differences over various matters, not least how they foresaw the post-Hitler future of Germany, on killing Hitler, and how an interim governmental phase could be worked through. If there were different opinions within each group, there were also many differences between the groups. Moltke's group held the higher moral grounds in their reasoning for resisting and the way they wanted it carried through; while Goerdeler and Beck's group was more nationalistic with some moral concerns; and the military resistance by wanting immediate action to save Germany from defeat. For it to be effective a substantial effort had to be made for a rebellion to encompass more areas of German life, and Moltke was more aware of this and ensured the SPD and many others, including the Churches were involved. This aspect will be explored in this chapter, but first to underline the moral issues the attitude of the resisters to extreme anti-Semitism must be explored.

Resisters and the Jewish Persecution

The vexed question of the motives of the various resistant drives between the nationalistic inclined conservatives, and those who resisted because of the immoral behaviour of the Nazi regime, becomes a complex problem. There is no doubt that among the major civilian resisters there was a distaste for Nazi barbarity, not just because they lived in a society repressed by the threat of the Gestapo and the feared SS security wing, but the Night of the Long Knives then *Kristallnacht*, followed by news of massacres of Jews and civilians in Poland concerned many and convinced some to resist. After the war many justified accusations were made, but eventually the Holocaust emerged as a major condemnation of Nazi Germany. For a time, it was popular to view the resistance as focused on the Jewish persecution, but as the resistance has been further scrutinised it has raised a few problems. Much of the civilian resistance was driven by condemning Nazi behaviour but how far gross anti-Semitism was central to their thinking remains something of an enigma.

There is no doubt that much of the Church resistance focused on the treatment of the Jews, but in some areas only for those Jews who had become Christianised, and it cannot be forgotten that some clergy were taken in by Nazism and some were anti-Semitic. There were those who believed the Jews were guilty of having Christ killed, neglecting the fact that their 'saviour' was Jewish as were the apostles. Nevertheless, as noted above, men like the Catholic Bishop Augustinus von Galen and Protestant pastor Dietrich Bonhoeffer were outstanding in their courageous opposition, and many others followed. Many clergy of all denominations were in concentration camps and many other figures of a Christian background attempted to help the resistance. Archbishop Josef Frings of Cologne condemned the liquidation of the Jews, knowing that in Nazi Germany his high status was no protection. Many clergy of all denominations died in the concentration camp system. One of the more neglected figures was the Jesuit priest Father Alfred Delp, who gave considerable time and effort to the Kreisau Circle, and he became a close friend of Moltke. Like Archbishop Frings, he was brave enough to ensure his passionate objections to Nazism were heard, roundly condemning the treatment and persecution of the Jews. Delp's Jesuit superior Augustin Rösch had suggested Delp join with Moltke indicating that most Christian leaders were against the Nazi regime. Delp, like Bonhoeffer was executed in the 20 July plot round up (though he was not directly involved) as a means of removing critics of the regime, and both men have left future generations with their books of prayers and thoughts written while in prison.

However, these Christian views were not shared across the group of resisters. Many still retained that social bigotry against Jews which was sadly prevalent across much of Europe. There were some who felt that it was only Himmler who behaved in this manner, but the Wannsee Conference (20 January 1942) was a clear indicator this was a Nazi policy, not just the SS. There were others who thought or hoped that it would not last long and would quieten down, but to the last months of the war train transport essential for troops was still being used to carry more victims to the extermination camps, and in the end days of the Third Reich, frantic efforts were made to hide the atrocities causing yet more suffering.

The reality has to be faced that in the overall resistance groups the question of the Nazi persecution of the Jews was not at the top of their list of priorities, although there is a case to be made that the Kreisau Circle regarded the Jewish issue as a prime concern. Outside this group it could not be regarded as a motivating factor, let alone a major one. Amongst the conservative elite resisters anti-Semitism had been part of their lives long before Hitler rose to power. This had increased in 1918 with the 'stab-in-the-back' nonsense, and the association of the dreaded Bolshevism with Judaism. The bigotry against Jews had increased, and even the respected German General von Fritsch, expelled from the army by Nazi intrigue had been known to claim that for 'Germany to become great again' there were three battles to be won, the first 'against the workers, Rome's domination of the Catholic Church and one against the Jews'.[4] Many were inclined this way with the exception of Hans Oster, Moltke, and a few others who became more disturbed having witnessed the cruel attacks on their own streets and avenues, followed by the disappearance of their Jewish neighbours.

Goerdeler was a by nature a civilised man, he had protested about the attack on Jews in his city of Leipzig, and in 1934 had tried to persuade Hitler towards moderation, mainly based on his fear of German reputation overseas. He had argued for a Jewish state abroad somewhere in South America or Canada, he wanted exemption for those Jews who fought in the 1914–18 conflict, and he had been appalled by news of the atrocities in the east. He was probably anti-Semitic in the social sense, and whether his ideas for Jews going overseas indicated this or whether he saw it as a safer alternative is ambiguous. It is known that in his group, as with the Kreisau Circle, they wanted the attacks on Jews to stop. Others were more bigoted, and unlike his deputy Oster, Canaris always demanded racial segregation if progress were to be made. Even von der Schulenburg wanted Jews out of public service and government, but he was appalled to hear of the crimes against Jews in the east, and like so many Germans who tended to distrust Jews, it took time for them to realise the nature of the Nazi barbarity. On this issue of taking a moral stand, especially in the issue of the Jews, one conservative resister, Johannes Popitz (1884–1945), a lawyer by training and finance minister, after *Kristallnacht* was so furious about the pogroms that he offered his resignation, which was refused. He had joined Goerdeler's group, but he had already affiliated himself with another right-wing group called the Wednesday Society, which had evolved from a debating club to become another centre of conservative opposition. Later he used his expertise to draw up a provisional post-Hitler constitution, which given his traditional background was somewhat authoritarian. However, the major point is that Popitz was originally driven by moral motives stimulated by the treatment of Jewish people.

Amongst the resisters in the military camp, it could now be generally accepted that the moral arguments played a lesser role in their motives, and some of them had undoubtedly been involved in some of the Jewish atrocities in the post-battle scenarios. General von Stülpnagel and other military resisters had been indoctrinated to equate Bolshevism with Jewry, long implanted since 1918, and they were often associated with Jewish atrocities by following Hitler's criminal orders. Others often associated Jews with partisans which in German military terms was illegal. Some military resisters such as General Hermann Karl von Tresckow and many other military commanders also have serious question marks over their views and actions. It is tempting to say that for many of them it was confusing to run with the fox as well as the hounds, and frequently it took revelations of places like Babi Yar and Auschwitz to cause them to ponder their past attitudes. In an overall explanation it has to be accepted that for many resisters, moral issues dealing with Jews, PoWs, and civilians in occupied areas was never a prime motive. So embedded was the mindset of this generation it would take the shock of the disclosure of the camps, remote massacres, the numbers involved, and the horror of outside observers to change such deep bigotry.

Apart from resistance shown by some Church leaders and clergy most of the civilian and military resisters tended to be right-wing conservatives, although Moltke had worked hard to bring in other political elements to make the overthrow of Hitler a national effort. If any plot were to be successful it had to have plans ready for a government after the death of Hitler and overthrow of the Nazi regime, as any form of anarchy would be potentially dangerous. This was to prove divisive as the only view most agreed upon was not to return to the Weimar Republic, while some wanted a military type of dictatorship, others the return of the monarchy, some a return to the days of Bismarck, and few wanted a president, chancellor, and limited elections.

Social Democratic Party Resistance

Julius Leber

Moltke who appeared to hold the higher moral grounds within these groups was always trying to recruit people to widen the brief of the proposed future, and he became of interest for many who were outside the conservative box. One of these was the Jesuit Father Alfred Delp mentioned above, another more politically orientated person was Julius Leber (1891–1945) who had been the editor of the Social Democratic newspaper *Lübecker Volksbote* (People's Messenger). After Hitler had come to power there was an attempt on Leber's life, and he was eventually arrested in March 1933, and detained at Sachsenhausen camp until 1937. He survived and proved to be both courageous and strong, because the Gestapo, with their unlimited means of cruel persuasion, failed to break him. After his eventual release he worked as a coal dealer which acted as his cover for his developing role in resisting the regime. It has been noted that he was 'one of the few plotters who could win the confidence of the people', something of which Moltke more than others knew to be essential.[5] Leber's aims were clear and uncluttered, he wanted the Nazi regime with all its horrors and injustices overturned, and also demanded a return to social justice for all. When he had been in the concentration camp, he had no influence as personal survival was imperative, the interrogators never changed his mind, but he started to realise that there was no realistic way Hitler could be toppled by a man of the people like him. It was this factor that brought him first into touch with Moltke, then Goerdeler, and thereby came into touch with the 20 July plotters. It is a curious aside, but it was apparent that Leber was able to pick up information about the Kreisau Circle, and although an ex-political prisoner watched by the Gestapo, which despite its reputation, had to await until the 20 July plot to wade in and arrest suspects.

Moltke welcomed Leber's arrival, as he wanted Germans of all political persuasions involved. Leber was uncomplicated in his views, he was not overly interested in the long-term plans, but like Schulenburg wanted Hitler dead, which led him to a close friendship with Stauffenberg. This became a firm friendship because both men were driven by the need for action as soon as possible, and as such he became one of those who was involved in the intricate planning. He eventually came around to working on the plans for a provisional government and Stauffenberg tended to listen to him. Leber was not a man lost in a dream world, he was dedicated to the death of Hitler and the destruction of the Nazi regime. Sadly, he was betrayed by an informer and executed in January 1945.

Carlo Mierendorff

A second Social Democrat who became involved was Carlo Mierendorff (1897–1943) who is often associated with the 'Socialist Action Plan' of the SPD during the Weimar days. He was an intellectual activist and had played a key role in the anti-fascist Iron Front.* At first, he had fled to Switzerland for safety, but on his return was arrested, and tortured in concentration camps before being released in 1938. He immediately became part of the resistance, but like others kept a safe distance because he knew he was closely watched after he left the concentration camp, and often used a man called Haubach to represent his views.[6] Later he was killed in an Allied bombing raid of Leipzig. The major conservative resisters were wary of him because it was known that he called on his followers for armed insurrection, and he had made contacts with other left-wing groups including the dreaded KPD (German Communist Party) hoping they could overthrow the Nazi regime without involving party politics. Moltke normally sought out other classes and parties saw it more as a splinter group, but he welcomed Mierendorff. Moltke was aware that Mierendorff wanted prompt action against the figure of Hitler, whereas he tended to hope that the regime would collapse from internal problems, which was mere wishful thinking. On the other hand, Goerdeler's group wanted action as soon as possible. It could be said the Kreisau Circle, sometimes described as a paramilitary resistance, was more philosophical and looking at political theories to find the solution. There was some amalgamation of thought in proposed future plans, but they were quite different forms of resistance. However, the arrival of SPD members acted as a reminder of the need to have a wider appeal in the public arena, especially from the workers. It could be argued that Mierendorff's concept of a non-party popular uprising, having the consent of the masses must have made some think it was the best way forward, but time was running short as the military crisis was gathering momentum.

---

* The Iron Front was a paramilitary organisation aimed at attacking right-wing totalitarianism and the extreme left-wing looking to democratic socialism and liberal democracy, always in opposition against the SA.

Wilhelm Leuschner

Another Social Democrat who became involved was Wilhelm Leuschner (1890–1944) who had been the chairman of the Darmstadt Unions and a member of Hesse Legislature for the SPD in 1924. In 1933 he had been elected to the board of the General German Trade Union Federation, but he was forced to resign when the Nazis came to power. True to Nazi policy of crushing possible political opposition he then spent a year incarcerated in two concentration camps. However, despite the lessons the Nazis tried to teach him, by June 1934 he started to build up his own resistance network by taking over a small manufacturing workshop which was his cover for resistance. It was at this stage he contacted the Kreisau Circle, and then from 1939 with Goerdeler.

He was welcomed by Moltke as a representative of the labour unions, previously much despised by the traditional German conservatives, but Moltke considered his presence as invaluable, not least because such a person could help the thinking of the elite conservative resisters to remember the importance of keeping the workers onside. He was considered to be safe because he did not share the same views as the communists and left-wing, who were constantly talking of mass action. Leuschner was a man dedicated to free trade unions, and he had only wanted them treated fairly by the Nazi regime which he soon realised was a daydream, especially when Robert Ley, who headed the German Labour Front, confiscated all the union assets. Leuschner cared for the outlawed unions bringing him again under the attention of the Gestapo. He described Germany as 'one vast prison in which rebellion was tantamount to suicide'.[7] To Leuschner's despair, elections were banned, and he knew that most workers had resigned themselves to the new regime, which in their opinion was there to stay. However, he had had many links with Christian labour leaders which brought him into contact with the major conservative type of group resistance cells, especially Goerdeler.

Leuschner was soon deeply involved in recruiting men for a planned German Labour Movement, but Goerdeler was annoyed with him when he had made direct contact with Stauffenberg, whom he undoubtedly saw as dedicated to prompt action. Leuschner was well aware that the army was traditionally right-wing, and during the Weimar years had often clashed with unions as the government wanted a ban on strikes. All this background of bias and to a degree a sense of enmity was not easy for Leuschner or men like Goerdeler. However, Leuschner persuaded the Kreisau Circle to accept the German Labour Union, which was generally widely accepted by 1942, but few were keen on a multi-party system.

It was generally agreed that the only way of disposing of Hitler was through the military, there could be no other way, and Leuschner saw no point in trying to enlist the masses. Not only could this lead to needless slaughter, but some of the so-called masses were Nazis, and confidentiality would become an impossible task, and the denouncing of resisters would be an even more dangerous prospect. Later the Gestapo had called the chief resisters the 'overage union team' – probably justified, because the leaders had existed before the Nazis had seized power.[8]

There had been discussion in the hope of overthrowing the Nazi regime by institutional reform, but quite how this could be achieved in the heavily policed Nazi state is impossible to conceive. All these various thought processes and ideas led to factional disputes with Leuschner tending to side with Goerdeler and the Christian unions. He did, however, manage to persuade the old conservative resistance leaders to give more prominence to social justice in the new Germany, hoping for a more just society. In this alone he achieved something for the future to ponder, and he was heroic in his efforts for working people. He brought with him a better balance and made himself acceptable to the conservative groups, and when he was executed, his last statement was a cry for unity which was lacking throughout the German resistance.

Adolf Reichwein

These various members of the SPD played a potentially valuable part in terms of the conservative resistance, reminding them of the possibility of seeing more value in the sense of democracy than they had hitherto managed. Much of their impact was dependent on their personalities. If they were wanting prompt action, they would tend to find favour with Goerdeler, if they had thoughts for the future post-Hitler era, then they would be more fitting for the Kreisau Circle and Moltke. An educational expert with SPD leanings was Adolf Reichwein (1898–1944) who as early as 1930 had warned about the dangers he foresaw in Hitler and the NSDAP. However, it soon dawned on him that the popularity of the Nazi regime was immense, that it was likely to be in existence for some considerable time, and so having moved to Berlin to take a post in the Museum of Anthropology he soon contacted Moltke sometime in 1942–3. He was soon a member of the Kreisau Circle, and he and Moltke became such good friends that when Reichwein's home was bombed, he was invited to stay on the Moltke estate. Many of these contacts encouraged one another to become recruits, with Moltke's wife recalling how Reichmann had won over Carol Mierendorff who had connections with Leuschner.[9] Such was the resentment about Hitler's regime it took only one activator to set the ball rolling.

Reichmann had in common with Moltke the hope the Nazi regime would self-destruct as military success seemed unlikely, and did not see the necessity of assassinating Hitler, although he may have had a change of mind later. Like other SPD resistant members, he was good at recruiting members, agreed with Moltke's vision of a united Europe, but became more desperate for Hitler's immediate death.

Military Resistance

The military aspect of the resistance has had the most historical study applied, for the same reason that Goerdeler's group recognised that it would need the military to accomplish this and take prompt control. One resolute person may have been able to kill Hitler, but it would need military resources to bring down the whole Nazi structure. Many of the SPD would have agreed with this as they recognised that even if they managed to start a popular people's insurrection, it would have probably led to a serious civil war and bloodshed. The general theme in most studies is to try and establish a connection between the civilian and military resisters, and while it is true that Goerdeler in particular had a long-standing relationship with Beck and a few others, the military had their own motives and intentions, and would have been wary of the civilian groups for a variety of reasons. Barely mentioned is the highly likely fear of the vulnerability of the civilian groups to Gestapo interest, who were all too able to make their victims talk. The military officers were not immune from this, but it was easier for military officers to know who to trust, and when for personal safety to stand apart. It would have been easier to identify a Gestapo agent in the officers' mess than in a civilian meeting. For the safety of their position and rank many knew of various proposed conspiracies, but knew silence was the best way, and it was also safer not to betray a fellow officer. The number of officers involved, and those who knew something was going on, remains an enigma in so far that numbers are impossible to verify, based on the dictum that 'when you have a secret to keep, keep it a secret'.

Just as the civilian resisters had different plans and varying motives it was the same with the military. Generally, they had first welcomed Hitler on the grounds of overturning the Versailles Treaty. Some had reservations about Nazi anarchy-type behaviour, not least the growing presence and ambitions of the SA. Because of his theory of *lebensraum* in the East many of those in the Junker class were interested in their plans as it appeared to be that the eastern territories were of interest to them. When he met the military command in February 1933, the meeting was polite and so was the applause, and 'Hitler remarked afterwards that he felt as if he were "talking to a wall all the time"'.[10]

There is no question that some of the military continued to be concerned in the uncivilised behaviour of the Party, not least the Night of the Long Knives (June 1934) and *Kristallnacht* (November 1938) amongst many other moments which the traditional generation found appalling. The Night of the Long Knives must have warned the more astute that Hitler was ridding himself of anyone who might stand up to him, and senior military men could also be included, as was seen in the Blomberg and Fritsch affairs. The first stirrings of serious unease in the military arose as early as 1938, when Goerdeler and Beck first became united, as they were concerned about Hitler leading them into a major war (as noted in the previous chapter), but the initial military successes in Poland and France changed the whole atmosphere, so even early military doubters became loyal to the dictator, though many were disturbed by the brutal treatment of Jews and Poles by the SS and even some of the Wehrmacht units following Hitler's orders. However, because of these successes Hitler's popularity was enhanced beyond measure with Goebbels' help, and many realised that an attack on him was virtually impossible. Franz Halder (Chief of Staff 1938–1942) once critical of Hitler distanced himself from the resisters like so many others, either because they started to admire Hitler's seeming military ability, or thought overthrowing him was now impossible, or it might influence their career ambitions. This scenario narrowed down the would-be military resisters to a few, notably in the Abwehr with men like Oster, Canaris, and Beck still in touch with people like Goerdeler, Hassell, and Johannes Popitz.

Even at this early stage there were indecisive plans with the civilians expecting the military to carry out the coup and then hand over to the new civilian government, but Beck was to be seen as head of state and commander of the military. Whether it was seen as a long-term and hopefully benign military dictatorship or for a short changeover period, remains unknown. Nevertheless, there were some who stayed in touch with Beck and Oster, notably General Henning von Tresckow who remained staunchly anti-Hitler. After the success in France, Tresckow realised Hitler had no intentions of stopping his plans of aggression, and he had developed a distrust of Hitler's war of racial extermination and being overly ambitious about wanting to rule Europe. Tresckow was hyper-active in finding military colleagues who might join the resistance. At one stage he even approached Erich von Manstein who told him that Prussian officers did not behave in this way. However, it is believed that like many others he stayed in touch with some resisters, though one historian noted that for Manstein it 'was quite delusional, and von Manstein never fully grasped the extent of the plot and its possible consequences'.*

* For more information of Manstein's attitudes see: Forczyk, Robert, *Erich von Manstein* (Oxford: Osprey, 2010), pp.46–57 and Lemay, Benoît, *Erich von Manstein: Hitler's Master Strategist* (Newbury: Casemate, 2010), pp.213–250.

However, Tresckow was equally determined to hold onto his military identity and the respect of his troops, which may account for the question marks over his racial attitudes mentioned above. However, he could not persuade Generals von Bock and von Kluge to his way of thinking, so he started to recruit his own group as a form of opposition to the regime. He was probably, like many other officers, not driven primarily by moral reasons, but for the safety of the military. He could see the military resources were becoming seriously over-stretched, but he knew he had to be careful as many of his fellow officers had been mesmerised by Hitler. He also, knew that most senior officers lacked the courage to challenge Keitel or Jodl. Keitel as Chief of the OKW would not hold with any criticism of his revered master, and Jodl was a staunch Prussian traditionalist who followed orders without question.

It has been claimed that the military had recognised that unless Hitler was put out of action Germany was heading for catastrophe, but by this stage it was too late, even if the plot had succeeded. Not only had Roosevelt announced unconditional surrender, but the Soviet army could not be beaten by the weakened Wehrmacht suffering from manpower and lack of essential resources. Had the civilian resisters tried more effectively and earlier to arrive at a common plan of post-Hitler government, confirmed that their motives included moral considerations, and ensured that the military agreed it would, despite the failure to kill Hitler, have left a better impression of the resistance. However, it must not be overlooked that many in the resistance were prepared to become martyrs in the cause, but their courageous sacrifice was forgotten by May 1945, and only resurrected post-war to remind everyone that not every German was a Nazi, and some were brave enough to resist.

Chapter Six

Resistance Efforts

__Author's Notes:__ The penultimate chapter concludes with the situation prior to the famous 20 July plot. There had been further but useless efforts by the German civilian resistance to contact the enemy, and while Hitler's popularity had risen after occupying France, the Eastern Front with the failure of Stalingrad and constant bombing by the West began to make many aware of a forthcoming disaster, especially in the German military. It was during this time of uneasiness that Tresckow, always deeply active in agitating for the disposal of Hitler, started to conceive the use of the German plan known as Valkyrie (originally a proposed operation for defence) to be used by the resistance. It was a clever idea as the plot could be more easily concealed from prying eyes as it was initially a Nazi scheme. However, Tresckow found himself moved to a post on the Eastern Front, and he entrusted Stauffenberg with the task. It was not an easy commission planning the coup, as even finding explosives was a delicate issue as such weapons were always under surveillance. Even more complex was finding a willing assassin prepared to risk life and limb. They were hindered in various efforts, mainly because Hitler's guards were constantly alert as there had been rumours of a plot, and because of the dictator's erratic behaviour. After a few visits Stauffenberg found that the agreement that Himmler should be present was making matters overly complex, so he decided to go ahead. Stauffenberg planted only one of the two prepared bombs at Hitler's Eastern HQ, and such was the explosion Stauffenberg assumed he must be dead. There followed a period of total confusion both in the Wolfschanze and the Bendlerstrasse in Berlin where the conspirators met. News had reached the planners that according to Keitel, Hitler was still alive, and now they faced Stauffenberg assuring them the Führer was dead. General Fromm, aware of the plot, took Keitel's word and was locked under guard in his office. The plot quickly collapsed after Goebbels managed to arrange for Hitler to speak by phone to an officer called Remer. Shots were exchanged in the Bendlerstrasse, and Fromm allowed Beck to shoot himself, but the others, including Stauffenberg, were executed under Fromm's orders. There were thousands of executions following the People's Court, and this chapter concludes by raising the issue of how many military officers had known of the plot even after ignoring some post-war self-justifying memoirs.

Reaching out Internationally

Resistance efforts after Hitler's victory in France did not cease but became more dangerous, as for a time Hitler had become immensely popular within Germany because he had appeared to the more nationalistically inclined to have fulfilled his promises, not least he had overturned the Versailles Treaty, and he had made Germany into a formidable military power supported by Italy and Japan. The Axis was a charade, as Japan was the other side of the globe with its own imperialistic ambitions, and Italy was not strong, but in 1940–41 Germany felt successful. Despite this popularity amongst many, the resistance in Germany continued, albeit with mixed motives, but above all to bring about the downfall of the regime.

Amongst the initial moves were efforts by the conservative civilian elite to establish contacts with the enemy, at the first stage of the war the only main determined opponent had been Britain, albeit as a country militarily unprepared and under-resourced. One of the lesser-known initiatives came from Albrecht Haushofer whose family contacts had brought him into touch with Rudolf Hess, Hitler's deputy since 1933. Hess found Haushofer useful because of his knowledge and contacts with the British. Hitler at this stage had turned his eyes towards Soviet Russia and would have preferred some sort of peace with Britain, and it may be speculated that Hess agreed and believed he could help. Haushofer had explained to Hess that he knew the British would not trust any agreement with Hitler and would fight until Germany's eventual defeat. Hess initially approached Haushofer's father, a famous and knowledgeable professor, who suggested a meeting with the Duke of Hamilton which might help such arrangements. It was later agreed that Albrecht Haushofer should try and make contact. It was first suggested that a meeting in a place like Portugal would be the best answer, but while Hess was happy with a letter, he rightly saw no sense in Haushofer travelling to Portugal and thus Hess's strange flight to Britain which Haushofer thought indicated that Hess was unbalanced.

At this stage Albrecht Haushofer was not anticipating a German defeat, although he had warned the regime that the USA would eventually support Britain which would have dangerous ramifications. Others also realised that the German position was not so good and anticipated a defeat, not least Moltke, and as noted above Hassell made desperate efforts on the international front with both Britain and America, testing the waters as to any arrangements which could be made if Hitler were toppled from power. Like others, as mentioned above, the theme of their proposals was that Germany should retain some of Hitler's gains which was not well received. As Hoffmann noted, 'the questionable nature of certain of these points leaps to the eye. It must be remembered that, when the memorandum was drafted, Germany's military situation was not completely hopeless' occupying territory 1,000 miles deep into Soviet Russia.[1] In many ways at this stage the resistance was wanting an end to the war, especially with the west, and keeping a sense of German dignity and respectability by ridding themselves of the Nazi regime. As noted above men like Goerdeler, Hjalmar Schacht, Moltke, the diplomats Adam von Trott zu Solz, von Hassell, and Erich Kordt had made many efforts to warn the outside world of Hitler's intentions and his madness. They continued to make these efforts when it was safe for them to travel and communicate through mutual friends, especially in Sweden.

In 1941, Bonhoeffer travelled to Switzerland, to use Church contacts to try and discover if the Allied side had any hints about making peace. He managed after considerable efforts to contact Bishop Bell of Chichester, and Bonhoeffer showed his trust when asked by the bishop for some names of the main resisters, he selected a few. Moltke, as previously mentioned maintained his international contacts where possible. There were many such connections by many German resisters, but it was a hopeless task. As far as the Allies were concerned any form of agreement would demand the death of Hitler a man they never trusted, they found it impossible to believe this could be achieved, they were uncertain how far the resisters could be trusted, the brutality of the regime had been noted, and despite the arguments of various resisters the occupied territories had to be restored; the chances of any agreement were negligible and totally non-existent. It was equally pointless turning towards Stalin, although there had been peace feelers at one stage when Stalin was desperate, and it was good for him in terms of his political and somewhat tense arrangements with the West, but he was no different from Hitler in his imperialistic covetousness for more territory. Hassell had once considered these peace feelers a possibility, telling both Russian and German sides 'That the preservation of Germany was in their interests'.[2] Both Hassell and Haushofer thought that Stockholm was a good place for meeting Western allies and could also be useful for contacting the Soviets. It is now known there was no real contact between Stalin and Hitler or the German opposition.

The resistance efforts overseas were fruitless, full of mixed motives, badly spelt out and poorly presented, but it must be recalled it was a form of active resistance, because if their activities were known then their lives and those of their families, were at stake.

After the Victory over France

The military efforts to avoid a major war had failed and France had been swiftly defeated with the British retreating home through Dunkirk. Everyone, including the Germans were taken by surprise at the outcome, and many believed that Hitler was either vindicated or he had proved to be a great military leader. However, the sudden victory had been achieved by the professional skills of the German military and their innovative tactical use of planes and tanks. It was later dubbed Blitzkrieg war, based on the military reconstruction under von Seeckt much more than Hitler, whose only input was to demand it should happen. Nevertheless, this had the effect of dampening internal opposition, especially from the military point of view. Many, as noted, had tried to dissuade Hitler from a war which now appeared as a total victory. The Versailles Treaty had been demolished, and the traditional enemy France defeated, while the British had been put back in their island box. Field Marshal von Witzleben who had long been a Nazi opponent acknowledged this factor, but there were still many who decided their efforts to overturn Hitler and the Nazi regime should not falter, despite the increased risks. Hitler for many had reached the top of his popularity and this factor alone would have increased the number of potential informants. His popularity could be seen on newsreels of massive crowds (often organised by Goebbels) massing around Hitler's car or stage, as if greeting a successful Roman emperor, and for some with the adulation usually kept for a deity.

However, various plots and plans are still known about which intended the downfall of the messianic Führer despite his popularity with the crowds. Dr Eugen Gerstenmaier who had been an official in the Evangelical Church, with von der Schulenburg mentioned above, worked together with the plan to find officers and others to arrest Hitler in Berlin, and shoot him if there were resistance. They never found an opportunity to be close enough to the dictator, but clearly indicated there were resisters even at the time of victory prepared to be martyrs to bring down the regime which they recognised as criminal and fundamentally evil. Members of Field Marshal von Witzleben's team had also devised various plans to assassinate Hitler in France, but the opportunity never arose, and attention was soon being drawn to Hitler's intentions against Soviet Russia. For many Germans and other countries, the fear of Bolshevism was almost magnetic. The same fear pervaded the English government, but in time, as is well known, the Nazi regime pushed Churchill into an alliance with Stalin, and in Parliament Churchill wished Stalin well, upon which, when he was teased for this apparent volte-face he replied, 'if Hitler were to invade Hell, I would try to send some words of encouragement to the Devil'.

Halder and Brauchitsch who had been in touch with some resisters now busied themselves with military matters, they ignored the news of the barbarities committed under Hitler's orders even when the notorious Commissar Order was issued, they continued to follow his instructions. There were some mild protests, but the top men worked on. They had been brought up in the tradition of obeying orders seeing insubordination as a deadly sin, but many others recognised the Commissar Order and the way it was exercised in the field as immoral. This is emphasised to demonstrate that many military men, although noted for not wanting war or wanting a new commander in chief were also deeply concerned about the moral deterioration which they knew was wrong and would smudge German honour.

One such man was Tresckow, mentioned many times above. He came from a staunchly traditional Prussian background and found himself being asked to follow orders he found obnoxious. He became increasingly pro-active in trying to find men who would be prepared to take the risk of toppling Hitler, whose early successes in Russia were increasing the dictator's popularity. Tresckow made a staggering number of contacts too numerous to name in this study, but men who agreed the Nazi regime had to fall. Tresckow even tried to persuade General von Bock to fly to Hitler to ask him to revoke the Commissar Order, but he directly refused.

Much of the resisters' discussion was now changing from post-Hitler times and why they had to accomplish the coup, to how it could be achieved. Explosives were looked at, especially some clever British small bombs taken from the French resistance, and even attacks by pistol. Many of his contacts were men at the top end of senior officers close to major figures such as Field Marshals von Bock and von Kluge. Much of this military build-up emanated from Tresckow and tended to be focused in the HQ of Army Group Centre. It was a matter of timing from the point of view that many, including those in the ranks, regarded it as a time of success and no one wanted to be seen as a traitor. Men like General Thomas, Hassell, Goerdeler, Beck, Oster, and others continued to talk between themselves as to the various ways forward, always hoping that more and more army commanders would refuse to carry out the barbaric orders. It was sadly the fact that the ranks of ordinary soldiers and junior officers had been long indoctrinated in conducting orders, many of the younger ones influenced by their years in the Hitler Youth. The civilians mentioned above remained active but knew they had to rely on the military if the coup were to have any chance of success. Tresckow again tried to work on von Bock who, once he realised what Tresckow was suggesting lost his temper. He managed to gain the attention of General Olbricht who pledged himself to the cause, but Tresckow and others always remained concerned at Olbricht's stability. In these preparations they were constantly looking out for more recruits, men prepared to assassinate and how it could be done successfully. They managed to establish a mobile force of dependable men for when the opportunity arose.

Impending Military Disaster

In 1943 the overall picture of German military success started to deteriorate badly, and for many military commanders the future looked bleak. There were worrying signals, the Allies' growing success in the Mediterranean and North African area, with the more disconcerting news of the disaster at Stalingrad, caused by Hitler's hopeless directions imposed upon and accepted by General Paulus. There had been a total failure to make any fruitful contact with the Western Allies, and the demand for Unconditional Surrender had been an unwelcome surprise. The security surrounding the Führer was intense if not paranoid, and Schmundt, Hitler's army adjutant, had told Tresckow and his fellow resister Rudolf von Gersdorff that Hitler wore a bullet proof waistcoat and hat. All kinds of plans were discussed ranging from a bomb to a pistol shot, to arrest, but the need for immediate action was, for some, becoming urgent, Tresckow for one was determined that Hitler should be killed as soon as possible. The problem with a bomb was managing to find a place close enough to Hitler, with the additional issue of who may be in his company, as they might be potential resisters or necessary personnel for the post-Hitler era. The critical issue centred on the Eastern Front where discontent was growing. The conspirators deemed it essential that the plans should include consideration as to how all communication systems could be cut between Hitler's HQ at the Wolfschanze and Berlin. The OKW were always at the HQ, but the political Nazi regime was in Berlin, which remained a critical factor.

On 13 March 1943 Hitler was at Smolensk on a flying visit. Tresckow persuaded one of Hitler's accompanying officers (Lieutenant Colonel Heinz Brandt) to take back to Berlin two bottles of Cointreau Brandy for a Berlin friend. They were bombs timed to detonate during the flight, the operation was known as *Flash* (which became a general code word for Hitler's death) but they failed to work. One of Tresckow's subordinates retrieved the bottle on the excuse it was the wrong type of brandy, and he discovered the fuses had not worked. It had proved difficult finding appropriate explosives, evading the tight security, and Hitler was known for suddenly changing arrangements and this failure would have been a major blow for the resisters.

However, soon after they planned another effort when Hitler was viewing an exhibition of captured Soviet flags and banners. An officer called Rudolf von Gersdorff was asked to carry and set the bomb off while close to Hitler because it was realised the security was too tight to set a bomb up in the room before he arrived. This amounted to a suicide mission as the bomb fuse was only ten minutes. Those allowed to be near the Führer were carefully selected and watched, but Gersdorff managed this on the pretext that in some matters he was an expert, and he could explain to Hitler what he was looking at. At the last moment, and without warning, Hitler left the room with Gertsdorff dashing to the bathroom area with seconds left to defuse the bomb. Hitler often believed that providence was looking after him, but his erratic behaviour was his main saving device. Whether Hitler had suddenly picked up a sense of panic or potential danger will never be known, what was understood was Hitler's erratic behaviour. How far the civilian resisters were aware of these attempts is unknown, and Tresckow probably kept these possibilities between himself and his closest officers.

Tresckow, whose major role is often overlooked in many history books, failed to convince Manstein, he tried seeking the cooperation of General von Kluge, who showed more interest, but this transpired to be merely superficial curiosity. Plots and plans grew exponentially during 1943, mainly because of the desperate situation of which everyone was acutely aware. Meanwhile, the keen activator Tresckow (July 1943) was transferred to OKH command reserve and in October 1943 took over as commander of the 442 Infantry Regiment.

Other planners desperately tried to gain support by asking Hitler to stand down, and Goerdeler volunteered, but it would have been a dangerous and useless effort. He harassed the military to do something, pointing out that millions of civilians had already been executed, but they understood the dangers of making a wrong move in a police state under the tightest possible security.[3] Many of them were by now under suspicion, and they knew they were being watched by Himmler's SD and Gestapo. The Abwehr were being investigated over some form of currency scandal, and this led to uncovering some of their resistance efforts, not least Dohnányi who had been assisting Jews (and who had some Jewish origins himself), and Oster's support raised further Gestapo suspicions. Dohnányi and Bonhoeffer (with his sister) were arrested, Oster and his acquaintances were under constant surveillance, and Keitel ordered that Oster had no other business with the Abwehr. Those who were arrested never let any secrets out, and those under suspicion knew they had to keep low profiles and do nothing to expose their resistance, but it was a serious blow to the opposition. Canaris continued for a time but their work, official and unofficially, virtually ground to a halt.

The situation was so desperate that Bock thought the coup could only be successful if Himmler were involved, and Popitz had the bravery to talk with him. It was not only dangerous to talk with Himmler, but it verged on an act of sheer recklessness. It also indicated that firm leadership was missing, and by considering Himmler it undermined all moral considerations because Himmler was as criminal as his Führer. Time was running out in terms of the military situation, and it was a mere daydream to hope the Allies would talk of peace or some form of settlement at this stage. Tresckow talked to Goerdeler pointing out the urgency that within months the Soviet Red Army could be on Germany's borders. Tresckow was the leading light of the opposition, and tried to explain to Goerdeler that the situation was such that some of the generals were beginning to see the sense of what had to be done.

At one stage when Tresckow had contemplated arresting Hitler in Vinnitsa in Russia (July 1943) he started to plan and develop the coup called *Valkyrie*. Once again there were mixed plans and few amongst the civilians would have been aware of the details. It is a distinct possibility that Oster may have known about Tresckow's plans, but how far he understood his ideas to establish a military dictatorship with the help of General Olbricht remains uncertain. It is known that when Tresckow was posted elsewhere, he left the central plans with Stauffenberg to which Popitz added some guidelines, but they were very different from the plans and thoughts of the civilian thinking. It is virtually impossible to know to this day what discussions between Tresckow and Goerdeler took place, if any did, as Goerdeler was closer to Beck than Tresckow. Such was the desperate need for secrecy that written documentation was rare, and the sense of urgency was increasing. There were some reports of a meeting between Goerdeler, Tresckow, and Olbricht, at which the latter promised to carry out the coup with the reserve army, but by this time Tresckow was mainly dependent on Stauffenberg. Tresckow and Stauffenberg were driven men, and they were dedicated to removing Hitler as soon as possible. For both these officers the military crisis was the paramount motive, and they were planning this to avoid military disaster with Hitler bringing ruin on the German people. The military and lead civilians were intent on keeping the army intact and avoiding defeat; this was their paramount motive. Reflecting the attitudes of the day the fear of Bolshevism was top of their list, it appeared they were not intent on destroying Russia but the Soviet system. This explained their many efforts to use Russian volunteer units such as the Vlasov Army to help them win.* It has been claimed that Stauffenberg once said the eradication of Bolshevism had to happen first before Hitler could be toppled, but they were opposed to the treatment inflicted on the Russian prisoners, especially the civilian population by the SS.[4] The motives of the military varied, but they were somewhat removed from those of the civilian resisters. For the military it was the care of their units and blocking Hitler's interference in military matters. There is no question that Hitler's constant demand of no retreat and 'stand to the last man' had led to the catastrophe of Stalingrad and elsewhere. There is also no doubt that Hitler's

* The Vlasov Army was called the Russian Liberation Army, a mixture of Russians fighting under German command. Andrey Vlasov was a Red Army general who had defected.

management of the armed forces was a gift to his Western and Eastern enemies. Many of his commands had not only led to confusion because of their sheer stupidity, but many had caused outrage. There were divisions of opinion on how to deal with Partisans, prisoners of war, the shooting of commissars and civilians. Stalin and communism were not always welcome within the Soviet lands, and its fear influenced many neighbouring countries. Instead of Hitler's brutal commands the German army for some people could have been seen as a liberating force, but Hitler's orders made him appear far worse a prospect than Stalin.

The army commanders were mainly focused on military motives, and humanitarian principles for many took second place. As noted above Generals von Stülpnagel and Eduard Wagner although in the resistance, were still involved in killing some prisoners and Jews, and it has been noted that Tresckow also cooperated with *Einsatzgruppen*. Many of them were also by their own positions and status involved in the barbarity of starving Russian prisoners to death. There is no reliable evidence of any serious discussion between military and civilian resisters, Stauffenberg saw Beck as head of state and replacing Goerdeler with Juluis Leber as Chancellor. 'Nonetheless, it seems doubtful that, had Valkyrie been successful, any use would have been made of the political appeals that Goerdeler had prepared, as a government statement and for a speech to be broadcast to the nation'.[5]

The Original purpose of Valkyrie

There have been many books and films about Valkyrie, which was a codeword for reserves or units to fill gaps in the field armies in the various designated military districts across Germany (known as *Wehrkreis*). Curiously, before he fell from grace, it was Admiral Canaris who had sold the idea to Hitler.[6] The nature of this policy changed following a series of new command orders. As the war unfolded with increased Allied bombing raids there were fears of internal disturbances, not least the possible dangers of some form of insurgency by the vast numbers of slave labourers and PoWs, possible parachute troops landing, and Valkyrie was to hold and defend critical areas and buildings. The idea of slave labourers or PoWs revolting was unlikely, as was a parachute drop by the enemy. However, these new instructions demanded a rapid response and assembling combat groups for which training was provided; the key was the need for rapid mobility. In overall charge of this operational scheme was General Fromm, the Chief of Army Equipment and Commander in Chief of the Replacement Army. Fromm was the key because only on his orders could the waiting troops be activated.

In October 1943 Olbricht, having become a more determined resister signed an order for more reinforcements. In February 1944 Stauffenberg who was now Olbricht's Chief of Staff issued further orders about making the combat groups more efficient. Valkyrie was now being used for the planned coup without the Nazi powers realising what was happening. Because of the nature of the original plans for this policy Stauffenberg was able to impose a strict security on their work. The only problem was although it was a Wehrmacht project in some *Wehrkreis* areas, Party and SS personnel were involved. Nevertheless, the resisters had cleverly adopted a scheme which, if the assassination were successful, may well have worked, the critical aspect was using the correct code word. The major issue was ensuring General Fromm cooperated which would probably succeed if Hitler were dead. The major preparational issues were rehearsals but without inviting suspicion, but it could be done in Berlin constantly suffering bombing raids. The idea was that combat troops could be moved without arousing hints that 'something else' was happening. Tresckow before he left had worked hard on this aspect and was able to share it with Stauffenberg before being posted away to the Eastern Front. Stauffenberg had known Tresckow since 1941 and there was a mutual trust and understanding between the two men. It was also agreed that Field Marshal von Witzleben was to assume command of the Wehrmacht to which he readily agreed.

Stauffenberg

When Tresckow was posted to the Eastern Front his place was taken by the now famous Count von Stauffenberg, whose ancestors included two Prussian field marshals, making him very aware of his traditional background. In the early years he was, by all accounts, a supporter of Hitler, and like many young Germans of his class believed Austria and the Sudetenland were German, and after the victory in France believed Hitler had a mastery over military strategy, which soon rapidly changed during Operation *Barbarossa*. He had been approached by the resister Schulenburg who told him of the barbarities committed during the Polish occupation, but at this stage Stauffenberg appeared disinterested, although some historians note this had a major effect on his thinking.[7] What was raising doubts for him was the poor German military command in Russia, along with his critical view of Göring's failed promises about the Luftwaffe.

Stauffenberg was educated in the classics and enjoyed discussing them to the boredom of many colleagues, especially on the subject of politics. There have been many views and criticisms of Stauffenberg over the years, some claiming he felt he was called to be famous and was driven by ambition, some that he was only interested in military success, while others, with some justification, that he was a highly moral person who disliked the facts first brought to him by Schulenburg. There is no doubt he had a dynamic personality and was seen as an activator. It was known that he had little time for the socialists and trade unions, but this changed in time either because he was seeing life from a wider perspective, or somewhat cynically, out of necessity.

It was in North Africa he was badly injured in a strafing attack by a British fighter-plane and lost his right hand, with three fingers left on the remaining hand, and lost his left eye.* After surgery and recovery, he was posted in September 1943 as Chief of Staff to the General Army Office under General Olbricht where he met Tresckow who was by now a dedicated resister looking to the downfall of Hitler.

The Search for Assassins

Trying to acquire the right kind of bomb with which to kill Hitler was not easily achieved, but it was also dangerous as senior officers asking for such weapons would not just raise a few eyebrows but create deep suspicion. It was against regulations to hold explosive weapons at home or in the office whatever the rank, and the captured British devices for some reason were often selected. This may have been because an answer for holding them could be based on curiosity, and they may have been considered more effective for their purpose. To this day anyone in most national military units must sign out for weapons and bombs, and avoiding this in Nazi Germany could swiftly lead to Gestapo interest. It was also a problem as to how to conceal a bomb and detonating it was not straightforward; finding permission to be close to Hitler was unbelievably complex, and not helped by Hitler's erratic habits and custom of rearranging matters at the drop of a hat. Hitler may possibly have behaved this way out of habit, or he may have sensed that he was in danger. He was constantly guarded by SS men trained to be suspicious of anyone who was not part of their fabric, and even a hand reaching into a pocket would draw their instant attention. Following the investigation into the Abwehr it was probably the case that all the security guards were alert even to senior officers. Even more difficult was finding a person willing to carry out the act of an assassin, as this had to be suicidal and conducted by sheer nerveless determination. The conspirators had many discussions over bombs, the use of pistols, and whether it would be easier simply to arrest Hitler by attacking his HQ. Pistols demanded a dedication beyond normal human courage, and according to one

---

* Although Shirer suggests he may have driven into a minefield, see Shirer, William, *The Rise, and Fall of the Third Reich* (London: Mandarin, 1997) p.1029.

account, when a junior officer was asked why he had not used his pistol to kill Hitler, he replied 'I will tell you exactly why. In the first place I was afraid, it would have been the end of me, and, secondly, as a colonel, I did not really feel it was my mission to interfere with fate in this way'.[8] It is not difficult to have some sympathy for any person asked to go on a suicide mission. It may have been this realisation that made some think another way was to lead an attack on Hitler's HQ with guns aimed at Hitler, but it was an unrealistic plan and never used. Detection by the many suspicious and resolute guards was the main problem, and it was eventually decided that Hitler had to be killed by a bomb. Stauffenberg approached many, who although sympathetic, either refused or could not see how they could get close enough. Stauffenberg needed to find a person who was so angry martyrdom was acceptable. His first find was Major Axel Freiherr von dem Bussche who was highly decorated for personal valour, and well known by Tresckow. He was a soldier who had been totally disgusted at watching Ukrainian SS troops systematically murder thousands of Jews. He had stood helplessly by knowing he could not stop it, and even considered joining the queue to be part of their suffering. He was evidently a highly moral person, and he turned at once against the man and the regime who had given such barbaric orders. Bussche had been personally trusted by Olbricht to ensure that in the regiment there were no fanatical Nazis, and he immediately agreed to volunteer to kill Hitler even though it meant himself as well. Various means of arranging for Bussche to have an excuse to be close to Hitler were explored. One such idea was for a show of new uniforms and equipment, and as Bussche was so highly decorated, it was believed it might work for him to present this to Hitler. There were problems arranging a bomb device, but Bussche virtually organised the bomb for himself using German hand grenades. Because Hitler could not or rather would not be tied down to specific times and dates it failed, and Bussche was recalled to the front. Stauffenberg promised to call him back the next moment it arose, but when he did, Bussche's commander refused, and later Bussche was wounded. After the war he studied law, married an English woman, worked hard in Germany and was a member of the German Evangelical Church Congress, dying in January 1993.

Having failed with Bussche through no fault of the volunteer, Stauffenberg turned to Lieutenant Edward von Kleist, who asked his father first, who had been constantly anti-Nazi, and who replied that something had to be done. At this stage there was some faltering by other resisters, but Olbricht convinced the waverers that German's military plight was so serious that to avoid total disaster and save the country, a coup was essential. This underlined Olbricht's motives which tended to be military inclined. It was back to the uniform demonstration, but the code word never arrived because there had been a failure to find the necessary bomb to do the job. Tresckow even offered to carry out the task himself, but finding the right bomb, the right place, and placing oneself close enough to Hitler remained a serious problem.

The third attempt involved Captain Arthur Eberhard von Breitenbuch, who preferred to use a pistol rather than a bomb, but he was persuaded otherwise with a device which could be hidden in his tunic, but still insisted in a concealed pistol in his pocket. For once it seemed as if all were going well, but at the last moment an SS guard stopped him entering the room as aides were not allowed entry. This aborted attempt, understandably put him off trying again. He survived the war, became a forester, and died in 1980.

Planning the Coup

Planning the death of Hitler was frustratingly complex, but there were other even more difficult concerns which had to be worked through, all in a time of deep uncertainty. If Hitler were killed or arrested it was essential that what happened afterwards should be carefully thought through first. There were many loyal military men such as Jodl, Keitel and Dönitz, perhaps even more dangerous than the Nazi henchmen such as Göring, Himmler, and Goebbels. It was understood for a long time if the coup were to take place it would be at one of Hitler's military HQ and not in the political capital of Berlin. The OKW would be with Hitler, and it was therefore essential that once the deed had been carried out the HQ had to be isolated from the rest of Germany, during which the new government would come into force with the necessary explanations and plans for the future. Somehow the communications system had to be taken under strict control. General Erich Fellgiebel, who had long despised Hitler and the regime, had full authority over all army communications. The year before Fellgiebel had assured the other plotters he would have a firm clamp on all signal communications. However, as events were to prove it would necessitate closing down the entire HQ because radio, teleprinters, and phone systems could all be used. With the benefit of hindsight, it could be argued that the entire system should have been blown up, and Fellgiebel has been unfairly criticised for this failure. This would have needed considerable cooperation and understanding by the hundreds of people gathered in the HQ area. There were many senior and junior officers who were by now resisting the regime and hoping for its downfall, but the Hitler Youth machine had indoctrinated many of the youngest soldiers, making the outcome even more tenuous. The fall of Stalingrad was causing serious fragmentation in the military, but there was no large, unified resistance body to challenge Hitler, and so it was down to those who had long been dedicated to this overthrow. The charismatic nature of Hitler's leadership now supported by the police state and the Nazi structure indicated that the coup would have to rely on some good fortune, even though his support was dwindling because of the military setbacks. During his interrogations in the Nuremberg Trial, Göring had explained that he thought there was no chance of a coup because of the large structure surrounding Hitler.[9]

As noted in the previous chapter, the various groups of civilian resisters had long been talking about how to reform Germany after Hitler's regime was overturned. However, as noted, there were disagreements, but by July 1944, the situation had changed drastically with the Russians appearing unstoppable and the Western Allies were now fighting in France. It must have felt as if all the previous plans needed to be reprocessed into a state of necessary rearrangement. Beck had demanded a full script of the civilians prepared to step into what was hoped would become the forthcoming breach, because without that assurance the military might feel stymied. There were many resisters, but the key personnel were critical, even looking to control outside Germany as in occupied Paris, where Schulenburg had already been active. They tended to agree that a semi-authoritarian regime would be a pro tem necessity, and at this stage even the Kreisau Circle became more in touch with Goerdeler's group. Plans for a future government were agreed. These had been worked on since 1943 and many of the plans had undergone several revisions. They were later exposed from Gestapo files and the historian Peter Hoffmann provides a full and extensive list.[10] Beck was to be head of state, Goerdeler the Chancellor, and other major resisters were given other major posts, but these were only working documents. Not all agreed on the assassination, some wanting an arrest and a full trial, others were morally concerned that killing Hitler would be seen as deploying his methods, and at one time even Beck and Goerdeler wanted killing avoided. As the months progressed it soon became clear that only assassination would work, and even many in the Kreisau Circle agreed it was the only way forward, as did the Churchmen Bonhoeffer and Delp. Even Moltke was against a coup for the time, but his opposition became less staunch. Most of the active resisters on the civilian side had little choice and accepted that Hitler had to be killed.

The July Plot Unfolds

Stauffenberg knew the way that his civilian counterparts were thinking, and also knew that only the military could achieve this, and by July many realised the war could not be won and haste was essential. By this stage there were questions for some as to why bother with a coup, because defeat was on the horizon, with chatter about letting the Western forces through to the Eastern Front with Russian tanks moving some 50 miles close to Hitler's HQ. On the other hand, it was argued that Germany could only re-establish its dignity and future by being seen to rid itself of the criminal regime. It might also save hundreds of thousands of lives. These issues were raised by different individuals in various groups, but Stauffenberg's way of thinking was to stop talking and do something. When he decided to take on the role of assassin as well as the active leader, some tried to dissuade him. In the initial stages there was no sensible access to Hitler by Stauffenberg, and he had been seriously wounded with his right hand gone and limited fingers on this remaining hand. Then suddenly he was Chief of Staff to General Fromm which would give him access to Hitler's presence. Several reasons have been given as to why Fromm selected him, but they have to be pure speculation. Stauffenberg had the courage to point out to Fromm that military defeat was imminent, and it could only be averted in the political field, insinuating a coup d'état. Fromm said little one way or the other, which was an indicator that he was a man who wanted to hunt with the hounds unless the situation turned, and he remained vague on the subject until the bitter end. In the meantime, Tresckow from his position on the Eastern Front was pressing for immediate action. Stauffenberg was wondering whether there was any point now the Western Allies were already in France, but Tresckow pointed out that the assassination would prove to the world that there were Germans who were prepared to die for the country's honour and dignity. This was sufficient for Stauffenberg, who has gone down in history as the key figure in the plot, but it was Tresckow's long-term persistence which was a key factor in the resistance movement.

It was a tense moment as one resister, Julius Leber had been arrested by the Gestapo, followed by rumours that Goerdeler may well be next. This must have been nerve-racking news as it was well-known that the Gestapo used sophisticated torture methods which only a very few could resist. Arthur Nebe, chief of the Reich Criminal Police, also a resister warned that Himmler might strike against them, because many of the resistance were becoming known, and rumours were beginning to abound about a possible attack on Hitler. According to one source even Eva Braun 'wanted to talk Hitler into staying at the Berghof, because she was frightened that something would happen to him'.[11] There were constant rumours of a possible coup, and common sense would suggest that given the unpopularity of the regime, now facing military defeat, such an event was more likely in 1944 than in the years of success. It must have been felt by many resisters that they were all in grave danger.

On 7 June, Stauffenberg accompanied Fromm to a meeting with Hitler at the Berghof (Hitler's retreat in the Bavarian Alps) where he noticed the freedom of movement by the other visitors, allowing Stauffenberg to gain an understanding of Hitler's style and habits when in closed sessions. Later, when Stauffenberg's wife asked him about the impression he had made on Stauffenberg, he replied: 'Not at all, Nothing! …as if veiled. Hitler had shuffled the maps around with a trembling hand, continuously glancing at Stauffenberg; Göring had been wearing make-up. The whole atmosphere was rotten and degenerate'.[12]

It was a matter of holding one's nerves, and General Helmuth Stieff had offered to kill Hitler at a new uniform display but felt unable. It was, Stauffenberg decided, down to him. One of the demands most had agreed upon was that the bomb should be activated when Himmler and even if possible Göring were present. It was entirely unpredictable to know whether they would attend as they often sent their own personal representatives, as Stauffenberg was doing for Fromm. He was back in Hitler's presence on 7 July with Himmler present, but it is not known whether Stauffenberg had the bomb ready or was expecting Stieff to manage the assassination. On 11 July Stauffenberg was back and equipped with a bomb but Himmler was not present. This was a confusing issue as no one could be certain as to the whereabouts of men like Himmler and Göring. On 14 July he was back with Fromm and accompanied by Captain Klausing his aide. It was a brief meeting and with one hand missing and only a few fingers on his other hand, he had little opportunity of setting the fuse without drawing attention to himself. This drew his awareness to the fact that he would need to slip out of the room for a brief moment to activate the fuse for which he would need help from his aide. There was also the continuing problem of Himmler's whereabouts. He had anticipated setting the bomb off on 15 July but once again abandoned it in the light of Himmler's absence. Some of his fellow conspirators remained adamant that Himmler should be present rather than thinking that Himmler's death would only be icing on the cake. It has even been stated that Stieff actively interfered but whether it was to protect Stauffenberg, or a loss of nerve will never be known.[13] Meanwhile, in Berlin, the conspirators were awaiting for 'the flash' (the successful carrying out of the assassination) to be heard, and Olbricht, in anticipation, had alerted the prepared army units and later had to pretend it was a mere exercise. It was, curiously, the same day that Goerdeler's proposed arrest by the SS security was raised. It was not an easy day for the plotters, because in addition to all these problems doubts were raised as to the reliability of Major Remer who was the commander of the Berlin Guard Battalion, not knowing whether he was or would be onside, as he was essential to controlling central Berlin once 'flash' was announced, but at this stage it was a matter of simply hoping, while waiting to see what happened.

One thing was clear in Stauffenberg's mind that with all these emerging problems and rumours there could no longer be any delay, and even Himmler's presence could not be a critical factor.

20 July Plot Activated

There have been various accounts of the 20 July plot at Wolfschanze, many with different versions. One of the most thorough is by Peter Hoffmann who examines the minutest details.[14] This event has been explored so many times this study will summarise the event and immediate consequences, which will expose that there was a great deal of confusion and suspicion from beginning to end. Stauffenberg, it appears, cleverly attached himself to Keitel as they approached Hitler's conference, probably because such company would make entry into the sacred room less disconcerting for the watchful guards. He had as company his aide, Werner von Haeften, and on the excuse of needing to change his shirt they disappeared into the lavatory to fuse two bombs, while Keitel waited for them. It was not an easy task with Stauffenberg's disabilities and the undoubted tensions of the moment. It was not helped when a Sergeant-Major Vogel called in and asked them to hurry, and he stayed at the door. As a consequence, only one bomb was loaded into the briefcase as they hurried to catch up with Keitel already strolling towards the meeting. Keitel introduced Stauffenberg to Hitler informing the dictator he was there to update on the new formations, Hitler shook his hand then turned back to the briefing. Once inside more difficulties occurred as Stauffenberg, a minor visitor, had to somehow shuffle his way towards the table's edge and as close to Hitler as possible. He eventually managed to place the briefcase under the table where it was possible someone may have nudged it further in. He managed to leave the meeting which was not unusual for someone to leave the room for a variety of reasons, and outside to the car. There had been problems with the car, but they were resolved, and the driver Kretz told Stauffenberg he had forgotten his cap and belt, but this was pushed aside as of no consequence. As they drove away, they could see the smoke and sense of panic and had to pass through two gate checks. The first took Stauffenberg's natural sense of officer superiority to have the barrier lifted, but the second was more stubborn. Stauffenberg had to phone a Captain von Möllendorf before the gate was lifted. On the way to the airport the driver Kretz noticed that Haeften had thrown a parcel out of the car, which was the unused bomb and because of Kretz seeing this act of disposal it was later discovered.

As is well known today a few were killed, many injured with glass and wooden splinters, but Hitler survived. Like all the others the noise had caused him hearing problems and the explosion left him with torn clothes, some burns, and splinters, but it appeared that Keitel and Hitler had managed to escape the concussion from which the other survivors were nearly all suffering. It has been suggested that Hitler, having realised he had escaped death believed even more in his nonsensical idea that providence was caring for him giving him yet more self-boosting. It was also stated that 'at the beginning of August 1944 Hitler's health took a turn for the worse, as his fainting fits increased'.[15] Had the meeting taken place in the usual bunker the concrete walls would have contained the explosion, and everyone would have probably died. As it was, they had moved to a wooden structure because of the summer heat, and the explosion blew the room apart but outwards, and Hitler had been protected, as with some others by a huge solid wooden table. The second bomb, had it been used may have been more effective. It is not difficult to imagine the immediate after-effects of shock and panic and a time of total confusion. Fellgiebel used the codeword 'the signals equipment is leaving' which was slightly different (i.e., 'the signals equipment has left') but there is some confusion over how it was received. Fellgiebel had done all he could, but communications meant more than just signals, but by 1.30 Berlin was aware that 'flash' had occurred.

Not long afterwards a Sergeant-Major Adam noted that he had seen Stauffenberg leave afterwards. At first, the NCO was ignored, but then he spoke to Bormann who took him directly to Hitler. From that moment Stauffenberg was pinpointed and Adam was rewarded financially. Between two and three that afternoon, steps were taken to arrest Stauffenberg, and later in the afternoon an SS officer arrived at the conspirator's HQ in the Bendlerstrasse (a building complex in the Tiergarten district erected as a military centre) to arrest Stauffenberg only to find himself under arrest. Ironically, eleven years and six months before (February 1933) Hitler had gone to the Bendlerstrasse to pay his first formal call on the military leaders.

If it were confusion in the Wolfschanze it was the same in the Bendlerstrasse where the key problem was inactivity which has generated much speculation. They had perhaps become accustomed to Stauffenberg attempting Hitler's death in July, they knew something had happened, but were probably uncertain as to whether Hitler were dead. Communications were unsound and rare, and it may have been this anxiety which caused the lack of action. Meanwhile Stauffenberg was still flying, but with the added problem at which airport his plane would land, with his driver waiting at a different airport. When he landed, he eventually ordered a car and arrived at the Bendlerstrasse at about 4.30, to find the resisting generals moving with too much caution given what he had been through. Olbricht was caught between the deep-blue sea and the devil; on the one hand Fellgiebel and Keitel had announced Hitler was alive, on the other hand Stauffenberg stated he had seen him dead, leaving an atmosphere of doubt. The Wehrmacht had no control over post office communications, and the radio stations and telegraph offices had not been seized, and there was no entire blackout on all communications. Eventually Olbricht agreed to start the agreed action, and he took the necessary reports to Fromm for signing and sending out the necessary code word, and it was assumed that General Beck was now the Reich's leader. Fromm had apparently spoken to Keitel who said the Führer was still alive. Olbricht was probably aware of this conversation but had decided to move while the moment was ripe because of all the confusion. Fromm, who had knowledge of the plot was intent on staying alive and arranged for those staff he knew to be involved to be removed (a few by execution) because he needed clean hands. The missive to be sent announced Hitler was dead and 'an irresponsible clique of Party leaders divorced from the front had tried to stab the hard-struggling Army in the back and seize power'.[16] Others were sent with Fromm's name attached, although he did not know, and backed up with Stauffenberg's signature. The occupation or surrounding of SD and Gestapo offices, and other critical buildings on the excuse of protection was authorised.

Fromm remained a problem, because although he was acquainted with the plot, he had decided to play it safe and refused to join. He was told Keitel had lied but remained adamant he was going to stay neutral. His anger exploded, and he tried to assault Stauffenberg, but the two aides Kleist and Haeften drew their pistols which pacified Fromm immediately. Fromm was not going to change his mind, so he was locked in his office with a guard on the door. Olbricht put General Erich Hoepner in Fromm's place. Confusion seemed to be the order of the day, but Beck clarified the situation by pointing out that for him Hitler was dead, and everything should proceed on these grounds, and by the time Hitler's group could react the coup could take place. Beck ordered that Goerdeler should be contacted, but since his arrest warrant was known, he had understandably disappeared. What was curious at this stage was that there were no counter measures by the SS, which again has raised various theories about Himmler. Stauffenberg spent considerable time ensuring that the Valkyrie progress was being made in the various military districts (Wehrkreis) and in the Bendlerstrasse all seemed to be going to plan. However, the commander of district III having seen the orders turned up at the Bendlerstrasse demanding to see Fromm, as he had guessed a coup was taking place. After trying to escape once it dawned on that he was correct, he was, like Fromm, put under armed guard, and in the meantime various units were busy cordoning off various areas of importance.

In the outside world there was the same sense of confusion over what was happening and understandably a great deal of suspicion with rumours and counter rumours in abundance at every level. It was a question of lack of certainty, and senior officers demanded written orders rather than instructions via a courier or radio, which also occurred when it was understood that the Waffen SS was to be integrated into the Wehrmacht. When the broadcast came through that Hitler was dead some were suspicious and decided to wait and hear more, others seemed to rejoice, and although proceedings were beginning as anticipated, it was far from universal as scepticism is part of human nature. The critical issue was that the coup started at about the same time that Keitel had phoned claiming Hitler to be alive.

These problems of uncertainty pervaded the entire time of the attempted coup. Throughout the various military districts there were a variety of actions, some pleased because they knew of the coup, some happy to hear Hitler was dead, and many not knowing where they stood, and demanding to speak with General Fromm, with Stauffenberg constantly busy on the phone trying to ensure cooperation. However, from about mid-afternoon most of their teleprinted messages were not just going to the Wehrkreis HQ but were being routed through Wolfschanze. This meant that Keitel's officers could thereby challenge the coup and demand of the Wehrkreis HQ that they should only respond to orders from Keitel or the Reichsführer. Even those men who had hoped for a coup could feel by late afternoon that matters were not running well, serious doubts were arising, those who did not know of a possible coup became more resilient to ignoring orders from the Bendlerstrasse, thereby creating a policy of 'wait and see'. In some cases where troops had been sent out, they were recalled to their barracks. Even Stauffenberg who had tried to impose the new authority and was impatient for success, must have realised the coup was not working in the way he had hoped, and by the late evening the Valkyrie orders were being ignored, and Hitler's control remained intact. It was a similar reaction in the occupied capitals of Prague, Vienna, and Paris, mainly involving some initial reaction to the orders, then doubt, followed by rejection and often leading to recriminations against those who had followed the Bendlerstrasse orders. The nearest to success was General Carl-Heinrich von Stülpnagel in Paris, who started the arrest of SS and Gestapo personnel, but after the failure of the coup he managed to talk himself back on the side of the government for a brief time. However, he knew when he was ordered back to Berlin what was happening, he tried to shoot himself, but only lost his eyesight, and was later executed after the People's Court session.

The Collapse of the Coup

It did not take long for the coup to collapse, although some men like General von Hase had worked their role quickly, the problem was that the orders came too late and at the same time as the news that Hitler was still alive. One of the key players transpired to be Major Remer who obeyed Hase's orders and had cordoned off some buildings. He was a highly decorated officer known for obeying orders, but the Valkyrie ones were so unexpected and unusual there is no question he was accruing some doubts. There have been various views expressed about Remer who appears to have been one of many who simply obeyed orders without question. It was known that after the war he became a Holocaust denier.[17] It was suggested that Remer should first visit Goebbels, although he was on the arrest sheet, the meeting was arranged and happened. At first the meeting was frosty as Remer remained uncertain and was obsessed with obeying orders, but he now found that he was faced by contradictory authorities with differing orders. The original intention was the arrest of Goebbels who made a phone call to the Wolfschanze where Hitler had been busy with a visit by Mussolini, but by 7.00 that evening, Remer found himself talking to Hitler over the phone. This resolved for Remer the conflict of orders which signified a turning point as Hitler's authority remained intact. Remer followed Goebbel's advice, the roadblock and cordons were withdrawn as Remer spoke to other officers that the Valkyrie orders were nothing more than a coup. The following hours continued with the atmosphere of confusion both for the conspirators and those loyal to the regime, but it must have been clear that the coup was seriously foundering. Witzleben who headed the Wehrmacht for the coup and whose direct chief was now Beck, was furious at how matters were turning out, and refused to believe Beck and Stauffenberg who claimed that the rumour that Hitler was still alive was false. Shots were suddenly heard as the Nazi loyalists had entered the Bendlerstrasse. According to one account Olbricht had been asked about his guards around the Bendlerstrasse and whether they would defend him from attacking loyal SS troops to which he replied, 'I don't know', and it was now clear they would not.[18] The fighting closed in and Stauffenberg in the exchange of fire was slightly wounded. It ended with Fromm being released and Stauffenberg, Haeften, Beck, Olbricht, and others under arrest. Matters moved too fast even for a kangaroo court, and they were ordered to be executed, Beck was allowed to commit suicide but bumbled it and then shot, while the others were executed outside with Stauffenberg crying out at the last moment 'Long live Sacred Germany'.

It was a time of confusion with no one certain as to what was happening. One young officer wrote in his autobiography that 'the next several days were total chaos through Germany. Nobody knew what would happen next…there were endless rumours, whispered names…it was at least a week before the situation showed any signs of abating'.[19] Even as this was happening arrests were being made elsewhere; the plot had failed. Fromm was arrested later under suspicion, he was not treated as badly as most, but finally executed by firing squad on 12 March 1945. The revenge on the others started with Keitel holding a court of honour when the military personnel involved were sacked, so they could be tried with the non-military by the People's Court under Roland Freisler.

The executions were intentionally barbaric and slow, with the process being filmed so Hitler could watch it at leisure. The list of convicted resisters was long and varied, and 'according to one source it numbered some 4,980 names. The Gestapo records a list of 7,000 arrests', some given figures vary but it was long.[20] There were, of course, many senior commanders shocked by the attempt, many rushed to congratulate Hitler on his survival, how far this was a safety measure to avoid suspicion or genuine is not always clear. It certainly led to a tightening up of the security reins, and a quick review by the propaganda offices which reflected happiness at the Führer's survival, but on the other hand a Joe Bloggs was hardly likely to say otherwise. According to Ian Kershaw 'more than two-thirds of prisoners of war in American captivity indicated their belief in Hitler' after the failed plot, but again it is understandable that many would not want to please their captors, and group pressure could be presumed, but a third disagreed.[21] In Britain, where high ranking officers were kept in Trent House Park where their private conversations were secretly monitored, there were some who were sad that Stauffenberg had not shown his usual efficiency, and the bomb had failed. However, most were more puzzled how many had survived the blast, with some wondering whether the Nazis had rigged the moment to flush out possible conspirators.[22] The overheard generals were more concerned on hearing about the trials and the fact their contemporaries had been hanged and not shot. In another curious overheard conversation, the Luftwaffe officer Lieutenant Freiherr von Richthofen was glad the attempt had failed, otherwise it would have created another stab-in-the-back theory, and it was 'politically necessary for the nation to go down the road to the bitter end'.[23] He did not consider the possibility that had the coup worked it may have saved millions of lives, but the anger against the Nazi leadership was evident. One junior officer who survived Russian imprisonment, and who later lived in America, wrote that 'it occurred to me that Germany would not be enduring this terrible final battle [against the Soviets] if von Stauffenberg had succeeded'.[24] As with many post-war accounts they were written with hindsight, but it was also clear that many had turned against the regime.

It is often asked what the new government's plan would have been if the coup had succeeded. Some think they would have tried peace with the Western Allies and fought on in Russia, but by now the realists knew they could not win by this stage, and it may well have led to capitulation which would have saved millions of lives. One knock on effect caused by Hitler's growing distrust in the army was that his henchmen such as Himmler, Goebbels, Bormann were given more powers, and even Speer. No more thought was given to a regime change after this failure.

Military knowledge of the Plot

There have been many observations made about the 20 July Plot, both criticisms and adulation, but perhaps one of the most interesting features was not its failure or success but the sheer number of generals and high-ranking officers who knew of its existence. There were those who stated categorically they wanted nothing to do with a political assassination but were trained to obey orders; they turned their backs, but there is little evidence of them rushing to inform the Gestapo. There were those who were curious but decided it was somewhat risky in the Nazi state to oppose. Some showed an interest, stood in the margins, and offered help if necessary. General Fromm reflected this style of support, but once he knew the plot was unlikely to succeed distanced himself and tried to clear any evidence connecting him with the possible coup. The danger, as Fromm was to discover, the slightest connection was later used at the People's Court where no mercy was shown.

Even the top fighting generals appeared to know something, but post-war memoirs have to be read with care, as after the war it was obviously advantageous to be associated with the conspiracy. Even some biographers have fallen to this weakness as with Rommel, a German hero often highly regarded by the British. Rommel's ties with the anti-Hitler resistance have been largely exploited in the creation of his post-war myth, with the intention of transforming him not only as an exceptional commander, but also in the anti-nazi conspiracy. However, there is little if any evidence of Rommel's involvement with the anti-Nazi resistance plot of 20 July. Most informative was the file which eventually led to Rommel's own end. On 28 September 1944, Martin Bormann, Hitler's secretary, put together a series of events suggesting that Rommel might have been involved in the 20 July plot. This file started with a simple statement: many of those involved, including some which had been put under trial and hanged, had mentioned Rommel who 'was in the frame', who had supposedly said that he would put himself at the disposal of the new government in the aftermath of the attack. The names included General Stülpnagel and Field Marshal von Kluge's nephew, Colonel Rathgens. The claim was read somewhat sceptically, Bormann recalling Rommel's service as commander of Hitler's headquarters and the many ties with Hitler and the propaganda ministry. However, Rommel's defeatist attitude in Italy could not be ignored, and Bormann (who also had cast doubts on Rommel's achievements as a military commander) claimed that Rommel had never been a Nazi. Most importantly, Bormann highlighted some traits of Rommel's personality. His ambition, which made him grasp any opportunity to be photographed along with Hitler, and his vanity which made him remove his glasses when photographed. A further proof of Rommel's attitude was his critical remark towards the conduct of the war, as reported by Gauleiter (district leader) Murr. This comment, which attracted the attention of Himmler's security, was explained as a complaint about Hitler's absence from the Western Front, and criticising his colleagues, such as von Rundstedt, von Kluge, and Göring, all of which amounted to mere hearsay but also possible heresy.

The critical point is that no actual evidence of Rommel's involvement was ever found, even though Rommel was compelled to commit suicide allowing some, after the war, to automatically enlist him in the anti-Hitler movement. General Speidel's post-war memoirs sanctioned this, only to be challenged by David Irving's biography whose thesis was that Rommel never opposed Hitler, not knowing of the attack, all of which was resumed later by David Fraser and Hans Georg Reuth. Others argued that Rommel was in fact aware of the anti-Hitler opposition, like other top-notch commanders such as von Manstein and Guderian, but they were opposed to killing Hitler. The simplest explanation is that Rommel was too close to people involved in the 20 July plot not to have been sounded out. Almost certainly he knew of the anti-Hitler circle and of their plans to overthrow his regime, even though he may not have been informed of the actual 20 July plot. Undoubtedly, Rommel would have been available and more than willing to put himself at the disposal of the new government, an attitude he certainly shared with the other generals who merely kept a 'wait and watch' attitude, waiting for the conspirators to take their steps. From the evidence claiming Rommel was an anti-Nazi, or that he even opposed the regime is too much of a leap. Rommel's ambition was probably the real driving force behind his successes and the reason behind his failures. This probably explains why he was compelled to commit suicide, while others, including his accusers, survived thanks to the lack of proof. Hitler was certainly aware of Rommel's ambition, but he could not risk facing him at the moment of crisis knowing that the myth he had helped create had a popular influence amongst German soldiers. In a way, Rommel's myth which he himself contributed to create, and which he unquestionably enjoyed was also the reason behind his eventual downfall and death.[25]

After the Stauffenberg 20 July bomb-plot, nearly all generals claimed ignorance, including Kesselring who fought to the very last hours of the war. However, in his memoirs he mentioned that Dr Karl Goerdeler had tried to 'approach me in 1942, but unsuccessfully, as I could not then be reached'.[26] However, Dollmann confirmed this and referred to Goerdeler as 'a ringleader.'[27] After the war Kesselring admitted to his son that he was aware 'that something was afoot'.[28] Generals Westphal and Senger knew about the plot, and Senger had informed Kesselring's son that he owed his life to his father's intervention at that difficult time.[29] It is known that General von Senger's Chief of Staff was a friend of Stauffenberg.[30] It also appears that Kesselring had saved another staff officer, two in all, it may have been Westphal.[31] The 20 July plot involved many, but Kesselring never seemed to come under suspicion because of his undoubted loyalty. He had proved a success in defence, never questioned Hitler and remained obedient to the regime. How much he knew about the plot if anything, like many other survivors long since dead, is impossible to verify, but is seems speculatively he knew something 'was up'. These examples of post-war analysis and the memoirs demonstrates the quagmire of finding the true facts, and undoubtedly many died in Plötzensee prison merely because someone had spoken to them.

Although there are no available provable statistics it appears that the majority of the Wehrmacht's most senior officers were aware that something was afoot, though most of them stayed hidden in the background upon a 'wait and see' policy, probably out of safety and ambition. Those involved actively in the plot, the leading 'conspirators lacked the sophistication of normal criminals or traitors, but they were self-sacrificing and heroic rather than cunning. Anyone, therefore, who tries to write off the conspiracy as naïve culpable imprudence is guilty of failure to recognise its true worth or level'.[32] Their motives may have been mixed, often with the military the fear of Hitler's mismanagement and ridiculous orders, but also with many of them having serious objections to the lack of acceptable morality and the issuing of criminal orders. Like many others they died at Plötzensee prison under the most humiliating conditions knowing there was no way out. Many others from teenage students to resisting civilians had gone the same way, by the guillotine and hanging, but while they may have failed, they had left a memory of courageous resistance which helped restore the traditional dignity of Germans and their country post-war.

Chapter Seven

Final Observations

Author's Notes: *In this chapter a brief summary of the study is made, and some conclusions are offered. For this writer, a huge question mark hovers over the accusation of Collective Guilt, and the warning that what happened in Germany can happen again.*

When in Britain the agricultural revolution was followed by its industrial counterpart it set a pattern which affected future generations. A social pattern was established between a growing working class often living in poverty, whereas the few rich landowners lived in wealth and on their own planet. This division of classes, despite the emergence of a white-collared middleclass remained a feature of British life into the twentieth century, where trade unions were viewed as dangerous by the governing elite. After the Great War, the situation remained the same, highlighted by incidents such as the General Strike (May 1926) and the Jarrow March (October 1936). France had a major revolution in 1789, but the social structure was similar to that in Britain. It was the same in Germany, with its Junkers landowning rulers, the same class divisions and unbalanced distribution of wealth. In Russia, the communist revolution appeared to have ironed the problem out, but although it created universal fear across Europe's elite, Stalin soon replaced the traditional upper classes with its own form of class system and wealth distribution. All this can be found in many history books and is referred to at this point to indicate that a country often finds it difficult to change the ramifications of its immediate history.

In Germany there were always the rich and poor, and since modern Germany had come into existence in the late nineteenth century, it had been governed by authoritarian rule and had established itself as a major player on the European scene, of which most if not all Germans, rich and poor were aware. It was the same in Britain with their pink coloured empire maps showing their overseas territories. The first chapter of this study outlined this feature of the German mindset which was turned upside down and inside out, when after the Great War it must have felt as if Germany had lost its identity, and this pervaded all classes, from the Junkers to the farmworkers and factory floors. The year 1918 was a disaster for Germany augmented by the retributions of the Versailles

Treaty and the subsequent economic downfall, and this was not helped by the world monetary crisis of 1928–9. The poverty, as elsewhere in Europe recovering from war, hit the working classes the most. The Weimar Republic had at first looked like the democratic ideal, but they were unfairly blamed for the post-war treaty, the economic downfall and ensuing deprivation, and none of this was helped by the new system having too many political parties. The German mindset also played its part when the Weimar Republic fell, because many would have looked forward to better days with an authoritarian regime returning Germany to greater security and comfort, as it had done in the past.

It was an accumulation of these problems which made Hitler's rise to popularity so quick, winning the hearts of the masses by promising a better future and shouting at them with a determination which many found attractive. His success was his oratory, and Hitler and his photographer Heinrich Hoffmann pored over his photographs so he could prepare the best stances and poses when speaking in public. His appeal was wide as he asked the crowds to cast their eyes back to when Germany had been great, a proud country stressing its power, glory, and honour. He projected himself as the saviour of Germany, told the crowds he was one of them and would tear down the social barriers making one people. He was almost able to produce a sense of religious fervour when he arrived on the public stage promising a bright future. It was understandable that he was popular as there was no talk of war, and this popularity increased when German troops walked into the Saar (1935), occupied the Rheinland (1936), regained the Sudetenland (1938), Czechoslovakia (1939), and when war was started against Poland (1939), the public were informed the Poles had opened fire first. When the old and traditional enemy of France was occupied in a matter of a few weeks, Keitel and others saw Hitler as the greatest military leader in history. However, it must be recalled that some Germans started to accrue doubts about the war, the treatment of Jews, prisoners of war, but by 1940 Hitler was seen by many as the nation's saviour.

It is comfortable with the benefit of hindsight to condemn the German public for their support of Hitler, even for being hoodwinked by him. However, after the 1918 humiliation and Hitler's assurance of a more prosperous landscape it should be, in human behavioural terms, easy to understand if not be somewhat sensitive to the public reaction. As noted in Chapter Two of this study, the sense of nationalism was rife across Europe, and Hitler took it to its extreme boundaries with his maniacal obsession with ethnic races such as Jews and Slavs being sub-human. Under the guise of holiday camps for youth the regime produced the colours of the Hitler Youth dancing their way across the Alps and singing around happy bonfires. It had always been Hitler's intention to bring young Germans to his side, and they were indoctrinated and militarised to fit in with the military clandestinely rebuilt during the Weimar years. The Hitler youth was painted in glowing pictures by Goebbel's brilliant propaganda, which was continuously used to illustrate Hitler as Germany's greatest leader.

The dangers of propaganda are better known today, often because of the way Goebbels used this clever political machine to make people think the way he dictated. Again, it is easy to condemn the German public for being influenced by Goebbels, and they only started accruing doubts about him when the tides of war changed, and bombs were dropped on their towns and cities. To this day many people believe what they read in newspapers, hear on the radio and television news, and never doubt the veracity of what they are told. It is widely known that politicians tell lies, and although it is tempting to list some recent incidents, such as weapons of mass destruction in the Iraqi war, it is over to the reader to reflect on this all-too-common issue. Although many more thoughtful Germans started to realise that the propaganda was misleading, many still hoped to the very last minute in the lies of wonder weapons, which when in extreme distress, was understandable.

The number of doubters about the Nazi regime and those who tried or wanted to oppose it started to grow, especially with the recognition that war could lead to destruction, and for many the immoral and criminal conduct of the regime was highly questionable. However, by this stage Germany had become a tightly controlled police state, and speaking critically of the regime to a neighbour, colleague and even a family relative could lead to a concentration camp and death in the worst-case scenario, at the lesser end one could lose one's job or position having endured a Gestapo interrogation. Fear became the dominating factor even in the factories and working-class areas. The mass of workers had to tread with care because although some were communists, while others also objected to the Nazi regime, there were many Nazi supporters, and because informing on others could bring its own rewards, this habit became a feared way of life for most people.

In short, the Nazi regime won less than 40 per cent of the votes, and shortly after the time Hitler had manipulated the democratic process to make him the sole leader, many of his opponents were in Dachau and other prisons or dead. Less than half the population had offered him support, and many of these soon changed their views, some joined the opposition while most, understandably, deemed it safer to keep one's mouth shut trying to survive. By 1942 it could be claimed that Hitler was less popular, and his public appearances dwindled to a time when he rarely appeared in public.

Nevertheless, some observers still hold to the collective guilt imposed on the whole German people. When today the slave trade is raised there is a sense of corporate guilt that one's country participated in this immoral and criminal trade, but there are three factors which have to be considered. First, that a feeling of guilt is right because the country and some of its citizens benefited from the crime. Secondly, it must be recalled that most of the trade and its financial benefits did not involve the entire population, usually less than 3 per cent who were mainly the wealthy landowners. Finally, it was another generation, and the current one can only react by apologising, compensating, and ensuring it never happens again. The slave trade is a serious smear on the history of many European nations, America, and elsewhere in the world. It is a stain on the country's historical fabric which justifiably cannot and should not be wiped clean because it stands as a stark warning from the past.

It is the same with Germany's Holocaust history, as the archival photographs of piled bodies at numerous concentration camps has left a terrible stain on German history, recalled to this day by the massive tomb-like and unavoidable Holocaust Memorial in Berlin. The war produced stains on the historical fabric of many countries during the twentieth century, but they must be kept in context. As the slave trade is a national slur it must be recalled this was the outcome of greedy people and not the whole population. The Holocaust was brought about by the Nazi regime, and the facts revealed by archival investigations and histories 'beggars belief'. It has cast a shadow over both Germany and humankind because of the depths of depravity it reached. There is no apologia possible for the Nazi regime and those who adhered to its policies to the end, but in terms of the whole German population the condemnatory 'collective guilt' must be kept in context.

Germany had a criminal gang leading it from 1933 onwards, they had cleverly hoodwinked many with their promises of a better future, and they used barbaric repression to ensure their leadership remained secure. This has happened in other countries, notably under the Russian Stalin, who had manipulated a society of Marxist ideals into a totalitarian state where, like Nazi Germany, fear, and repression blocked opposition. In Spain, Franco the dictator was still executing republicans years after he had grasped total power, and in China Mao Zedong was killing more Chinese than the invading Japanese. Today it has been claimed that there are more dictatorships than democracies, small but dangerous North Korea, a religious grip by religious fanatics in Afghanistan, a military one in Myanmar and the list is endless.

It is easy and reasonable to condemn the leadership of corrupt dictators and the high-level support they used, usually the military. It is unreasonable to blame the Joe Blogs who simply want to live their lives and care for their families, and who do not have the power or means to change the leadership, corrupt as it may be. In Chapter Three of this book two German 'Joe Blogs' managed to keep diaries which reflected their anti-Nazi views, but also offered insights into the reactions and thinking of other ordinary Germans from judges to shopkeepers. In a democratic society if something is considered wrong it is possible to start a petition which, on reaching a certain level, should be discussed by the government in power. To do this in a Nazi type state would mean serious persecution.

In Germany there grew many forms of protest, opposition and eventually resistance. This aspect, alongside the helplessness of the 'Joe Blogs' casts further doubt on the judgement of collective guilt. As discussed in Chapter Three there are descriptions of how opposition and resistance can best be described. However, it must be recalled that making any form of opposition in a dictatorship controlled by its own policing system, with no holds barred, is very different from today's democracies. In most democracies anyone or group can stand in opposition, and usually say what they want unless it incites racialism or hatred. In Nazi Germany as in any police state, any reaction such as a mild protest would be dangerous, and this is known to be all too true by people who have endured such circumstances. Despite this, opposition occurred many times in Nazi Germany, and probably more often than are known about.

Not every act of opposition can be noted as many are unknown and are just ashes in some concentration camp area. There were individuals who quietly objected to the regime, and the well-known attempt by Georg Elser to kill Hitler and his cohorts in Munich. There was even rebellion amongst some teenagers who for a variety of reasons objected to the Hitler Youth movement, and a group of university undergraduates who eventually gave their lives in protesting at the work of what they called a criminal government. There were many such groups often neglected at the time and since because they were communists. This study illustrated the lives of some of the better-known resisters at the top end of German life. They consisted of senior Churchmen, diplomats, economists, civil servants, and many others from all walks of life, some of whom held positions within the regime.

As noted in this study, their motives and intentions often differed, in a broad sweep of the brush they moved from those who had moral issues with the way the regime conducted itself, to motives of not wanting war, then winning a battle, or avoiding defeat. They are not clear-cut divisions as in many individuals both moral and military reasons stood side by side. The approach to the Jewish persecution (and Jewish reaction) was explored not least because the Holocaust has left a stain on German and on world history. The grim fact has to be accepted that some of those who opposed Nazism had anti-Semitic attitudes, but not as degraded as those of the regime. The civilian resisters plotted and planned for a better post-Hitler Germany, but they knew that only the military could bring down the regime. There were many attempts which failed or had to be aborted by military officers, resulting in the famous 20 July Plot noted in the final chapters. The instant retribution which followed this failed coup, interestingly revealed the massive numbers of military personnel who were involved or knew about what was likely to happen. There were many activists involved, with Stauffenberg being the most well-known, but it should not be forgotten that many like Tresckow were tireless in their efforts and risked their lives many times.

Over the years there has been considerable debate as the whether the resistance was of any value at all. The German historian Joachim Fest suggested that a final 'reason for the reluctance of most officers to assist the resistance was its lack of support among the general population' and their fear of Hitler's ability to sway them when necessary.[1] For this writer, as much as he admires Fest' work and experience this raised several questions. The first was that the senior military had little to do with the working masses until they provided gun fodder for the military. Public feelings for them at this stage could only be pure speculation, and it should not be forgotten that many were subdued by living in a vicious police state. In 1939, Fest may have been right, but by 1942–3 there had been substantial changes. Many of the most ardent Nazi supporters had started to have a change of mind as witnessed in the diaries of Kellner and Klemperer examined earlier in this text. Kellner had noted that some judges in the court system where he worked, had believed in Hitler, but when the war turned, they lost their sense of adulation for the leader and his regime. This had started with the growing public knowledge of the barbarities of the SS and even some Wehrmacht, and this feeling of despair increased rapidly with the Allied bombing of their homes, and the ever-present threat of the Russians because many feared Stalin as much as Hitler's regime. Fest also argued that the bombing had strengthened public resolve, which, as with the British, was probably true, but this for many would not have meant boosting their adoration of Hitler or Göring who had promised no enemy planes over Germany, they probably only wanted the war to finish. Even for the more cynical members of the public there was possibly even the thought that Hitler was losing the war, and possibly Russia could be held back by the military expertise while not being handcuffed by the Führer.

The problem the German resistance faced was very different from resistance in occupied countries, they had the almost impossible task of bringing down a totalitarian regime, which had for nearly a decade, established a system of total control over every strand of German life, and backed it with fear if not sheer terror. When Anthony Eden told Bonhoeffer's friend the Bishop of Chichester that the German resistance was not as good as the French, the Bishop pointed out that the French had been offered liberation, the German resistance unconditional surrender. In occupied countries resistant fighters or partisans faced recriminations against their families and executions of members of the public, so many fought in areas away from home and with different names. To resist in Germany there was no safety valve if caught, and the Nazi adoption of the medieval policy of charging kith and kin was well known and feared. It was this fear which often meant that even the most active resisters had to walk a tight-rope and not be seen conversing or attending meetings with the ever-observant Gestapo and their informers, making a united resistance very difficult. In Nazi Germany there was no form of immunity they could rely on, as Rommel had to face.

Because the plot failed it has been easy to find fault and lack of zeal, with some accusing the resisters of being mere romantics. If they were romantic in this sense, they still left a symbol or 'act' which cast some light in the abyss of darkness. Even had the plot succeeded it was clear that this would not stop the invasion but, importantly, their effort, symbolic as it was, demands a place on one of history's pedestals. History is not just about recording battles lost and won, or significant events, but also the deeds of men and women who put morality and the plight of fellow human beings at the top of their priority list.

It has also been claimed that the civilian resisters were just talking shops and had no realistic chance of overturning the regime, that the military had left it far too late, and the whole act of resistance by 1942 was a senseless enterprise because the enemy was not going to cooperate, and only unconditional surrender was acceptable. The resister Moltke was one of the few who recognised the reality of the situation, namely that only an international alliance could bring Hitler down, thus his hope and plans for a post-war European union. In many ways these critics were correct, the Nazi regime was so deeply embedded the chances of a successful coup were minimal, and although it may have worked had the bomb killed Hitler, it would still have been too late as far as the Soviet and Western Allies were concerned.

However, it must not be neglected that many Germans from all walks of life, from the working classes, through the intellectual circles to the elite and military there was opposition and resistance. The Plötzensee prison and other sites became places of martyrdom, as countless Germans were guillotined, brutally hanged, or were shot for opposing the regime, adding to the countless thousands who had died in the previous years for the same reasons. In the immediate post-war years such was the Holocaust, the barbarity of the concentration camps, and the numberless massacres made public by the Nuremberg Trials, that this all created a sense of shame and revenge on the name Germany. This would last for decades, and the film industry revelled in the horrors of the war, even affecting the generation born during and immediately after the war years. Apart from one or two films about the 20 July Plot in later years, the resistance to Hitler has only received historical interest.

When the July plotters were wondering whether Hitler had survived or not, they sought advice from Tresckow who replied:

> The assassination must be attempted at any cost. Even should it fail, the attempt to seize power in the capital must be undertaken. We must prove to the world and to future generations that the men of the German Resistance Movement dared to take the decisive step and to hazard their lives upon it. Compared with this objective, nothing else matters.[2]

This singular message underlined not only the required courage, but the conspirators knew their actions in July 1944, would send a message to future generations, namely that not all Germans were prepared to accept Hitler and his regime. The coup failed, but despite this it must be seen that the concept of collective guilt was generally unfair based on the evidence of this study. The Nazi regime was as evil as any in history, and given it occurred in the twentieth century must claim to be top of the tree in criminality, immorality, corruption, and sheer cruelty. To achieve this, it gathered its selected fanatics and indoctrinated them, but many remained subdued by fear, many opposed in the ways they could, and others resisted. The accusation of collective guilt was hardly reasonable, thousands of anti-Nazis had been killed from the 1930s, and although the resistance inevitably failed it now provides an act of martyrdom and remembrance that not all Germans were tainted, and this must be kept in perspective. Historians hold diverse opinions, but the central issue is that it could happen again, and as noted in the preface, the Jewish historian Zimmermann stated that history is more than a story, because the historian needs to infer from the past about the present.

Notes

Foreword

1. Taylor, A.J.P., *The Course of German History* (London: Methuen, 1961), p.248.

Chapter 1

1. *Fragen an die deutsche Geschichte* (*Questions on German History*) (German Bundestag Press, 1984), p.202.
2. Ibid., p.203.
3. Tipton, Frank B., *A History of Modern Germany Since 1815* (London: Continuum, 2003), p.243.
4. *Fragen an die deutsche Geschichte*, p.209.
5. See Tipton, Frank B., *A History of Modern Germany Since 1815*, p.249.
6. Ibid., p.258.
7. *Fragen an die deutsche Geschichte,* p.238.
8. Tipton, Frank B., *A History of Modern Germany Since 1815*, p.303.
9. Colville, John, *The Fringes of Power* (London: Hodder and Stoughton, 1985), p.26.
10. Churchill, Winston, *The Second World War Volume 1: The Gathering Storm* (London: Cassell, 1948), p.34.
11. Bryant, Mark, *World War II in Cartoons* (London: Grub Street, 2009), p.11.
12. See Tipton, Frank B., *A History of Modern Germany Since 1815*, p.332.
13. Ibid., p.343.
14. Housden, Martyn, *Resistance and Conformity in the Third Reich* (London: Routledge, 2006), p.158.
15. See Tipton, Frank B., *A History of Modern Germany Since 1815*, p.370.
16. Ibid., pp.382–3.
17. *Fragen an die deutsche Geschichte*, p.250.
18. Tipton, Frank B., *A History of Modern Germany Since 1815*, p.404.
19. Fulbrook, Mary (Ed.), *Twentieth Century Germany: Politics, Culture and Society 1918–1990* (London: Arnold, 2001), p.43.
20. Ibid., p.19.
21. Ibid., p.94.
22. Keegan, John and Wheatcroft, Andrew, *Who's Who in Military History* (London: Hutchinson, 1987), p.279.
23. Haigh, R.H., Morris, D.S. and Peters, A.R., *German-Soviet Relations in the Weimar Era: Friendship from Necessity* (Aldershot: Gower, 1985), p.165.
24. Ibid., p.63.
25. Ibid., p.63.
26. Ibid., p.115.
27. Ibid., p.177.
28. Kershaw, Ian, *The End: Hitler's Germany, 1944–45* (London: Allen Lane, 2011), p.303.

29. Citino, Robert M., *The Path to Blitzkrieg: Doctrine and Training in the German Army, 1920–39* (Mechanicsburg: Stackpole Books, 2008), p.7.
30. *The Rise and Fall of the German Air Force 1933–45* (The National Archives, Air Ministry Pamphlet, issued by the Air-Ministry 1948, 2008), pp.1–2.
31. Boyne, Walter J., *The Influence of Air Power Upon History* (New York: Pelican, 2003), p.153.
32. Ibid., p.153.
33. Liddell Hart, B.H., *The German Generals Talk: Startling revelations from Hitler's high command* (London: Harper, 2002), p.10.
34. Ibid., p.13.
35. Westphal, Siegfried, *The German Army in the West* (London: Cassell, 1951), p.3.
36. Liddell Hart, B.H., *The German Generals Talk*, p.18.
37. Westphal, Siegfried, *The German Army in the West*, p.5.
38. Caddick-Adams, Peter, *Monty and Rommel: Parallel Lives* (London: Arrow, 2012), p.177.
39. Vagts, Alfred, *A History of Militarism: Civilian and Military* (New York: The Free Press, 1959), p.295.
40. Janowitz, Morris, *The Professional Soldier: A Social and Political Portrait* (New York: The Free Press, 1971), p.8.
41. Haigh, R.H., Morris, D.S. and Peters, A.R., *German-Soviet Relations in the Weimar Era*, p.64.
42. Ibid., p.159.
43. Ibid., p.160.
44. Maycock, Ian, 'Poland 1939 – What really happened?', *Military History Monthly* (Issue 36, September 2013), p.37.
45. Wheeler-Bennett, Sir John, *The Nemesis of Power: German Army in Politics, 1918–1945* (New York: Palgrave Macmillan, 2005), p.81.
46. See Tipton, Frank B., *A History of Modern Germany Since 1815*, pp.410–11.
47. Ibid., pp.421–3.
48. See Tipton, Frank B., *A History of Modern Germany Since 1815*, p.428.
49. Catalogue, *The Topography of Terror* (Berlin: Stiftlung Topographies des Terrors, 2014), pp.24–5.
50. Ibid., p.27.
51. Hoffmann, Peter, *The History of the German Resistance 1933–1945* (Massachusetts, MIT Press, 1977), p.19.
52. Ibid., pp.30–1.
53. Fest, Joachim, *Plotting Hitler's Death: The German Resistance to Hitler 1933–1945* (London: Phoenix, 1997), p.24.
54. See *Fragen an die deutsche Geschichte*, p.302.
55. Evans, Richard J., *The Coming of the Third Reich: How the Nazis Destroyed Democracy and Seized Power in Germany* (London: Penguin Press, 2004), p.188.

Chapter 2

1. Welch, David, *The Third Reich: Politics and Propaganda* (London: Routledge, 1993), also quoted in Housden, M., *Resistance and Conformity in the Third Reich*, p.3.
2. Zimmer, Oliver, 'Nationalism in Europe, 1918–1945' in Breuilly, John (Ed.), *Oxford Handbook of the History of Nationalism* (Oxford: OUP, 2013), p.415.
3. This theme generally reflects the insights of Oliver Zimmer in Zimmer, O., 'Nationalism in Europe, 1918–1945', pp.414–31.
4. Zimmer, O., 'Nationalism in Europe, 1918–1945' (Oxford: OUP, 2013), p.416.

5. Ibid., p.426.
6. Hassell, Ulrich von, *The Ulrich von Hassell Diaries, 1938–1944: The Story of the Forces Against Hitler Inside Germany* (London: Frontline Books, 2011), p.44.
7. Ferguson, Niall, The War of the World: History's Age of Hatred (London: Allen Lane, 2006), p.32.
8. See Sangster, Andrew, *The Roots of Nationalism in European History* (Newcastle: Cambridge Scholars, 2019), p.215.
9. Rauschning, Hermann, *Hitler Speaks: A Series of Political Conversations with Adolf Hitler on His Real Aims* (London: Thornton Butterworth, 1939), pp.246–7.
10. Focke, Harald and Reimer, Uwe, *Alltag unterm Hakenkreuz: Wie die Nazis das Leben der Deutschen veränderten [Everyday Life Under the Swastika: How the Nazis Changed the Lives of Germans]* (Hamburg: Rowohlt, 1989), pp.88–91.
11. Housden, M., *Resistance and Conformity in the Third Reich*, p.73.
12. Focke, H. and Reimer, U., *Alltag unterm Hakenkreuz*, pp.87–8.
13. Lloyd, Alexandra, *Defying Hitler: The White Rose Pamphlets* (Oxford: Bodleian Library, 2022), p.2.
14. Roberts, Stephen H., *The House That Hitler Built* (London: Methuen, 1938), p.27.
15. Ibid., p.29.
16. Kershaw, Ian, *The End: Germany 1944–45* (London: Penguin Books, 2012), p.23.
17. Manvell, Roger and Fraenkel, Heinrich, *Doctor Goebbels: His Life and Death* (Barnsley: Frontline Books, 2010), p.33.
18. This was an entry for 14 June 1926, *The Goebbels Diaries 1942–1943* (edited by Louis P. Lochner) (New York: Doubleday and Company, 1948), p.7.
19. See Heiber, Helmut, *Goebbels* (New York: Hawthorn Books, 1972), p.38.
20. Manvell, R. and Fraenkel, H., *Doctor Goebbels*, p.116.
21. Longerich, Peter, *Goebbels* (London: Penguin Vintage, 2016), p.215.
22. Ebermayer, Erich and Meissner, Hans-Otto, *Evil Genius: The Story of Joseph Goebbels* (London: Allan Wingate, 1953), p.97.
23. See Longerich, *Goebbels*, p.223
24. Reimann, Viktor, *Joseph Goebbels: The Man Who Created Hitler* (London: Sphere Books Ltd, 1979), p.221.
25. Shirer, William L., *The Third Reich* (London: Mandarin, 1960), p.241.
26. Heiber, H., *Goebbels*, p.136.
27. Reimann, V., *Joseph Goebbels*, p.249.
28. See Welch, D., *The Third Reich: Politics and Propaganda*, and quoted in Housden, M., *Resistance and Conformity in the Third Reich*, p.5.
29. Quoted in Ebermayer, E. and Meissner, H.-O., *Evil Genius*, p.182.
30. Reimann, V., *Joseph Goebbels*, p.311.
31. Kershaw, Ian, *The End: Hitler's Germany, 1944–45*, pp.164, 243 and 281.
32. Ibid., p.244.
33. Lucas, James, *Last Days of the Reich: The Collapse of Nazi Germany, May 1945* (London: Arms and Armour Press, 1986), p.151.
34. Moltke, Freya von, *Memories of Kreisau and the German Resistance* (Lincoln: University of Nebraska Press, 2003), p.13.
35. Housden, M., *Resistance and Conformity in the Third Reich*, p.8.
36. Ibid., p.6.
37. Toland, John, *The Last 100 Days: The Tumultuous and Controversial Story of the Final Days of World War II in Europe* (New York: The Modern Library, 1996), p.133.
38. Padfield, Peter, *Himmler Reichsführer-SS* (London: Macmillan, 1990), p.103.

39. Ibid., p.105.
40. Manvell, Roger and Fraenkel, Heinrich, *Heinrich Himmler* (London: Skyhorse Publishing, 2007), p.27.
41. Ibid., p.36.
42. Housden, M., *Resistance and Conformity in the Third Reich*, p.13, quoting Rauschning, H., *Hitler Speaks*.
43. See Stargardt, Nicholas, *The German War: A Nation Under Arms, 1939–45* (London: Vintage, 2015), p.71.
44. Evans, Richard J., *The Third Reich at War 1939–1945* (London: Allen Lane, 2008), p.530.
45. Padfield, P., *Himmler Reichsführer-SS*, p.185.
46. See Longerich, Peter, *Heinrich Himmler* (Oxford: OUP, 2012), pp.236–7.
47. Quoted in Davies, Norman, *No Simple Victory: World War II in Europe, 1939–1945* (London: Viking, 2006), p.375.
48. Kershaw, Ian, *The End: Hitler's Germany, 1944–45*, p.23.
49. Fest, J., *Plotting Hitler's Death*, p.8.
50. Housden, M., *Resistance and Conformity in the Third Reich*, p.23.
51. Ibid., p.25.
52. Ibid., p.31.
53. Ibid., p.37.
54. See Housden, M., *Resistance and Conformity in the Third Reich*, p.39.
55. Moltke, F., *Memories of Kreisau*, pp.7 and 29.
56. Housden, M., *Resistance and Conformity in the Third Reich*, p.19.
57. Evans, R.J., *The Third Reich at War*, p.456.
58. Taylor, A.J.P, *The Course of German History*, p.248.

Chapter 3

1. See more on this in Peukert, Detlev J.K., *Inside Nazi Germany: Conformity, Opposition and Racism in Everyday Life* (London: Penguin, 1993), pp.222–3.
2. See Gordon, Sarah, *Hitler, Germans, and the "Jewish Question"* (New Jersey: Princeton University Press, 1984), p.195.
3. Steinhoff, Johannes, Pechel, Peter and Showalter, Dennis (Eds), *Voices from the Third Reich: An Oral History* (Washington: Regnery Gateway, 1989), pp.292–3.
4. Michalka, Wolfgang, *Das Dritte Reich Vol. 1* (Munich: DTV, 1985), p.169.
5. See Hilberg, Raul, *The Destruction of the European Jews* (London: Holmes and Meier, 1985) pp.662–8.
6. For more on this see Barkai, Avraham, *From Boycott to Annihilation: The Economic Struggle of German Jews, 1933–1943* (London: University Press of New England, 1989), p.141.
7. Koonz, Claudia, *Mothers in the Fatherland: Women, the Family and Nazi Politics* (New York: St Martin's Press, 1987), p.363.
8. Barkai, A., *From Boycott to Annihilation*, p.46 and see p.149.
9. See Hoffmann, P., *The History of German Resistance 1933–1945*, p.252.
10. Sangster, Andrew, *The Unfolding Agony of Oppression: Victor Klemperer, Nazi Germany and Soviet Communism, 1933–1959* (Cambridge: Cambridge Ethics Press, 2023), p.54.
11. Ibid., p.61.
12. Ibid., p.71.
13. Ibid., p.49.
14. Ibid., p.50.
15. Ibid., p.60.

16. Ibid., p.71.
17. Ibid., p.74.
18. Kellner, Robert Scott (Ed.), *My Opposition: The Diary of Friedrich Kellner – A German Against the Third Reich* (Cambridge: CUP, 2018).
19. Ibid., p.12.
20. Ibid., p.30.
21. Ibid., p.179.
22. Ibid., p.182.
23. Ibid., p. 211.
24. Ibid., p.217.
25. Ibid., p.286.
26. Ibid., p.68.
27. Ibid., p.69.
28. Ibid., p.100.
29. Ibid., p.170.
30. Ibid., pp.202 and 351.
31. Ibid., p.279.
32. Ibid., p.95.
33. Ibid., p.99.
34. Ibid., p.261.
35. Ibid., p.265.
36. Ibid., p.72.
37. Ibid., p.73.
38. Ibid., p.74.
39. Ibid., p.75.
40. Ibid., p.93.
41. Ibid., p.125.
42. Ibid., pp.108, 123 and 163.
43. Ibid., p.54.
44. Ibid., p.146.
45. Ibid., p.155.
46. Ibid., p.203.
47. Ibid., p.117.
48. Ibid., p.229.
49. Ibid., p.329.
50. Ibid., p.49.
51. Ibid., p.56.
52. Ibid., p.60.
53. Ibid., p.79.
54. Ibid., p.79.
55. Ibid., p.106.
56. Ibid., p.109.
57. Ibid., p.249.
58. Ibid., pp.251 and 272.
59. Ibid., p.307.
60. Ibid., p.312.
61. Ibid., p344.
62. Ibid., p.399.
63. Ibid., p.386.

64. Ibid., p.27.
65. Ibid., p.29.
66. Ibid., p.33.
67. Ibid., p.35.
68. Ibid., p.97.
69. Ibid., pp.111–12.
70. Ibid., p.120.
71. Ibid., p.191.
72. Ibid., p.67.
73. Ibid., p.122.
74. Ibid., pp.120 and 171.
75. Ibid., p.48.
76. Ibid., p.242.
77. Ibid., p.228.
78. Ibid., p.65.
79. Ibid., p.256.
80. Ibid., pp.44–5.
81. Ibid., p.83.
82. Ibid., p.193.
83. Ibid., p.36.
84. Ibid., p.39.
85. Ibid., p.41.
86. Ibid., p.78.
87. Ibid., p.124.
88. Ibid., p.127.
89. Ibid., p.130.
90. Ibid., p.131.
91. Ibid., pp.167 and 169.
92. Ibid., p.233.
93. Ibid., p.231.
94. Ibid., p.239.
95. Ibid., p282.
96. Ibid., p.395.
97. Ibid., p.376.
98. Ibid., p.59.
99. Ibid., p.89.
100. Ibid., pp.89–90.
101. Ibid. p.145.
102. Ibid., p.164.
103. Ibid., p.168.
104. Ibid., p.272.
105. Ibid., pp.275 and 300.
106. Ibid., p.345.
107. Ibid., p.348.
108. Ibid., p.155.
109. Ibid., p.178.
110. Ibid., p.407.
111. Ibid., p.407.
112. Ibid., pp.410–11.

Chapter 4

1. A view shared by Mommsen, Hans, *Germans Against Hitler* (London: I. B. Tauris, 2009), p.25.
2. Mommsen, H., *Germans Against Hitler*, p.132.
3. Hassell, U. von, *The Ulrich von Hassell Diaries*, p.157.
4. Tödt, Heinz Eduard, *Authentic Faith: Bonhoeffer's Theological Ethics in Context* (Michigan: Eerdman's Publishing, 2007). Digitised by the Internet Archive in 2022 with funding from Kahle/Austin Foundation, p.169.
5. See Mommsen, H., *Germans Against Hitler*, p.36.
6. Ibid., p.2.
7. Ibid., p.16.
8. See Hoffmann, P., *The History of German Resistance 1933–1945*, p.253.
9. Hoch, Anton and Gruchmann, Lothar, *Georg Elser: Der Attentäter aus dem Volke – Der Anschlag auf Hitler im Munich Bürgerbräu 1939* (Frankfurt am Main: Fischer Taschenbuch, 1980), p.171.
10. Goebbels, Joseph, *The Goebbels Diaries, 1939–41* (translated by Taylor, Fred) (London: Hamish Hamilton, 1982), p.47.
11. See Bundesarchiv Koblenz, *Interrogation Report* (November 1939) signature-R 22/3100.
12. Kellner, R.S., *My Opposition*, p.53.
13. Padfield, P., *Himmler Reichsführer-SS*, p.282.
14. Longerich, P., *Heinrich Himmler*, p.473.
15. For more details on these more obscure individuals see Hoffmann, P., *The History of German Resistance 1933–1945*, pp.251ff.
16. See Ibid., p.252.
17. See Housden, M., *Resistance and Conformity in the Third Reich*, pp.84–5.
18. Peukert, W.H., *Die Edelweiß Piraten. Protestbewgungen jugendlicher Arbeiter im 'Dritte Reich'* [*Protest Movements of Young Workers in the 'Third Reich'*] (Bonn: Bund, 1988), p.106.
19. See Housden, M., *Resistance and Conformity in the Third Reich*, pp.50–1.
20. Report of an Oberstaatsanwalt from Trier quoted in Focke, H. and Reimer, U., *Alltag unterm Hakenkreuz: Wie die Nazis das Leben der Deutschen veränderten* [*Everyday Life Under the Swastika: How the Nazis Changed the Lives of Germans*] (Hamburg: Rowohlt, 1989), pp.111–12.
21. Hassell, U. von, *The Ulrich von Hassell Diaries*, p.131.
22. Conway, John S., *The Nazi Persecution of the Churches, 1933–1945* (London: Weidenfeld and Nicolson, 1968), p.175.
23. Housden, M., *Resistance and Conformity in the Third Reich*, p.59.
24. Conway, J.S., *The Nazi Persecution of the Churches, 1933–1945*, p.175.
25. Housden, M., *Resistance and Conformity in the Third Reich*, p.55.
26. Ibid., p.58.
27. See Metaxas, Eric, *Bonhoeffer: Pastor, Martyr, Prophet, Spy* (New York: Thomas Nelson, 2011), p.113.
28. Ford, David, *The Modern Theologians: An Introduction to Christian Theology Since 1918* (London: Wiley-Blackwell, 2005), p.38.
29. See Kelly, Geffrey B. and Nelson, F. Burton (Eds), *A Testament to Freedom: The Essential Writings of Dietrich Bonhoeffer* (San Francisco: Harper, 1990), p.19.
30. Raina, Peter K., *Bishop George Bell: A Portrait in Letters* (London: CTBI Publications, 2006)
31. Ibid., p.284.
32. Housden, M., *Resistance and Conformity in the Third Reich*, p.47.

33. Schmidt, Dietmar, *Pastor Niemöller* (London: Odhams Press, 1959), pp.90–5.
34. Kellner, R.S., *My Opposition*, pp.229 and 142–3.
35. Butler-Gallie, Fergus, *Priests de la Résistance! The Loose Canons Who Fought Fascism in the Twentieth Century* (London: One World, 2021), p.52.
36. Ibid., p.59.
37. Ibid., p.53.
38. Zahn, Gordon Charles, *German Catholics and Hitler's Wars: A Study in Social Control* (London: Sheed and Ward, 1963), p.79.
39. Lloyd, A., *Defying Hitler*, p.19.
40. Ibid., p.47.
41. Ibid., p.91.
42. Ibid., p.97.
43. Ibid., p.109.
44. Ibid., p.115.
45. Ibid., p.29.
46. Hassell, U. von, *The Ulrich von Hassell Diaries*, p.23.
47. Ibid., p.32.
48. Ibid., p.34.
49. See Manvell, Roger and Fraenkel, Heinrich, *The Men Who Tried to Kill Hitler* (New York: Skyhorse, 1964), pp.43–4.
50. See Koch, H.W. (Ed.), *Aspects of the Third Reich* (London: Macmillan, 1985), p.148.
51. Hamerow, Theodore, S., *On the Road to the Wolf's Lair: German Resistance to Hitler* (Cambridge: Belknap Press, 1997), p.185.
52. Hassell, U. von, *The Ulrich von Hassell Diaries*, p.129
53. Ibid., p.38.
54. Speer, Albert, *Inside the Third Reich* (London: Weidenfeld & Nicolson, 1995), p.181.
55. Moltke, F., *Memories of Kreisau*, p.26.
56. Ibid., p.x.
57. Balfour, Michael and Frisby, Julian, *Helmuth von Moltke: A Leader Against Hitler* (London: Macmillan, 1972), pp.171–2.
58. Moltke, F., *Memories of Kreisau*, p.12.
59. Ibid., p.18.
60. Roon, G. van, *German Resistance to Hitler: Count von Moltke and the Kreisau Circle* (London: Van Nostrand Reinhold, 1971), pp.373–4
61. Moltke, F., *Memories of Kreisau*, p.21.
62. Ibid., p.23.
63. Lloyd, A., *Defying Hitler*, p.48.
64. Mommsen, H., *Germans Against Hitler*, p.137.
65. Ibid., p.53.
66. Ibid., p.55.
67. Ibid., p.51.
68. See Rothfels, Hans, *The German Opposition to Hitler* (London: Oswald Wolff, 1961) pp.112–114.
69. Moltke, F., *Memories of Kreisau*, p.30.
70. See Delp, Father Alfred, *The Prison Meditations of Father Alfred Delp* (Martino Fine Books, 2021).
71. Moltke, F., *Memories of Kreisau*, p.32.
72. Ibid., p.35.
73. Sangster, Andrew, *The Futile Pursuit of Power* (Caithness: Whittles, 2023), p.36.

74. Hassell, U. von, *The Ulrich von Hassell Diaries*, p.2.
75. Ibid., p.9.
76. Ibid., p.10.
77. Ibid., p.23.
78. Ibid., p.28.
79. Ibid., p.24.
80. See Wheeler-Bennett, John, *The Nemesis of Power: The German Army in Politics, 1918–1945* (2nd Edition, London: Macmillan, 1967), pp.416–17.
81. Hassell, U. von, *The Ulrich von Hassell Diaries*, p.224.
82. Blet, Pierre, *Pius XII and the Second World War: According to the Archives of the Vatican* (New York: Paulist Press 1999), p.256.
83. Mommsen, H., *Germans Against Hitler*, p.154.
84. See Ibid., p.163.
85. Ibid., p.152.
86. Ibid., p.153.
87. Ibid., p.176.
88. May, Ernest R., *Strange Victory: Hitler's Conquest of France* (New York: Hill and Wang, 2000), p.37.
89. Reynolds, Nicholas, *Treason Was No Crime: Ludwig Beck, Chief of the German General Staff* (London: William Kimber, 1976), p.43.
90. See Koch, H.W. (Ed.) *Aspects of the Third Reich* (London: Macmillan, 1985), article by Müller, Klaus-Jürgen, p.64.
91. Hassell, U. von, *The Ulrich von Hassell Diaries*, p.76.
92. See Koch, H.W. (Ed.), *Aspects of the Third Reich*, p.162.
93. Hassell, U. von, *The Ulrich von Hassell Diaries*, p.72.
94. Ibid., p.150.
95. Hoffmann, P., *The History of German Resistance 1933–1945*, p.255.
96. See Bassett, Richard, *Hitler's Spy Chief: The Wilhelm Canaris Betrayal* (New York: Pegasus, 2011), pp.97–8.
97. Ibid., p.99.
98. See Höhne, Heinz, *Canaris: Hitler's Master Spy* (New York: Doubleday, 1979), pp.216–17.
99. See Fest, J., *Plotting Hitler's Death*, pp.3–4.
100. Ibid., p.94.
101. Ibid., p.109.
102. Hoffmann, P., *The History of German Resistance 1933–1945*, p.129.
103. Ibid., p.142.

Chapter 5

1. Hoffmann, P., *The History of German Resistance 1933–1945*, pp.175ff.
2. Steffahn, H., *Stauffenberg* (Hamburg: Rowohlt, 1994).
3. See Mommsen, H., *Germans Against Hitler*, p.187.
4. Ibid., p.256.
5. Ibid., p.194.
6. Moltke, F., *Memories of Kreisau*, p.26.
7. Mommsen, H., *Germans Against Hitler*, p.208.
8. Ibid., p.212.
9. Moltke, F., *Memories of Kreisau*, p.24.
10. Fest, J., *Plotting Hitler's Death*, p.38.

Chapter 6

1. Hoffmann, P., *The History of German Resistance 1933–1945*, p.217.
2. See Ibid., p.244.
3. See Ibid., p.292.
4. Mommsen, H., *Germans Against Hitler*, p.247.
5. Ibid., p.251.
6. Shirer, William L., *The Rise and Fall of the Third Reich* (London: Mandarin, 1997), p.1034.
7. Ibid., p.1029.
8. Rees, Laurence, *The Dark Charisma of Adolf Hitler: Leading Millions into the Abyss* (London: Ebury Press, 2012), p.383.
9. See Kershaw, Ian, *The End: Hitler's Germany, 1944–45*, p.30.
10. Hoffmann, P., *The History of German Resistance 1933–1945*, pp.367–9.
11. Eberle, Henrik and Uhl, Matthias (Eds), *The Hitler Book: The Secret Dossier Prepared for Stalin* (London: John Murray, 2005), p.151.
12. Hoffmann, P., *The History of German Resistance 1933–1945*, p.380.
13. Ibid., p.384.
14. Ibid.
15. Eberle, H. and Uhl, M., *The Hitler Book*, p.163.
16. Hoffmann, P., *The History of German Resistance 1933–1945*, p.419.
17. See Rees, L., *The Dark Charisma of Adolf Hitler*, p.387.
18. Ibid., p.385.
19. Knappe, Siegfried, *Soldat: Reflections of German Soldier, 1936–1949* (London: BCA, 1993), p.254.
20. Shirer, W., *The Rise and Fall of the Third Reich*, p.1072.
21. Kershaw, I., *The End: Hitler's Germany, 1944–45*, p.32.
22. Neitzel, Sönke (Ed.), *Tapping Hitler's Generals: Transcripts of Secret Conversations 1942–45* (Barnsley: Frontline Books, 2007), p.58.
23. Kershaw, I., *The End: Hitler's Germany, 1944–45*, p.53.
24. Knappe, S., *Soldat*, p.37.
25. See Fraser, David, *Knight's Cross: A Life of Field Marshal Erwin Rommel* (London: Harper Collins, 1993), pp. 514–52, and Butler, Daniel Allen, *Field Marshal: The Life and Death of Erwin Rommel*, Chapter 14 (electronic edition). Hart, Russell A., *Rommel and the 20 July Bomb Plot* in Beckett, Ian F.W. (Ed.), *Rommel* (electronic edition) and Lieb Peter, 'Erwin Rommel: Widerstandkämpfer oder Nationalsozialist?', *Vierteljahrshefte für Zeitgeschichte* 3 (2013), 303–343.
26. Kesselring, Albert, *The Memoirs of Field-Marshal Kesselring* (London: William Kimber, 1953), p.209.
27. Dollmann, Eugen, *The Interpreter: Memoirs of Doktor Eugen Dollmann* (London:
28. Macksey, Kenneth, Kesselring: German Master Strategist of the Second World War (London: Greenhill, 1978), p.217.
29. Ibid., p.217.
30. Senger und Etterlin, Frido von, *Neither Fear Nor Hope* (London: Macdonald, 1963), p.200.
31. Dollmann, E., *The Interpreter*, p.330.
32. Hoffmann, P., *The History of German Resistance 1933–1945*, p.359.

Chapter 7

1. Fest, J., *Plotting Hitler's Death*, p.335.
2. Schlabrendorff, Fabian von, *They Almost Killed Hitler: Based on the Personal Account of Fabian Von Schlabrendorff* (New York: Kessinger Publishing, 1947), p.103.

Bibliography

Balfour, Michael and Frisby, John, *Helmuth von Moltke: A Leader Against Hitler* (London: Macmillan, 1972)

Barkai, Avraham, *From Boycott to Annihilation: The Economic Struggle of German Jews, 1933–1943* (London: University Press of New England, 1989)

Bassett, Richard, *Hitler's Spy Chief: The Wilhelm Canaris Betrayal* (New York: Pegasus, 2011)

Blet, Pierre, *Pius XII, and the Second World War: According to the Archives of the Vatican* (New York: Paulist Press 1999)

Boyne, Walter, *The Influence of Air Power Upon History* (New York: Pelican, 2003)

Bryant, Mark, *World War II in Cartoons* (London: Grub Street, 2009)

Bundesarchiv Koblenz, *Interrogation Report* (November 1939) signature-R 22//3100 Butler, *Field Marshal*, Chapter 14 (electronic edition)

Butler-Gallie, Fergus, *Priests de la Résistance! The Loose Canons Who Fought Fascism in the Twentieth Century* (London: One World, 2021)

Caddick-Adams, *Peter, Monty and Rommel: Parallel Lives* (London: Arrow, 2012) Catalogue, *The Topography of Terror* (Berlin: Stiftlung Topographies des Terrors, 2014) Churchill, Winston, *The Second World War Volume 1: The Gathering Storm* (London: Cassell, 1948)

Citino, Robert M., *The Path to Blitzkrieg: Doctrine and Training in the German Army, 1920–39* (Mechanicsburg, Stackpole Books, 2008)

Colville, John, *The Fringes of Power* (London: Hodder and Stoughton, 1985)

Conway, John S., *The Nazi Persecution of the Churches, 1933–1945* (London: Weidenfeld and Nicolson, 1968)

Davies, Norman, *No Simple Victory: World War II in Europe, 1939–1945* (London: Viking, 2006)

Delp, Father Alfred, *The Prison Meditations of Father Alfred Delp* (Martino Fine Books, 2021)

Dollmann, Eugen, *The Interpreter: Memoirs of Doktor Eugen Dollmann* (London: Hutchinson, 1967)

Eberle, Henrik and Uhl, Matthias (Eds), *The Hitler Book: The Secret Dossier Prepared for Stalin* (London: John Murray, 2005)

Ebermayer, Erich and Meissner, Hans-Otto, *Evil Genius: The Story of Joseph Goebbels* (London: Allan Wingate, 1953)

Evans, Richard J., *The Coming of the Third Reich: How the Nazis Destroyed Democracy and Seized Power in Germany* (London: Penguin Press, 2004)

——, *The Third Reich at War 1939–1945* (London: Allen Lane, 2008)

Ferguson, Niall, *The War of the World: History's Age of Hatred* (London: Allen Lane, 2006)

Fest, Joachim, *Plotting Hitler's Death: The German Resistance to Hitler 1933–1945* (London: Phoenix, 1997)

Focke, Harald and Reimer, Uwe, *Alltag unterm Hakenkreuz: Wie die Nazis das Leben der Deutschen veränderten* [*Everyday Life Under the Swastika: How the Nazis Changed the Lives of Germans*] (Hamburg: Rowohlt, 1989)

Forczyk, Robert, *Erich von Manstein: Leadership, Strategy, Conflict* (Oxford: Osprey, 2010)

Ford, David, *The Modern Theologians: An Introduction to Christian Theology Since 1918* (London: Wiley-Blackwell, 2005)

Fragen an die deutsche Geschichte (*Questions on German History*) (German Bundestag Press, 1984)

Fraser, David, *Knight's Cross: A Life of Field Marshal Erwin Rommel* (London: Harper Collins, 1993)

Fulbrook, Mary (Ed), *Twentieth Century Germany: Politics, Culture and Society 1918–1990* (London: Arnold, 2001)

Goebbels, Joseph, *The Goebbels Diaries, 1939–41* (translated by Taylor, Fred) (London: Hamish Hamilton, 1982)

——, *The Goebbels Diaries, 1942–1943* (edited by Louis Lochner) (New York: Doubleday and Company, 1948)

Gordon, Sarah, *Hitler, Germans, and the "Jewish Question"* (New Jersey: Princeton University Press, 1984)

Haigh, R.H., Morris, D.S. and Peters, A.R., *German-Soviet Relations in the Weimar Era: Friendship from Necessity* (Aldershot: Gower, 1985)

Hamerow, Theodore, S., *On the Road to the Wolf's Lair: German Resistance to Hitler* (Cambridge: Belknap Press, 1997)

Hart, Russell A., *Rommel, and the 20 July Bomb Plot* in Beckett, Ian F.W. (Ed.), *Rommel* (electronic edition)

Hassell, Ulrich von, *The Ulrich von Hassell Diaries, 1938–1944: The Story of the Forces Against Hitler Inside Germany* (London: Frontline Books, 2011)

Heiber Helmut, *Goebbels* (New York: Hawthorn Books, 1972)

Hilberg, Raul, *The Destruction of the European Jews* (London: Holmes and Meier, 1985) Hoch, Anton and Gruchmann, Lothar, *Georg Elser: Der Attentäter aus dem Volke – Der Anschlag auf Hitler im Munich Bürgerbräu 1939* (Frankfurt am Main: Fischer Taschenbuch, 1980)

Hoffmann, Peter, *The History of the German Resistance 1933–1945* (Massachusetts: MIT Press, 1977)

Höhne, Heinz, *Canaris: Hitler's Master Spy* (New York: Doubleday, 1979)

Housden, Martyn, *Resistance and Conformity in the Third Reich* (London: Routledge, 2006)

Janowitz, Morris, *The Professional Soldier: A Social and Political Portrait* (New York: The Free Press, 1971)

Keegan, John and Wheatcroft, Andrew, *Who's Who in Military History* (London: Hutchinson, 1987)

Kellner, Robert Scott (Ed.), *My Opposition, The Diary of Friedrich Kellner – A German Against the Third Reich* (Cambridge: CUP, 2018)

Kelly, Geffrey B. and Nelson, F. Burton (Eds), *A Testament to Freedom: The Essential Writings of Dietrich Bonhoeffer* (San Francisco: Harper, 1990)

Kershaw, Ian, *The End: Hitler's Germany, 1944–45* (London: Allen Lane, 2011)

Kesselring, Albert, *The Memoirs of Field-Marshal Kesselring* (London: William Kimber, 1953)

Knappe, Siegfried, *Soldat: Reflections of German Soldier, 1936–1949* (London: BCA, 1993)

Koonz, Claudia, *Mothers in the Fatherland: Women, the Family and Nazi Politics* (New York: St Martin's Press, 1987)

Koch, H.W. (Ed.), *Aspects of the Third Reich* (London: Macmillan, 1985)

Lemay, Benoît, *Erich von Manstein: Hitler's Master Strategist* (Newbury: Casemate, 2010)

Liddell Hart, B.H., *The German Generals Talk: Startling revelations from Hitler's high command* (London: Harper, 2002)

Lieb, Peter, 'Erwin Rommel: Widerstandkämpfer oder Nationalsozialist?', *Vierteljahrshefte für Zeitgeschichte* 3 (2013)

Lloyd, Alexandra, *Defying Hitler: The White Rose Pamphlets* (Oxford: Bodleian Library, 2022)
Longerich, Peter, *Heinrich Himmler* (Oxford: OUP, 2012)
——, *Goebbels* (London: Penguin Vintage, 2016)
Lucas, James, *Last Days of the Reich: The Collapse of Nazi Germany, May 1945* (London: Arms and Armour Press, 1986)
Macksey, Kenneth, *Kesselring: German Master Strategist of the Second World War* (London: Greenhill, 1978)
Manvell, Roger and Fraenkel, Heinrich, *The Men Who Tried to Kill Hitler* (New York: Skyhorse, 1964)
——, *Doctor Goebbels: His Life and Death* (Barnsley: Frontline Books, 2010)
——, *Heinrich Himmler* (London: Skyhorse Publishing, 2007)
May, Ernest R., *Strange Victory: Hitler's Conquest of France* (New York: Hill and Wang, 2000)
Maycock, Ian, 'Poland 1939 – What really happened?', *Military History Monthly* (Issue 36, September 2013)
Metaxas, Eric, *Bonhoeffer: Pastor, Martyr, Prophet, Spy* (New York: Thomas Nelson, 2011)
Michalka, Wolfgang, *Das Dritte Reich Vol. 1* (Munich: DTV, 1985)
Moltke, Freya von, *Memories of Kreisau and the German Resistance* (Lincoln: University of Nebraska Press, 2003)
Mommsen, Hans, *Germans Against Hitler* (London: I. B. Tauris, 2009)
Neitzel, Sönke (Ed.), *Tapping Hitler's Generals: Transcripts of Secret Conversations 1942–45* (Barnsley: Frontline Books, 2007)
Padfield, Peter, *Himmler Reichsführer-SS* (London: Macmillan, 1990)
Peukert, W.H., *Die Edelweiß Piraten. Protestbewgungen jugendlicher Arbeiter im 'Dritten Reich'* [*Protest Movements of Young Workers in the 'Third Reich'*] (Bonn: Bund, 1988)
Peukert, Detlev J.K., *Inside Nazi Germany: Conformity, Opposition and Racism in Everyday Life* (London: Penguin, 1993)
Raina, Peter K., *Bishop George Bell: A Portrait in Letters* (London: CTBI Publications, 2006)
Rauschning, Hermann, *Hitler Speaks: A Series of Political Conversations with Adolf Hitler on His Real Aims* (London: Thornton Butterworth, 1939)
Rees, Laurence, *The Dark Charisma of Adolf Hitler: Leading Millions into the Abyss* (London: Ebury Press, 2012)
Reimann, Viktor, *Joseph Goebbels: The Man Who Created Hitler* (London: Sphere Books Ltd, 1979)
Reynolds, Nicholas, *Treason Was No Crime: Ludwig Beck, Chief of the German General Staff* (London: William Kimber, 1976)
Roberts, Stephen H., *The House That Hitler Built* (London: Methuen, 1938)
Roon, G. van, *German Resistance to Hitler: Count von Moltke and the Kreisau Circle* (London: Van Nostrand Reinhold, 1971)
Rothfels, Hans, *The German Opposition to Hitler* (London: Oswald Wolff, 1961)
Sangster, Andrew, *The Unfolding Agony of Oppression: Victor Klemperer, Nazi Germany and Soviet Communism, 1933–1959* (Cambridge: Cambridge Ethics Press, 2023)
——, *The Futile Pursuit of Power* (Caithness: Whittles, 2023)
——, *The Roots of Nationalism in European History* (Newcastle: Cambridge Scholars, 2019)
Schlabrendorff, Fabian von, *They Almost Killed Hitler: Based on the Personal Account of Fabian Von Schlabrendorff* (New York: Kessinger Publishing, 1947), p.103.
Schmidt, Dietmar, *Pastor Niemöller* (London: Odhams Press, 1959)
Senger und Etterlin, Frido von, *Neither Fear Nor Hope* (London: Macdonald, 1963)
Shirer, William L., *The Third Reich* (London: Mandarin, 1960)

——, *The Rise and Fall of the Third Reich* (London: Mandarin, 1997)
Speer, Albert, *Inside the Third Reich* (London: Weidenfeld & Nicolson, 1995)
Stargardt, Nicholas, *The German War: A Nation Under Arms, 1939–45* (London: Vintage, 2015)
Steffahn, H., *Stauffenberg* (Hamburg: Rowohlt, 1994)
Steinhoff, Johannes, Pechel, Peter and Showalter, Dennis (Eds), *Voices from the Third Reich: An Oral History* (Washington: Regnery Gateway, 1989)
Taylor, A.J.P, *The Course of German History* (London: Methuen, 1961)
The Rise and Fall of the German Air Force 1933–45 (The National Archives, Air Ministry Pamphlet, issued by the Air Ministry 1948, 2008)
Tipton, Frank B., *A History of Modern Germany Since 1815* (London: Continuum, 2003)
Tödt, Heinz Eduard, *Authentic Faith: Bonhoeffer's Theological Ethics in Context* (Michigan: Eerdman's Publishing, 2007). Digitised by the Internet Archive in 2022 with funding from the Kahle/Austin Foundation
Toland, John, *The Last 100 Days* (New York: The Modern Library, 1996)
Trunk, I., *The Attitudes of the Judenrats to the Problems of Armed Resistance Against the Nazis* in Yad Vashem, *Jewish Resistance During the Holocaust* (Jerusalem: Yad Vashem, 1971)
Vagts, Alfred, *A History of Militarism: Civilian and Military* (New York: The Free Press, 1959)
Welch, David, *The Third Reich: Politics and Propaganda* (London: Routledge, 1993) Westphal, Siegfried, *The German Army in the West* (London: Cassell, 1951)
Wheeler-Bennett, John, *The Nemesis of Power: The German Army in* Politics, 1918–1945 (2nd Edition, London: Macmillan, 1967)
——, *The Nemesis of Power: German Army in Politics, 1918–1945* (New York: Palgrave Macmillan, 2005)
Zahn, Gordon Charles, *German Catholics and Hitler's Wars: A Study in Social Control* (London: Sheed and Ward, 1963)
Zimmer, Oliver, 'Nationalism in Europe, 1918–1945' in Breuilly, John (Ed.), *Oxford Handbook of the History of Nationalism* (Oxford: OUP, 2013)

Index